THE THEOLOGY

OF A

SOUTH AFRICAN MESSIAH

OEKUMENISCHE STUDIEN

HERAUSGEGEBEN VON

PROF. D. DR. ERNST BENZ

Direktor des Oekumenischen Seminars der Philipps-Universität
Marburg (Lahn)

VIII

GERHARDUS CORNELIS OOSTHUIZEN

THE THEOLOGY
OF A
SOUTH AFRICAN MESSIAH

LEIDEN/KÖLN
E. J. BRILL
1976

THE THEOLOGY
OF A
SOUTH AFRICAN MESSIAH

AN ANALYSIS OF THE HYMNAL OF
"THE CHURCH OF THE NAZARITES"

BY

GERHARDUS CORNELIS OOSTHUIZEN

PHOTOMECHANICAL REPRINT

LEIDEN/KÖLN
E. J. BRILL
1976

First published in 1967

ISBN 90 04 04772 7

PRINTED IN THE NETHERLANDS

CONTENTS

Preface IX

Bibliography XI

Introduction 1

I. The Supreme Being 11
   1. uMvelingqangi 11
   2. uNkulunkulu 12
   3. uThixo 15
   4. umDali 18
   5. Simakade 19
   6. Guqaɓadele 21
   7. Yise: Uyise 22
   8. uɓaɓa 24
   9. umEndzi 27
   10. Jehova 28
   Conclusion: Shembe's concept of the Supreme Being 32

II. THE MESSIAH 35

   A. 1. Jesus Christ 35
     2. iNkosi [King, Chief, Lord] 37
       i. Names for the Supreme Being and iNkosi used
       together or interchangeably 37
       ii. Jesus as iNkosi 39
       iii. iNkosi as a term for a Paramount Chief 39
       iv. Shembe as iNkosi 39

     3. uMkhululi [Liberator] 41
     4. uMsindisi [Rescuer, Redeemer, Healer] 43
     5. uMkhokheli [Payer of debts] 44
     6. iNceku [Servant] 44
       i. The Bible and the iNceku 44
       ii. Shembe's call as iNceku 45
       iii. The iNceku and preaching 45
       iv. Shembe, the iNceku, as Africa's Moses 45

v. The iNceku as forgiver of sins 46
vi. The iNceku resurrects 46

7. iDwala [Rock] 47
8. uThumekile [The one sent] 48
9. Ingelosi [Angel] 49
10. Isikhonzi [Voluntary Servant, worshipper] 49

B. Other designations for Shembe I. 50
Conclusion: Shembe, the eschatological King or Black Christ 52

III. MAN AND THE SUPERNATURAL WORLD 57

A. uMoya [Numinous power, spirit] 57
1. Impersonal power 57
2. Personal being 62
3. As metaphor 65
What does the Izihla6elelo understand by uMoya? . . 67

B. Umphefumulo [Soul] 68

C. Inhliziyo [Heart] 73
1. Physiological 74
2. Metaphorical 74
i. The heart and the word 75
ii. The cleansing of the heart 76

D. A6angcwele [Saints] 77
i. Who are they? 77
ii. Who are not elected? 78
iii. The holy ones in 'heaven' 79
iv. The influence of non-christian concepts 80

E. Ingelosi [Angel] 81
i. The Chief Angel 82
ii. The Angels 83
iii. The Angels and shades 84

F. Izithunywa [Messengers] 85
i. As earthly messengers 85
ii. As supernatural messengers 85
iii. Their work of judgment 86
iv. Their account of Shembe 87

G. Amakhosi [Royal shades] 87

H. Umoya oyingcwele [Holy Spirit]. 90

IV. THE COMMUNITY 95

A. The Congregation 95
  1. iBandla lamaNazaretha: "The church of the Nazarites" 95
  2. Amakholwa [Believers]. 96
  3. Aɓangcwele [Saints] 99
  4. Izithunywa [Messengers] 99
  5. Izikhonzi [Worshippers or Servants] 99
  6. AɓaProfithi [Prophets] 100
  7. AɓaPostoli [Apostles] 100

B. The Building 101

C. The Scriptures 101
  1. Imibalo [Scriptures] 101
  2. Izwi [Word] 102
    i. Izwi as word 102
      a. The Word and the Sabbath 102
      b. The Carriers of the Word 103
      c. The word at Ekuphakameni. 104
      d. Preaching of the Word 104
    ii. Izwi as Voice 106

D. The Commandments. 107
  1. iSabatha [Sabbath] 107
  2. Imithetho [Laws] 108
  3. Imikhosi [Public Announcements] 109
  4. Imiyalo [Warnings] 110
  5. Isimemezelo [Proclamation, Notice] 110

E. The Festivals 111

F. Numinous power in the Congregation 113
  1. Holy Communion and the Cross 114
  2. Numinous power in the service of healing 117
  3. Inhlanhla [good fortune, luck] 118

G. Sin and Sinners 119
  1. Sin 119
    i. As weight 119

ii. As dirt   120
iii. As the works of darkness   121
iv. As bonds   121

2. What should be done with sin?   121
    i. Concealed.   121
    ii. Buried   122
    iii. Washed away   122
    iv. Confessed.   122

3. Sinners   122
    i. Forgiveness   122
    ii. Judgment   123

4. Biblical reminiscences with regard to Shembe's concept of sin   124
5. The Biblical concept of sin misunderstood   125

H. Baptism   126

I. Miscellaneous.   128
1. Decoration.   128
2. Dancing   129

V. Eschatology   130

1. Before thy face [eɓusweni ɓakho]   130
2. The Resurrection   131
3. The Gates   134
4. The Holy City   136
    i. Ekuphakameni.   136
    ii. Ekuphakameni in other terms   140

Conclusion   145

Appendix   157

PREFACE

This book is the result of an effort to analyse the hymnal of "The Church of the Nazarites". The fact that the theology implied in the hymnal shaped that of the movement makes a closer analysis of this significant book necessary. Although Shembe I is the main author of the *Izihlaɓelelo*, the hymns of Shembe II have also been discussed; he has however not changed the theological position. Eighty-six of the hymns and songs have been translated and appear in the *appendix*.

The time has arrived that the analysis of the sources should receive closer attention. Such an analysis, concentrating on the hymns, prayers, sermons and ritual of approximately three thousand movements, will reveal the complexity of the basis on which they flourish and any over-simplification based on *general* causes will be refuted as unrealistic. This task is too great for individuals and should actually be undertaken through teamwork.

In typical German tradition Prof. Ernst Dammann of the Philipps University, Marburg, suggested a closer analysis of the *Izihlaɓelelo* which could be accepted as the catechism of the Nazarites. I am grateful to Prof. Dammann for his untiring inspiration and help with regard to this study. I would also like to express my gratitude to Prof. Dammann's staff, especially Dr. H. Greschat, for their kind assistance in many ways. To Mr. V. Z. Gitywa B.A. (Hons), Curator of the F. S. Malan museum at Fort Hare for his invaluable assistance with regard to the translations, I am greatly indebted. In this connection I am also indebted to Miss D. N. Jafta B.A. (Hons), B.Ed., of the Department of Bantu Languages at the University of Fort Hare. For information and assistance received from Prof. O. F. Raum, the Rev. Dr. A. I. Berglund, Dr. E. J. de Jager, the Rev. S. D. Sibanyoni (B.A. Theol.) and Mr. F. J. van Wyk, B.A., I wish to express my gratitude. Mr. N. von Lyncker's kind assistance in typing the manuscript is greatly appreciated.

For the acceptance of this study in his most esteemed ecumenical series I wish to thank Prof. E. Benz of the Philipps-University, Marburg.

For the most generous financial assistance rendered by the Alexander von Humboldt-Stiftung which enabled me to work in Germany and which makes the publication of this book possible, I wish to express my sincere gratitude. Dr. Heinrich Pfeiffer, the general secretary and Dr. Thomas Beberich, his assistant, have been most helpful.

A special word of thanks to my wife and children, who with great understanding, enabled me to continue undisturbed with my work.

I wish to dedicate this book to the memory of the late Prof. J. H. Bavinck, well-known scholar in the field of the science of missions, who has directed my interest in this field of study.

SELECTED BIBLIOGRAPHY

Asmus, G., Die Zulu, Essener Verlagsanstalt, 1939.

Axenfeld, K., Aethiopianismus, Koloniale Abhandlungen 6, Berlin, 1906.

Barber, B., "Acculturation and Messianic Movements", American Sociological Review, Vol. VI, No. 5, 1941.

Bleek, W. H. I., [ed. Engelbrecht, I. A.] Zulu legends, Pretoria, van Schaik, 1952.

Bryant, A. T., A Zulu-English dictionary, Natal, Pinetown, The Mariannhill Mission Press, 1905.

—, "Zulu medicines and medicine men", Annals, Natal museum, 1909.

—, Olden times in Zululand, London, New York, Toronto, Longmans, Green a. Co, 1929.

Callaway, H., The religious system of the Amazulu, Cape Town, Juta a. Co, 1870.

Cameron, W. M., "The Ethiopian Movement and the order of Ethiopia", The East and West, 1904.

Dammann, E., Bezeichnungen für die Führer nachchristlicher Kirchen und Sekten Afrikas, Sonderheft der wissenschaftlichen Zeitschrift der Friedrich-Schiller-Universität, Jena, 1963.

Doke, C. M., and Vilakazi, B. W., Zulu-English dictionary, Johannesburg, Witwatersrand University Press, 1958.

Dube, J., uShembe, Pietermaritzburg, 1936.

du Toit, B., "Some aspects of the soul-concept among the Bantu-speaking Nguni-tribes of South Africa", Anthropological Quarterly, July 1960, Vol. 33, 3, 134–142.

Eberhardt, J., Messianisme en Afrique du Sud. Archives de Sociologie des religions, Vol. 4, 1957, 31–56.

Eiselen, W. M., and Schapera, I., "Religious Beliefs and Practices" in Schapera (ed.), The Bantu-speaking trives of South Africa, 1937[2].

Gardiner, A. F., Narrative of the journey to the Zoolu country in South Africa, London, William Crofts, 1836.

Knoob, W. F., "Ethnologische Aspekte der religiösen Bewegungen im südlichen Afrika" in Mühlmann (ed.), Chiliasmus und Nativismus, Berlin, Dietrich Reimer Verlag, 1961.

Krige, E. J., The social System of the Zulus, London, New York, Toronto, Longmans, Green a. Co, 1936.

Lautenschlager, P. G. M., Die sozialen Ordnungen bei den Zulu und die Mariannhiller Mission, 1882–1909, Reimlingen, St. Josefs-Verlag, 1960.

Lea, A., The Native Separatist Movement in South Africa, Cape Town, Johannesburg, Juta a. Co, 1926.

Linington, P. A., A Summary of the Reports of certain Pre-Union Commissions of Native Affairs: Church Separatist Movement, 1924.

Loram, C., "The Separatist Church Movement", International Review of Missions, Vol. XV, July 1926, 476–482.

Lugg, H. C., "Agricultural ceremonies in Natal and Zululand", Bantu Studies, Vol. III, No. IV, 1929, 357–383.

Mair, L. P., "Independent religious Movements", Comparative Studies in Society and History, Vol. 1, No. 2, Jan. 2, 1959.

Martin, M.-L., "The Church facing Prophetic and Messianic Movements", Ministry, Jan. 1963.

Mqotsi, L., and MKele, N., "A separatist Church, *iBandla lika Krestu*", African Studies, Vol. V, 1946, 106–125.
Nyem6ezi, C. C. S., Zulu Proverbs, Johannesburg, Witwatersrand University Press, 1954.
Pauw, B. A., Religion in a Tswana Chiefdom, London, New York, Toronto, Oxford University Press, 1960.
Samuelson, L. H., Zululand: its traditions, legends, customs and folklore. Mariannhill Press, 1930.
Samuelson, R. C. A., The King Cetywayo Zulu dictionary, Durban, The Commercial Printing Co, 1923.
Schlosser, K., Eingeborenenkirchen in Süd- und Südwestafrika. Ihre Geschichte und Sozialstruktur, Kiel, Mühlau, 1958.
Shepherd, R. H. W., "The separatist churches of South Africa", International Review of Missions, Vol. XXVI, Oct. 1937, 453–463.
Sundkler, B. G. M., Bantu Prophets in South Africa, London, New York, Toronto, Oxford University Press, 1948^1, 1961^2.
—, Propheten in Die Religion in Geschichte und Gegenwart, Tübingen, J. C. B. Mohr, 1961, 611–3.
—, "Black Man's Church", Libertas Magazine, Johannesburg, 1945.
Tempels, P., Bantu Philosophy, Paris, Presence Africaine, 1959.
Union Government Report, 39, 1925.
van Warmelo, N. J., Kinship terminology of the South African Bantu, Pretoria, Government Printer, 1935.
Vilakazi, A., *Isonto Lamanazaretha*: The Church of the Nazarites, Connecticut, Hartford Seminary Foundation, 1954, Unpubl. dissertation.
—, Zulu Transformations: a study of the dynamics of social change, Pietermartizburg, University of Natal Press, 1962.
Wanger, W., "The traditional Zulu names of God", The Catholic Magazine for South Africa, Cape Town, 1919.
—, "The Zulu notion of God", Anthropos, Vol. XXI, 1926.
Weman, H., African music and the church in Africa, Svenska Institutet för Missionsforskning, Uppsala, 1960.
Willoughby, W. C., The Soul of the Bantu, London, SCM, 1928.

Bibles

1. Incwadi engcwele etiwa i Bibele noma imibhalo, Hermannsburg edition, Empangeni, P.o.Moorleigh, Natal, 1924.
2. iBaibele eli ingcwele, Revised version, 1924. New York, American Bible Society.
3. i Testamente Elisha, London, The British and Foreign Bible Society, 1956.
4. i Bhayibheli elingcwele, London, The British and Foreign Bible Society, 1961.

Hymnal

Izihla6elelo zaManazaretha, Durban, W. H. Shepherd Co. (Pty.) Ltd., 527, Smith Street.

INTRODUCTION

The *Izihlaɓelelo zaManazaretha*,[1]) the hymnal of the *iBandla lama-Nazaretha*,[2]) published for the first time in 1940 in Zulu,[3]) is one of the most remarkable collection of indigenous hymns that has appeared on the continent of Africa and the most remarkable of its kind in South Africa.

Most of these *Izihlaɓelelo* (hymns, songs) were composed by Isaiah Shembe (further referred to as Shembe I) according to his son Johannes Galilee Shembe (further referred to as Shembe II) in the preface. The prayers in the first twenty-three pages of the book also hail from Shembe I.

The author of most of this book was born ± 1867[4], and died on the 2nd of May 1935 after standing for three hours in cold water in a river during baptism. Shembe I, the founder of the "Church of the Nazarites", the son of a farm labourer, was illiterate. He did not visit school, had no educational contact with the whites and thus developed no sense of spiritual dependence with regard to their culture.

He was a sickly child but developed into a healthy young man. As a boy he experienced several revelations. Through lightning he received his call. In a thunderstorm a *voice* told him to shun immorality (*ukuhloɓonga*)[5]);

---

[1]) Printed by W. H. Shepherd and Co. (Pty). Ltd., 527, Smith Street, Durban. The book will further be referred to as *Izihlaɓelelo*, the hymns as Isl. in sing. and Izl. in plural.

[2]) The designation iSonto lamaNazaretha is not used in the *Izihlaɓelelo*.

[3]) The edition used by the author includes Izl. written as late as 1948 (cf. Isl. 239) while the preface has been written in May 1940. This latter edition includes more hymns of Shembe II than the first. The *Izihlaɓelelo zaManazaretha* has also been published by the City Printing Works (Pty.) Ltd., Pietermaritzburg, (1948), Natal Press Ltd., in the same city; Atlas Printers, Durban, (1958); W. H. Shepherd & Co. (Pty.) Ltd., Durban (1963). Five thousand copies are usually printed at a time. The later editions omitted Isl. 220, the hymn Shembe I is supposed to have written after his resurrection.

[4]) Sundkler puts the date at 1870 (cf. Sundkler, B. G. M., Bantu Prophets in South Africa, Oxford Univ. Press, 1961[2] 110), while Dube is not so certain and puts it at pl.m. 1867. (cf. Dube, J. *uShembe*, Pietermaritzburg, 1936.)

[5]) *ukuhloɓonga*: to indulge in external sexual intercouse; limited external sexual intercouse was allowed in Zulu custom. The following dictionaries have been used in this book:
Bryant, A. T., Zulu-English dictionary, Pinetown, The Mariannhill Mission Press, 1905; *Doke*, C. M. and *Vilakazi*, B. W., Zulu-English dictionary, Johannesburg, Witwatersrand University Press, 1958[2]; *Samuelson*, R. C., The king Cetywayo Zulu dictionary, Durban, The Commercial Printing Co. 1923.

as a young man with four wives he was again admonished in a vision to cease immorality after he saw his own corpse in a rotten state[1]). Shembe I believed he saw Jehovah. When it was revealed to him during a third vision that he should leave his four wives he obeyed, although he almost committed suicide[2]). He was finally convinced of his calling when, after he was burned by lightning, Jehovah asked him in a vision "You care for your mother, do you not obey my word?" He left his mother also and refused to have the lightning burns healed by medicine as Jehovah revealed to him that he should only be healed by His word.[3]) Shembe I had thus many emotional conflicts as a young man.

According to Vilakazi his somatic type differed very little from the *isangoma* (diviner) which is different from the heavy type of the chief. He had the qualities of a seer (*oboniswayo*) and the selfassurance and personal magnetism of a diviner.[4]) He was however not a diviner. Very little is known of his contact with Christianity and the missionaries. All that is known is that he was baptized in 1906[5]) by the Rev. W. M. Leshega of the African Baptist Church and eventually ordained as a minister of this church. The Baptist Churches started their missionary activities very late in the nineteenth century in Natal. The Independent Baptist Mission entered Natal in 1892 and was assisted by the Swedish Baptists in the United States of America in order to extend its activities. The Baptist Church had only 1.18 per cent of the christian white population of South Africa in 1911[6]) when Shembe founded his movement together with a certain *Mlangeni*. Although these statistics refer only to full baptized membership it gives an indication how small this church was in South Africa. There were 4,697,152 non-white christians in 1911 in South Africa[7]). According to the census of this year 31.08 per cent of the African population *in the Cape Province* were christians; 23.15 per cent in *Transvaal*; 48.5 per cent *in the Orange Free State* and *only* 14.79 per cent *in*

---

[1]) In Isl. 29[4] he refers to this period of his life and states; "in the youth of my health you did not hate me". (*ebusheni bempilo yami awungicasukelanga*). He was a great lover of the opposite sex in his youth, an *isoka* but not an *isifebe*, which is a person who has indiscriminate relations with women. Vilakazi, *Isonto lamaNazaretha*, 32.

[2]) Dube, 21.

[3]) Sundkler, 110.

[4]) *Vilakazi, Absalom*, Isonto Lamanazaretha: The Church of the Nazarites, Hartford, Connecticut, May 1954, Diss., 37.

[5]) This was the year of the Zulu Rebellion when the Zulu Congregational Church greatly increased. cf. *Wells, J.* Stuart of Lovedale, Hodder and Stoughton, 1908, 287–299.

[6]) Official Year Book No. 9, 1926–1927, 289.

[7]) cf. *Gibson, A. G. S.* in: The East and West. A quarterly review for the study of missionary problems. Westminster, S. P. C. K., 1903–1927, Vol. XI, 389.

Natal. When Shembe founded his movement in 1911 over 85 per cent of the African population still practised their indigenous religion in Natal. Of the total African christian population in South Africa according to the same census, 40 per cent were Methodists, over 15 per cent Anglicans, nearly 11 per cent Lutherans, nearly 7 per cent Congregationalists and nearly 7 per cent Dutch Reformed. The Baptists were much less although one has to take into account that they only register full adult members. By the time Shembe was born there were about 70,000 baptized African christians in South Africa.[1]) This indicates the tremendous growth that took place before 1911 as well as the syncretistic dangers to be faced in such rapid expansion, when growth at the circumference affects christian depth in the centre. While the Baptist Church was relatively small amongst the African population, its influence was felt on the leadership of the independent movements. Pentecostalism, with its strong emotional tendencies and emphasis on "the Spirit" and faith healing gave however the greatest contribution to independentism. Shembe most probably joined the African Baptist Church because of its indigenous character, its literalism in Biblical exposition and the importance attached to baptism.

Before he became a member of the African Baptist Church he was already known as a healer. After his call he travelled by foot or oxwagon in Natal, very seldom by bus or train, keeping himself busy in driving out demons, giving people holy water as a way of healing or purification, preaching inspired by "the Spirit", and in rain making. He preached under the open skies, in kraals and alongside water pools. In 1911 he broke away from the Church fully convinced that Saturday, the Old Testament Sabbath, is the special day of Jehova and that it should be observed most meticulously, and founded the *iBandla lamaNazaretha*, claiming all verses in the Old Testament referring to Nazarites, for his movement. That antiwhite feelings were predominantly responsible for the formation of the movement is not evident from the history of the movement.

In 1913 he visited Nhlangakazi, which became their holy mountain, for the first time. Ekuphakameni, the holy city, was founded in 1914 about 18 miles from Durban. This is the very centre of the movement. Shembe I is a *Ntungwa*, a pure *Nguni* from which the Zulu nation originated.[2]) Some doubt this and maintain that Shembe, who came from the Orange Free State to Natal, is of Sotho or Tswana descent. But the preface to the

---

[1]) *Carlyle, J. E.*, South Africa and its mission field, London, James Nisbett and Co., 1878, 310.

[2]) *Bryant, A. T.*, Olden times in Zululand, London, Longmans, Green and Co., 1929, 8f.

Izihlaɓelelo states that Isaiah Shembe was the son "of Mayekisa, of Nhliziyo, of Mzazela, of Sokhaɓuzela, of Nyathikazi". The Shembes are "Ntungwa of Nhlanzi of Donsa". Shembe I was in his very being a Zulu and Vilakazi states about Shembe II that he is "deliberately and unapologetically Zulu".[1]) Shembe I hailed as poet, composer and singer, had a never failing sense of supernatural presence and lived an ascetic life and his life of celibacy had been considered to be one reason for his great spiritual strength. He interpreted the Bible in the context of the Zulu religion because much in the Bible, especially the Old Testament, resembled for him what he understood in his own society.

Shembe I is not only Mediator but is Messiah, the manifestation of God. Shembe II in a sermon stated *inter alia* that "Isaiah Shembe showed you a God who walks on feet and who heals with his hands".[2]) The listerners naturally had Shembe I in mind. To this association of the Supreme Being and Shembe I his Izl. contributed. Shembe I is to the Nazarites the personification of Supreme Power. The kingship pattern of Zulu society and its system of rank is deeply ingrained in his movement. Whether Shembe's deification is due to the frustration of that of Shaka, the national Zulu hero or not, the fact remains that he had been deified and still has divine status as other personalities in Africa, under more or less similar circumstances, had been deified. Where people consider themselves to be socially oppressed,[3]) messianism was never far removed, and where the substratum of the Zulu mind has not been changed by the christian message because it never penetrated the innermost being of the person syncretism develops, leading back to the traditional religious concepts which are now revitalized by the elements of the new. These same problems have led to the appearance of messianic figures elsewhere on the continent of Africa. Shembe II is also deified, but this has not gone so far as is the case with his father. This also is evident in the *Izihlaɓelelo*.

The leadership of the movement has become institutional. Shembe II, born 27th July 1904 in Natal, who received university training at the University College of Fort Hare and who was a teacher, took over from his father after his death in 1935. Enquiring about this type of succession the people maintained that "the old Shembe had always declared that although the old flesh might die one day, the essence of Shembe remains

---

[1]) *Vilakazi, Isonto Lamanazaretha*, 110. He adds that the movement has no particular concern for whites and Indians but is rather meant for "the children of Sendzangakhona", (Ibid. 111).

[2]) *Sundkler*, 278.

[3]) For the socio-economic difficulties the Zulu had to face especially during the first decades of this century see Sundkler, Bantu Prophets, 65 ff.

in the new flesh. In other words, he would 'cast his mantle' of power upon his son."[1]) This is actually expressed in Isl. 233[4]). Vilakazi states that the Zulu understands this "kind of talk", to them "the son is the extension of the father's personality", an idea expressed in Zulu as follows: *Ukuzala ukuzelula amathambo.*[2]) Vilakazi sees Shembe I as the mediator in the service of the Supreme Being; that the God prayed to or worshipped is the God of Shembe. According to Vilakazi this is meant when the expression *uNkulunkulu Shembe* is used.[3]) But the analysis of the Izl. proves clearly that Shembe I is more than a mere instrument in the hands of the Supreme Being, and so is his son.[4]) Through especially Shembe I revelation comes to the people and what is being revealed is his own divine will. This is no more the Supreme Being of the Zulu religion, neither that of the Christian faith. It is the Jehova of the Old Testament understood in terms of concrete revelation. To his followers Isaiah Shembe is the reincarnation of the Holy Trinity.[5]) Where the Supreme Being has come to the forefront it is difficult for the pre-christian Zulu to accept the doctrine of the Trinity understood in Biblical terms.[6]) Shembe I still remains the very essence of the existence of the community (cf. Isl. 221). They keep themselves busy with those forces nearest to them.

Of the various reasons for joining the movement the doctrine of the Black Christ is the most significant. Other reasons are: a sense of belonging is felt, ritual prohibitions satisfy the magical-oriented person, healing, the shades are honoured[7]), little inner or outer disturbance or change to become a member, indigenous liturgy, polygamists accepted[8]), those who are possessed by an evil spirit find healing; it is an act religion in which dancing, singing, hand-clapping play an important role; the atmosphere

---

[1]) *Vilakazi*, Isonto Lamanazaretha, 57.

[2]) Ibid., 72.

[3] For this same tendency amongst a Xhosa independent movement, the *iBandla lika Krestu* in which Limba, the late bishop, was referred to as *uTata* (the Father) and the Supreme Being as *uThixo ka Tata* (the Father's God), cf. *Mqotsi, L.* and *Mkele, N.* "A Separatist Church, *Ibandla lika Krestu*", African Studies, 1946, 124-5.

[4]) Sundkler relates a sermon of Shembe II who stated that his deceased father revealed himself to him, put a shirt on his body and he recovered. The crowd responded with "A-A-A-men". *Sundkler*, Bantu Prophets, 188.

[5]) cf. *Schlosser, K.*, Eingeborenenkirchen in Süd- und Südwestafrika, Kiel, Mühlau, 1958, 241.

[6]) In the context of social Zulu values it is difficult to see the Son as equal with God—the Trinity upsets these values. cf. *Vilakazi*, Isonto lamanazaretha, 28.

[7]) *Bryant, A. T.*, refers to them as the "Gods of society". cf. The Collector, No. 4. Mariannhill Press, 1913.

[8]) Shembe I rejects Paul's pronouncements on polygamy. cf. *Vilakazi*, Isonto lamanazaretha, 47.

is indigenous, women[1]) play a significant role as well as the youth, chiefs take a prominent place in the movement, nationalism found here self-expression; both holy communion and baptism received a practical meaning as purification rites. The holy city and holy mountain, the holy drum, the secret scriptures kept in Shembe I's house, festivals – all this contributes to the popularity of the movement.[2])

But it goes further than this. Shembe tried to establish a national religion for his people and he is in this sense their Moses. The African claims for himself the right to interpret the Bible as he understands it. Social cohesion could for the Zulu only be established through the shades, reacted against in the churches, but given prominence by Shembe. The *iBandla lamaNazaretha* serves in all respects the spiritual character of a large number of the Zulu people and Ekuphakameni itself has been elevated from the terrestial to the celestial. Also with regard to its organization Shembe built on old foundations.[3])

The *Izihlaɓelelo* should be considered as the Catechism of the movement and gives an insight into its theology. This book, much used during services, consists not only of prayers and hymns but also dance songs, in particular Zulu dance songs. Right at the beginning is a photo of Shembe I which is considered to have magical power. Members wear on their clothes photos of Shembe I and II.

The first eight pages of the *Izihlaɓelelo* are devoted to *Morning Prayers* which are interspersed with choruses as is the case also with the *Evening Prayers* which occupy the next six pages. The following nine pages contain *Prayers for the Sabbath* through which a clear indication is given of his interpretation of the law of which the Sabbath is central. There are many admonitions to fathers and mothers to inculcate in their children respect for their fathers (cf. Section 34, 20ff); not to take or cherish another man's girl (Section 31, 21); not to take medicine (Section 45, 22). There are many of these "thou shalt nots". Ps. 23 is put into his own words. The *Prayers for the Sabbath* are also interspersed with choruses and two Izihlaɓelelo; the last in particular refers to Nhlangakazi.

The rest of the book consists of Izl. (further referred to as *Isl.*[4]) in sing.

---

[1]) While woman outnumber men by far in most of the African churches the ratio is in this movement about 4 woman to 3 men.

[2]) The statistics differ considerably with regard to the adherents and varies from 5,000 to 80,000. Shembe II puts it at pl.m. 100,000. The figure is nearer to 80,000.

[3]) cf. *Vilakazi*, Isonto lamanazaretha, 43; *Schlosser*, 264ff.

[4]) Every mother invents for her child a lullaby called *isihlaɓelelo* which is sung for the first time again at the ear piercing ceremony and when the girl starts to menstruate. It is then sung again when her marriage takes place. The word is derived from the verb

and *Izl.* in pl.) mainly hymns. Shembe was in most cases awake when he received them. The first hymn was sung by children with whom he came to Natal in 1910, an Isl. in which the old Zulu religion and Jehovah are brought together; the second hymn came in 1913 as he started to ascend Nhlangakazi. According to the preface no hymns were composed from 1914 to 1919. But from 1920 he wrote much and started to write also the Morning, Evening and Sabbath Prayers. Shembe II states that these Izl. are to be used in church services, religious festivals and festivities.

These Izl. are remarkable when one takes into consideration the de-pressing fact that most of the hymns in the established churches are trans-lations of hymns used in the historic churches. The hymns in the so-called independent churches and independent movements are also taken over from the hymn books of which that of the American Board is the most popular, then follow in popularity the Methodists from whom Shembe has also taken hymns (cf. Isl. 185), then the Anglican and Lutheran. Vilakazi states that after P. J. Gumede and N. Luthuli's important con-tributions to the American Board Hymnbook, *Amagama okuhlaɓelela*, the influence of African composers is limited and he adds "the field of hymns seems to be dead".[1]) Vilakazi has however not taken the *Izihlaɓe-lelo* into consideration which although, not always of a high standard, reveals depth in religious experience and a true understanding of the existential situation. Shembe understands his people and their needs; his Izl. live in the Zulu situation, have to do with their anxieties, their hopes, their crises. No other Zulu had in this century such a lasting influence on the Zulu people in particular than Shembe I.

Shembe I has written Izl. 1–219 which consist of hymns, nationalistic and dance songs. Isl. 220 is supposed to have been written by Shembe I in May 1939 after rising from the dead. Vilakazi's judgment on this Isl. is

---

hlaɓelela meaning to sing or recite. These songs are considered to have in themselves magical power. The king has also his song which is supposed to bring rain and is sung at the Great Umkhosi. For magical songs e.g. to produce a storm see Callaway, H. The Religious System of the Amazulu, Cape Town, Juta and Co., 1870, 409. Dingaan spent much time in arranging new dances and composing new songs. Each sib had its *iHuɓo* (ceremonial or tribal song or hymn) which was directed to a spirit. Through singing contact is made with the supernatural and these songs are treated with very great respect by all members of the sib and are sung at very special occasions. The word *isihlaɓelelo* is also used for Psalm e.g. *Izihlaɓelelo zika David* (The Psalms of David). Another word used for singing, chanting, vocal music is *umculo* (sing. only) while *i(li)culo* (pl. *amaculo*) is used for a hymn, a chant, a song e.g. *Amaculo esonto* (church hymns), *amaculo omboloho* (jazz music). Shembe does not use *iHuɓo* or *iculo*.

[1]) *Vilakazi, B. W.* "The Conceptions and Development of poetry in Zulu", Bantu Studies, 1938, 125.

that it is not from Shembe I; this seems to be justified as it is different from
the others in style and greater depth is expected from a hymn written
after Shembe's resurrection! Such a person is expected not to be interested
in the nationalistic slogans evident in Isl. 220.[1]) A few of Shembe's Izl.
are surprisingly superficial but such superficiality is not expected after
his death. Thirty two of his 210 Izl. have choruses and they are very
effective in driving home his message. The prophet sings the verse as
precentor and the mass respond by singing the chorus. In the Izl. key
words, like *thuthuka* (increase, grow, become influential, Isl. 207[1]) are
used to drive home a specific idea. Others are mere dance songs (Isl. 182)
while in others the nationalistic element is strong (Izl. 17, 46) and becomes
stronger in the latter part of the book as will be seen in the analysis. Most
of the verses have four lines while in the same Isl. they may vary from
three to five or five to seven lines or even four to ten.

There is some confusion in the literature with regard to the number of
Izl. Shembe I is supposed to have written after his resurrection. It seems
two editions, the one later, were published, both carrying 1940 in the
preface as date. The edition used by the author includes a hymn written
as late as 1948.[2]) Sundkler ascribes Izl. 223–226 to Shembe II[3]) while
Izl. 1–222 are ascribed to Shembe I, the last three of which, according to
him, "are stated in black and white to have been written by him".[4]) But
the superscription "after his rising from the dead" is only attached to
Isl. 220 in the edition used by the author[5]) and does not refer to Izl. 221
and 222. Schlosser states that Izl. 220–222 was published after Isaiah
Shembe's death under his name after it was revealed by women in a
dream and that Izl. 223–243 are from Shembe II.[6]) In the edition used by
the author it is clearly stated in the superscription to Isl. 221 "This
Isihlaɓelelo was written by J.G. Shembe in Jan. 1938 on the mountain of
Nhlangakazi. It should be sung on the day of memory only". May 2, the
day of Shembe's death, is the day of memory and it is clear that this Isl.
has been written for this occasion.[7]) Both Isl. 221 and 222 differ in style
from those of Shembe I. The superscription to Isl. 222 written by Shembe

---

[1]) *Vilakazi*, Isonto lamanazaretha, 83.
[2]) *Schlosser*, 220, states that there are Izl. which Shembe wrote in 1945. This is true
but Isl. 233 was written in 1946; Isl. 236 in May 1946; Isl. 237 in May 1947; Isl. 239
in Jan. 1948—as also indicated in her book.
[3]) *Sundkler*, 194. The edition he uses has only 226 Izl.
[4]) *Sundkler*, 196.
[5]) See also *Vilakazi*, Isonto lamanazaretha, 82–3.
[6]) *Schlosser*, 276. Whether Schlosser follows Sundkler also in this case is not clear.
[7]) See appendix.

II states: "This hymn arrived as I was at Velaɓahleke in 1938. I had remembered a certain girl who very much wished to be converted but the parents stopped her." According to this edition *only* Isl. 220 was supposed to have been written after his resurrection.

Some of Shembe's Izl. show often real spiritual depth but everything circles later round his person which gives the later Izl. over to much superficiality especially when the nationalistic elements become stronger. Shembe II's Izl. are not without merit—in fact, they are less concentrated on his person than the later Izl. of his father. Apart from the fact that to him his father is the Supreme Being, Shembe II reveals much more Biblical understanding, for example, on sin. There is a specific christian doctrinal influence.[1]) Some of these Izl. were written not long after his fathers death. He is deeply dependent upon his father and is thus modest in his approach. It seems as if one could speak of a certain development with Isaiah Shembe on the basis of his Izl. The first section is clearer in its Scriptural reference, while the latter part is often interspersed with nationalistic and dance songs in which he refers to his supernatural birth, his call and to himself as their Liberator.

From Isl. 126 the date on which the Isl. was written is added to the superscription of no less than thirty-six of the Izl. written by Shembe I, and here a chronological order, with one exception, is followed. Isl. 126 was written on June 24, 1926, and Isl. 218, his second last, in December 1934. The continuous emphasis in this section on his person, on him as the Liberator, on Ekuphakameni, on Nhlangakazi, on the Sabbath, on the book of life, on judgment, on the nation affects the spiritual depth of many of these Izl. This is also the case with the dance songs. In spite of this, the Izl. in general carry within them deep concern and sincerity. Literalism prevails in his exposition of the Bible so that to him hell is a literal den of fire; that the name is protected only in the "book of life" to which *he only* has entrance, the Sabbath is literally the key that opens the heavenly door and he is the key holder. But Shembe is more than a papal figure on earth. Furthermore, symbol does not merely represent but brings forth that which it represents so that the sacraments, for example, do purify a person from sin.

There are strong syncretistic tendencies in the Izl.—a mixing of Zulu religion, Judaism and the Christian religion and in this syncretism the

---

[1]) Shembe II was, for example, inspired by the penitential Psalms as is evident in Isl. 234 which is quoted as having been written at Nhlangakazi on the 16th of Jan. 1945. Isl. 231 is his version of Ps. 23 quoted as having been written at Ekuphakameni in July 1945.

Zulu religion is basic. Vilakazi's judgment in this connection is worth repeating here as it expresses the very fundamental theological problem one faces in analysing the Izl. He states "Shembe modelled on the old, but brought in a considerable amount of christian elements".[1]) Schlosser states that Shembe I's religion is "an interesting mixture of redemption and legalistic religion".[2]) Here is not merely a *mixture* but here is a religion of which the old is the very basis and to which a "considerable amount" of christian elements have been added. As every religion is an organic whole, the danger is that one cannot remain standing with both feet in two religions. The one foot will be dragged over to the other. One cannot borrow a leg here, a foot there and so on. In Shembe's case it has been dragged over to the old religion of his fathers in which christian formalism plays a role i.e., literalism, legalism and the Messianic concept. Here is a Zuluized religion! Every religion has a creed, a cult and a culture, and as far as the creed is concerned no borrowing is possible for Christianity unless one wishes to establish a new religion. The cult and the culture could be taken into possession and regenerated through the work of the Holy Spirit, but the Christian creed cannot be changed. Shembe has absorbed into his world view what is adaptable to it, and he stands at the centre so that his followers maintain, "the only difference between the two men (Christ and Shembe), they say, is that one was white and the other was black".[3])

Nevertheless, the Holy Spirit has much to say to the mission and the historic churches through the Independent Movements which should be approached with the modesty that is fitting in any dialogue. The Churches have much to learn from Shembe, and the sooner the superior and superficial attitude is discarded and a serious study made of the church's own mistakes and theological superficialities, a dialogue will be possible even with the independent movements.

---

[1]) *Vilakazi, Isonto lamanazaretha*, 95. Vilakazi rightly criticizes Sundkler for his emphasis on the *isangoma* (diviner) as he is of the opinion that Sundkler gives the impression that the diviner is a leader of a religious cult and that every leader of an independent movement is a diviner. Important however is the way in which Vilakazi contradicts himself when he states: "To us, it looks like an example of the contemptuous attitude taken by the missionaries towards the separatist churches, and their desire to prove that they are not christian but pagan". cf. Isonto Lamanazaretha, appendix.

[2]) *Schlosser*, 240.

[3]) *Vilakazi*, Isonto Lamanazaretha, 90.

CHAPTER ONE

THE SUPREME BEING

Different names are used in the *Izihlaɓelelo* for the Supreme Being. These represent both Zulu terms, *uThixo* which is a loan word, and one which is only used in the Bible translations, namely, Jehova.

1. *uMvelingqangi*

Shembe uses this designation for the Supreme Being only once namely in Isl. 93[4]:

Siyakuɓonga Mvelingqangi.	We are praising you *uMvelingqangi*
Siyakuɓonga Nkosi yethu.	We are praising you our *Nkosi*.
Siyakuɓonga chibi* elihle	We are praising you the beautiful lake
Lokugeza izono zethu.	It washes away our sins.

* chibi, (i(li)chibi, amachibi, pl.) n. i. Large strech of water, pond, vlei, dam, lake. ii. Multitude. The reference here is to water.
(The translations are literal as far as possible)

Every religion has to do with myth and the best solution for the enigma of mythology lies in the etymological explanation of the names for Gods and heroes[1]). *uMvelingqangi* has mythical and not cultic significance and is a word by which Shembe I is also designated.[2])

This word could be broken up into *three* component parts namely 1. *Umveli* which is derived from *ukuvela* with the following meanings: a. Come forth, appear, come into view; b. Originate, come from and c. Gain distinction, stand out, be prominent; 2. *ngqa*, the nunnated form of *qa* which is used with *qala* mostly to express the superlative means a first sight, rare occurrence, beginning, commencement and 3. *ngi* is the first person singular.[4])

---

[1]) cf. Siecke, E., Max Müllers mythologisches Testament, Archiv für Religionswissenschaft, 1902, 108.

[2]) cf. Sundkler, Bantu Prophets, 286.

[3]) cf. Doke, C. M. & Vilakazi, B. W.: Zulu—English Dictionary, Johannesbury, Witwatersrand University Press, 1958, 832. *ngangi* obs. rt. of priority; *unqangi*: First born of twins. *uMvelingqangi*: Creator, the first being.

[4]) Wanger, W. "The Zulu notion of God", Anthropos, XXI, 1926, 353.

In its adverbial use the word means the *first* before *All*. According to
some of Gallaway's informants *uMvelignqangi* was even before the origin
(*uHlanga*) and out of *uHlanga* came *uNkulunkulu* and his wife.[1]) *uMvelingqangi* expresses *priority* and is considered to be the Creator.[2]) It is
amongst the non-christian folk that *uMvelingqangi* is mostly used for
Creator even today.

This name has not been used in the Bible translations and is surprisingly non-existent in Genesis 1. A closer analysis of Isl. 93 reveals that
uMvelingqangi is especially related to the Nazarite purification rite and
thus used in a broader context than creation, namely, also with man's *re*-
creation. The pre-christian Zulu could call upon *uMvelingqangi* without
the help of intermediaries which is not the case with *uNkulunkulu*.[3]) In
Isl. 93, which is a praise song, Shembe restores a Zulu designation for God
which the missions have neglected. This is grasping back to the beginning,
the source of Zulu mythology, i.e., to the Creator-god. This also means the
exclusion of Jesus Christ as the old purification rites are restored through
uMvelingqangi. He associates *uMvelingqangi* with himself as he has
brought the whole creation myth, which states that man came out of
uHlanga, a bed of reeds, with Ekuphakameni. This is clear from Isl 34.

Kunjaloke namhlanje	It is so today
Emagqumeni as'Ohlange	On the hillocks of *uHlanga*

uHlanga, intrinsically associated with *uMvelingqangi*, has also been
used as a designation for the Supreme Being but is mainly utilised for the
potential source of being, a bed of reeds, from which the first Zulu was
broken off.[4]) *uMvelingqangi* has created this bed of reeds and this whole
myth had been given historical value in Shembe's mind via the Biblical
history of creation and re-creation and transferred to Natal and the
20th century.

2. *uNkulunkulu*

This designation for the Supreme Being is first used in the prayers.

---

[1]) Callaway, H. The Religious System of the Amazulu, Cape Town, Juta and Co,
1870, 7, 44.

[2]) "Als der allererste aber und deshalb einzigartige, über den hinaus niemand gewusst
wird, noch genannt werden kann, von dem sie alle kommen und neben dem kein
Gleicher steht, heisst er nicht *uNkulunkulu*, sondern *Umvelinqangi* oder der Erste".Asmus
Gustav, Die Zulu, Essener Verlagsanstalt, 1939, 21. cf. Samuelson, R.C.A., The King
Cetywayo, Zulu Dictionary, Durban, The Commercial Printing Co, 1923, 287.

[3]) cf. Asmus, 33.

[4]) Callaway, op. cit. 7.

He begins with those terms which every Zulu would fully understand. He nevertheless uses it only a few times in the Izl. while Shembe II did not use it at all in his Izl. It is impossible to enter here on the problem whether this designation refers to the Great-great-One or to the first ancestor. Unkulunkulu is in any case lawgiver, associated with the ritual prohibitions.

Shembe repeats about a dozen times four lines in the prayers what he calls *Isilandelo sebandla* which literally means "Response of the Congregation". (cf. Morning Prayers, Section 2, 1)

Nkulunkulu[1]) *onamandla onke,*	Almighty *Nkulunkulu* (lit. *Nkulunkulu* with all power)
Yise wabobonke abamkhonzayo,	Father of them all who worship him
Busisa ukuvuka kwethu kwanamhlanje,	Bless our waking up of today
Usigcine ngomsa wakho[2]). *Amen.*	Keep us with thy kindness. Amen.

These lines are not repeated in the "Prayers for the Sabbath" where he uses mainly the name of Jehova. He nevertheless states that "*uNkulunkulu* loves them who observe the Sabbath". ("*uNkulunkulu uyabathanda abagcina iSabatha*"). (Prayers for the Sabbath, section 27, 19.) *uNkulunkulu* is deeply concerned with the law e.g. he wishes them to honour their parents. (cf. Isifundo, Section 34, 20; also Section 35, 21.) Shembe I did not reject the name *uNkulunkulu* as his followers did according to Sundkler, but states in the "Evening Prayers", (Section 33, that

Mina ngiphaphame ngikukhonze	I woke up, I served
Wena Nkulunkulu Thixo wethu	You *uNkulunkulu Thixo* of us.

The naturalised designation *uThixo*, also used in the Bible, now describes *uNkulunkulu*, a designation for the Supreme Being used by christians and non-christians. *uNkulunkulu* has two main characteristics in the *Prayers*: he is *powerful* and he is *lawgiver*.

Only very late in the *Izl.* is this name found and then in the sense of the *Great* and *All Powerful One* as seen in Isl. 89[4]:

---

[1]) Vilakazi rejects Sundkler's statement that *uNkulunkulu* is a high god. He states he is an Urancestor. cf. Vilakazi, A. *Isonto Lamanazaretha*; The Church of the Nazarites, Diss. Hartford Seminary Foundation, U.S.A. unpubl.

[2]) The heading to these prayers states:
Imini mayibenhle kwabangcwele   Let the day be good for the saints.

Aluɓe kuwe udumo* lwakho   Let thy fame be with you
Emhlaɓeni nasezulwini,   On earth and in heaven;
Kuma ɓandla** onke akho   The hosts all thine,
Kuwe ɓaɓa Nkulunkulu.   Thine, ɓaɓa Nkulunkulu.

* -dumo (u(lu)dumo, izindumo, pl.) i. Fame, renown, notoreity; ii. Crowd of people or animals (esp. when rushing).
** ɓandla (iliɓandla, amaɓandla) i. Assembly of men, ii. Congregation, company of believers, church, denomination. It is here better translated *hosts*.

In this Isl. they ask their *Nkosi* to stay with them. (*Hlala nathi Nkosi yethu*: Stay with us our *Nkosi*, verse 1) and *ɓaɓa Nkulunkulu* is here used so that it could also refer to Shembe I. This is clearer in Isl. 93[5]:

Siyakuɓonga Manueli   We are praising you Immanuel
Siyakuɓonga Nkulunkulu   We are praising you *Nkulunkulu*

Immanuel (God with us) is the term Shembe applies to himself and the distant *uNkulunkulu* of the Zulu religion is now one with them. He is specially related to the Zulu *nation*, cf. Isl. 111:

3. *Ungasiliɓali isizwe sakho*   Do not forget your nation
   Nkulunkulu wethu ...   Our *Nkulunkulu* ...
4. *Sikhumɓule isizwe sakho*   Remember your nation
   Nkululunkulu wethu;   our *Nkulunkulu*
   Indlu ka Sendzangakhona[1])   House of *Sendzangakhona*
   Nkulunkulu wethu.   Our *Nkulunkulu*.

The restoration of the Zulu nation is Shembe's aim. The emphasis on "our *uNkulunkulu*" is a direct reference to Shembe himself. *uNkulunkulu*, the traditional term for the Supreme Being interested in his progeny but distantly removed, is brought amongst them and is now *Immanuel*. Shembe I who made an attempt to restore the self-respect of the Zulu nation, also against the missions which divided the nation into different denominations opposing one another, is now hailed as the *uNkulunkulu* of the nation. As the essence of the father is in the son, so *uNkulunkulu* is in Shembe I. He is the one who honours the Zulu tradition.

True to Zulu tradition *uNkulunkulu* is not described as the one who

---

[1]) Sendzagakhona is the father of Dingaan, Mpanda and Shaka. cf. Bryant, A. T., Olden times in Zululand and Natal, Longmans, Green Co, 1929, 45 ff. Shembe stresses in Isl. 199[1] the unity that should exist amongst them, that the children of *uNkulunkulu* love one another:
Bangeke ɓahlukane   They will never part from one another
Futhi ɓangeke ɓaxaɓane   moreover, they will never quarrel among
                                   themselves.

created the world. He is the first outcomer. Shembe I is also honoured as
Creator so that the question arises: Who is the Creator? when he states
in Isl. 114[1]:

Wangidala Nkulunkulu	You created me, *Nkulunkulu*
Thixo Nkosi yamakhosi	*Thixo*, the *Nkosi* of the *amakhosi*.

uNkulunkulu is honoured as the only shepherd (*umalusi nguwe kuphela*,
Isl. 123[3]); he is the one they worship (Isl. 137[3]) and so the invitation
comes in Isl. 163[1]:

Sondelani ɓantu nonke	Come near all ye people
KuNkulunkulu[1]	To Nkulunkulu

In his later Izl. this designation is not found and Shembe II does not
use it at all in his Izl. *uNkulunkulu* is often circumscribed by authors as
the creator of the world but nowhere is this stated in Zulu mythology[2]).
He is the Creator (rather "beginner", the first outcomer) of man and
animals. Shembe is the *uNkulunkulu* of the restored Zulu nation. In their
midst they have Shembe who claims he came on the clouds. Why did
Shembe I not use this name in his later Izl.? The fact that the missionaries
used *uNkulunkulu* seems not to be a full explanation of what happened.
Was it due to the fact that *uNkulunkulu* was considered to be the first
Adam rather than the Supreme Being in Biblical sense? Is it because of
the association Jehova→Moses→Law?! "*uNkulunkulu* was not worshipped by the Zulus maintaining that he died so long ago that no one knows
his praises."[3]) Each clan rather worships its own *uNkulunkulu* than the
distant one. *uNkulunkulu* as a name for God, has been pushed into the
background and both Shembe I and II used *Baɓa* which appeals much
more to a closely knit community.

3. *uThixo*

Neither Krige nor Asmus mention this designation for God among

---

[1]) Sundkler's contention that the black Christ is not at all identified with *uNkulunkulu*
or *uThixo* is not applicable to the Izl. of Shembe I. (cf. Bantu prophets, 286.)

[2]) Three different translations at the author's disposal state in precisely the same
manner, while they often differ elsewhere: *Ekuqaleni uNkulunkulu wadala izulu nomhlaɓa* (In the beginning *uNkulunkulu* created the heaven and the earth. Gen 1[1]). Bleek
states "The Great-great-one came out of the earth beneath". cf. Bleek, Wm. H. I. (ed.
Engelbrecht I. A.) Zulu Legends, Pretoria, J. L. van Schaik, Ltd., 1952, 1. cf. Callaway,
op. cit. 1–2 *Unkulunkulu* is no longer known. It is he who was the first man... we do
not know his wife...".

[3]) Krige, 281.

the Zulu. Nor is it found in Bleek's Zulu legends which he gathered about 1855. Callaway refers to *uTikxo* as a name for Supreme Being adopted by the early missionaries from the Xhosas who, in their turn, borrowed it from the Hottentots.[1]) Doke and Vilakazi state that it is probably "derived from the Cape Hottentot *Tixwa* or *Tiqwa*, found also as *Tsui - oap* in Nama."[2])

Shembe I uses this designation about twice as many times in his Izl. as he uses *uNkulunkulu* and Shembe II refers to his father as *uThixo*. In the "Evening Prayers" (Section 17, 11) Shembe I states that "Jehova is your *uThixo*, your *uNkulunkulu*" ("*uJehova uThixo wakho, uNkulunkulu wakho*"). He explains here as it were to the non-christians that the Jehova of Scripture is the same as *uThixo* and *uNkulunkulu*, with whom they are familiar. *uThixo* is also used to emphasize the authority and acceptance of *uNkulunkulu* as "our *uThixo*"[3]) (*Thixo wethu*, Evening Prayers, Section 23, 12; see also Section 34, 14). In the "Prayers for the Sabbath'" *uThixo* is only used in conjunction with Jehova.

In Isl. 18[1] the heroes of *uThixo* are described as the selected ones. ("*Amaqhawe Ka Thixo ayazikhethela*".); a person is carried by *uThixo* (*uzoɓelethwa ngu Thixo* lit. carried on the back as a Zulu woman carried her child, Isl. 18[4]); *uThixo* is described as *uMkhululi* (Liberator Isl. 19[1]); in Isl. 21[2,3] the *uMkhululi* is the *Thixo Ka* (of) *Adam* and the *Thixo Ka* (of) *Abraham*. Shembe's position is thus higher than merely an *uNkulunkulu* or Adam or Abraham but as Liberator he is *uThixo*. In Isl. 66[5], referring to *uThixo*, and using the name again in conjunction with *uMkhululi*, he states:

Akakho uɓaɓa emhlaɓeni onothando	There is no other father on earth with love
Olunjengo lwakho.	equal to thine.

The association of *Thixo* with *uMkhululi* is also evident in Isl. 81 where *Thixo* is described as the *almighty one*. In Isl. 27[1] he was described as the *one with hope*. (*Thixo ulithemba lethu*, Thixo is our hope.); he is the sheep of *uThixo* (Isl. 123[1]), *uThixo* is their sun (Isl. 179[1])[4]); what appeals is that

---

[1]) Callaway, 105.

[2]) Doke & Vilakazi, 797. The acceptance of this name in Zulu Bible translations created much controversy. cf. Wanger, W. 667 ff. How speculation played its part with regard to names for God is clearly brought out by Colenso who stated that the unfamiliar "mean and meaningless name *uTixo*" should be replaced by *uDio* because it is near to the Greek and Latin names for God!

[3]) See also Isl. 111[1].

[4]) The word *ilanga* (sun) is often used by the Zulu in connection with the Supreme Being.

their *uThixo* does not select a *few* but *pities all*. Shembe I hails from a church in which the emphasis on the selected few prevailed while he was faced with the Zulu disposition that the whole tribe as tribe was the concern of them all. He states in Is. 151[5]:

uThixo yena akakhethi muntu*	*Thixo* himself does not choose anybody
Uyaɓahawukela ɓonke.	He pities them all.

* Khethi<khetha<Ur.B—Keta i. choose, pick out, select. ii. pick out from, take out, exclude, separate from, differentiate.

Here again the development into the Messianic figure is clear. He is *uThixo* and in him is the salvation of the world, cf. Isl. 159[5]:

Siyakuɓonga weNkosi yethu	We are praising you our *Nkosi*
Thixo was' Ekuphakameni,	*Thixo of Ekuphakameni,*
Bonganini wemaɓandla*	Utter praises ye hosts
Awahleli kweliphezulu	Who are staying up above
Nazo izixuku zalomhlaɓa	and the crowds of this earth
Seziyongena kweliphezulu.	they shall now enter above.

* *ijonga* i. Praise; ii. Give thanks; iii. worship, offer sacrifices to (*ukujonga amadlozi*, to worship the spirits).

Shembe I, the Messiah of the world, the manifestation of the Supreme Being, stands in full control of the eternal destiny of men. In the centre of the Zulu nation he stands calling all the descendants of *Shaka* (who already heard!) and the *Mabaca* to come. cf. Isl. 178[4]:

NguThixo yedwa	It is *Thixo* alone
Ongahlanganisa lezo zizwe	Who can cause those nations to come together
Wozani Mabaca	Come ye *Mabaca*
Nilizwe izwi lakhe.	(So that) you may hear his word.

Shembe II designates his father as *uThixo*, cf. Isl. 229[5] [1]):

Uyi ngcwele wena Thixo,	You are holy, you uThixo
Mawuɓongwe njalo.*	Let you be praised in such a manner.
Umusa wakho awupheli	Your kindness is without end
Kuɓo aɓantu ɓakho.	to them your people.

* Schlosser's translation "Man lobe dich immer" (345) does not give the correct meaning.

---

[1]) cf. Isl. 234[1]; 239[1,2].

To *Ekuphakameni* he refers as the house of *uThixo* (*wena uyindlu Ka Thixo*, Isl. 237².) and about the feasts his father introduced he states in Isl. 240³:

Amadili* akho Thixo	Your feasts *uThixo*
Angumoya omuhle	they are good *umoya*.

* -dili (i(li)dili, amadili) i. Large gathering of people; abundance of food; ii. Feast, festival; large dinner party. Schlosser's translation reads:
Deine Feste, Gott,
Sind gute Geister (= Menschen).   This is not true to the original.

Then again he addresses his father as son of *uThixo* (*ndodana Ka Thixo*, Isl. 241¹.) thanking him *as uThixo* in Isl. 242¹.

uThixo is used by Shembe I mainly in the sense of Liberator and in this strain Shembe II speaks about his father as *uThixo*.

4. *umDali* (sing. only). *The Creator*<*dala*: *create, cause, conceive*

The Zulu speaks about *umDali welizwe* or *wezwe*, the Creator of the earth or world; the one who in one version of the chameleon and lizard "created heaven and earth" (*wadala izulu nomhlaɓa*).[1] Shembe is not interested in Cosmology. His interest is in the darkness that disappears from the face of the earth (Isl. 51²); that lamentation will stop on it (Ibid, verse³); that the news has to be sent in all the earth (Isl. 53¹.); that Baɓa's will may be done on earth as it is in heaven (Isl. 58²), and Shembe II states that heaven and earth praise him who is above (Nguye o Phezulu, Isl. 229⁶.) which refers to the hosts praising his father.

Shembe I, who has elevated *Ekuphakameni* to heaven on earth and who calls people to *this* heaven, is not interested in the creation of the earth. In Isl. 57¹ he has only *Ekuphakameni* in mind:

Sifuna indlela	We want the way
Yokuya ekhaya	which goes to the home
Ku Jehova Inkosi yethu	to Jehova, our *iNkosi*,
Umdali wezulu.	the Creator of heaven.

Shembe sometimes reveals Manicheistic tendencies, but he does not draw this to its extreme as he states in Isl. 73¹ that he believes in the Father, Creator of heaven *and* earth. Shembe I is considered by his followers to be Creator also and in Isl. 57¹ they find enough evidence for this supposition. In Isl. 225¹ Shembe II states Jehova has created him. The question

---

[1] cf. Wanger, 354.

is: Who is Jehova here? Shembe II keeps himself busy with his father in Isl. 234[5]:

Makuɓe iphunga elimnandi	Let it be a pleasant scent
Kuwe wedwa ongu Mdali	to you alone who is the Creator.

The omission of the name of uNkulunkulu where they specifically speak about creation is interesting.

5. *Simakade*

This significant term in the *Izihlaɓelelo*, which is not used in the *Prayers*, but twice as many times as *uNkulunkulu* in the Izl. takes Shembe's followers right back to the Zulu royal ancestry and is thus of special significance in the context of the movement. *Simakade* lit. means "he who is standing firmly stationary from ever". *Isimakade* (< - ma+ kade, lit. "what *stands* long ago") is thus an ancient being or thing. A common appellation of the Zulu King was *Isimakade sezwe*, the ancient of the land. When this term is used in the Izl. one continuously asks: Does it refer to Shembe or the Supreme Being? It will be more correct to maintain that it refers to Shembe I, the manifestation of the Supreme Being. cf. Isl. 50:

1. *Bonani uvela emafini*	Look he is coming from the clouds
uzoɓiza aɓantu ɓonke	he will call all people
2. *Amaqhawe ngaka Jesu*	The heroes *belong to* Jesus
Anhliziyonye naye,	they are one heart with him
Amehlo aɓo ayizinti	Their eyes are wide open
Ngokubeku Simakade...	through seeing Simakade...

In this Isl. Shembe I keeps himself busy with his own coming to this earth when the stars fell (verse 3); the dead came out of the graves (verse 4), the nations will appear before him their conqueror, even Satan will eventually appear before him (verse 5), they will burn in fire (verse 6) and then he concludes in verse 7 as follows:

Jaɓulani nina ɓantaɓami	Rejoice ye my children
Uyokusho njalo kwaɓanye	So he will say to others
Shiyanini umhlaɓa	Leave ye the earth
Wozanini Ekuphakameni.	Come ye to *Ekuphakameni.*

They are made to sing that *Simakade* is their *hope*, the hope of their *souls* and the "father of light". (*SoKhanyiso*, Isl. 15[1].); the heaven (the earth as such is not mentioned but the mountains, hills and fountains)

the sun and the moon praise *Simakade* Isl. 110,[1]) the stars of heaven kneel
down on their knees before him (*guqa ngamadolo* verse[2]) [2]) and say
according to verse 3:

Zithi uyingcwele   They say: you are holy
wena Simakade.   You *Simakade.*

In Isl. 158[1] *Simakade* is described as the one who brings rain and
associated with *Jehova*; a *voice* was heard, the word came with the
messengers, the trumpet sounded and the earth quaked as in so many
instances (Ibid. 2–4). *Simakade* is now the central figure at *Ekuphakameni*
cf. Isl. 164[4] [3]):

Ilanga nenyanga   The sun and the moon
Alikhanyi khona,   it does not shine there,
USimakade kuphea   it is *Simakade* only
*Ilanga lakhona**.   the sun of there.

    * This Isl. is composed for those who go to *Ekuphakameni.*

Simakade rejoices as a result of the resurrection of the dead. The Zulu
finds it difficult to accept the passivity of souls. The crowds that pass via
Simakade "enter up above" and do not stay in the grave. cf. Isl. 159.

4. *Wajabula uSimakade*   He rejoiced, *Simakade*
Ngokuvulwa kwamathuna,   As a result of the opening of the
....   graves
....
5. *Nazo izixuku zalomhlaba*   And they the crowds of the earth
Seziyongena kweliphezulu.   they will now enter up above.

When he uses the name *Simakade* in Isl. 200[1] in connection with the
Sabbath the reference is obviously to the Supreme Being. Shembe's intimate association with the deity, and himself being divine, makes it difficult
to discern when he speaks about himself and when about the Supreme
Being. But when Shembe II uses this name one is not in doubt as to whom
it refers. cf. Isl. 221[3]:[4])

---

    [1]) cf. Isl. 187[3,4] Simakade is often brought in association with *nature*.
    [2]) His followers knelt before Shembe I as they still do in the case of Shembe II.
    [3]) All those in trouble are invited to him at *Ekuphakameni*. Isl. 15[5].
    [4]) The superscription to this Isl. reads: "This Isl. was written by J. G. Shembe in
Jan. 1938 on the mountain of *Nhlangakazi*. It should be sung on the day of memory
only." Shembe I died on May 2, 1935 and one of the important days for the movement
is this date which is observed in memory of their founder.

Wena muzi okhethiweyo,   You the city that is chosen
Wase Mikhayideni*   of *Mikhayideni*
Ma wu hloɓe ngeziqhama   Let it dress up with blankets
Umsinele uSimakade.[1])   let it dance for *uSimakade*
U yi Nkosi yamakhosi,   He is the *iNkosi* of the *amakhosi*
Wena Mkhululi wami.   You my *uMkhululi.*

* It may refer to Micah, a book which takes a prominent place with independentists (cf. Micah 4[13]).

Shembe I has been elevated by his son to the "*iNkosi* of the *amakhosi*", an expression used in Scripture; in this case filled with the contents of the Zulu religion in which the *amakhosi* (royal ancestors) play a prominent role. This Isl. in memory to Shembe I ,or *Simakade*, gives a convincing insight into the canonisation of Shembe I and their dependence on him as seen in verse 6.

Nkosi yamazulu nomhlaɓa   *Nkosi* of the heavens and earth
Masinyane uzongiɓiza;   Soon you will call me;
Ungaɓaliɓali aɓantu ɓakho   Do not forget your people
AmaNazaretha ayingcwele.   the holy Nazarites.
Ngu mthandazo way' iNkosi   It is the prayer of the *iNkosi*
Nxa ishiya lomhlaɓa.   when he left this earth.

For the complete dependence on his father as *Simakade* see Isl. 233[3,5]. He uses this term in his very last Isl. stating: cf. Isl. 243[1]:

Nkosi yethu Simakade,   *Nkosi of us, Simakade,*
Simi phambi kwakho;   We stand before you;
Siyacela uɓekhona   We are asking that you be present
Nawe kanye nathi.   Even you with us.

6. Guqaɓadele

This Zulu praise name for the Supreme Being, which Shembe I applies to himself, had been explained in various ways.

Bryant held that it is of christian origin, a praise name for the Supreme Being on account of his answering prayers for rain and he gives the literal meaning as "he to whom one kneels and get his heart desire".[2]) Callaway

---

[1]) Dancing for *Simakade* is also referred to in Isl. 182.

[2]) Bryant, Zulu-English dictionary, 753–4. A big chief was approached on one's knees (*ukuguqa*), they crawled to him, while for a prophet they *guqa* (Kneel down).

gives the word as *ukugqaɓadela*[1]) while Doke and Vilakazi give the
derivation of the word from *guqa* and *ɓadele* lit. "he who stoops and they
are satisfied", a praise name also for *Cetshwayo*, the Zulu king.[2]) Callaway
states that kneeling, for the Zulu, is a sign of strength "if a man wishes to
make himself very firm, and avail himself of all his strength: he kneels,...".[3]
Wanger states in connection with this name that "if one wishes to
throw his spear with all his might, he, in the very act of throwing it, goes
down on his right knee to give himself a firm support".[4]) This is one of
the traditional titles used by the *aɓafana* ir *aɓelusi ɓezulu* (sons or herdsmen of heaven),[5]) the lightning magicians who contact directly, and not
via the ancestors, the *Inkosi ephezulu*, considered by some to be the high
god of the Zulus.[6])

In Isl. 124 Shembe I describes how people go to *Ekuphakameni* to be
blessed and in the *chorus* they are made to sing:

Ngiyahamɓa we Guqaɓadele	I am going, oh, *Guqaɓadele*
Ngaloluhambo lwakho;	by this journey of yours;
Yelula isandla sakho	Stretch out your hand
Uluɓusise uhambo lwami.	and bless my journey.

In Isl. 93[2] he states:

Siyakuɓonga Guqaɓadele,	We are praising you *Guqaɓadele*
Siyakuɓonga Nkosi yethu.	We are praising you our *Nkosi*.

He is thus the one before whom they kneel, yes, even the stars of
heaven. (Isl. 115[2].).

Both *Simakade* and *Guqaɓadele* are not used in the Bible translations.

7. *Yise: Uyise*

This name used by Shembe I for the Supreme Being could have the
following meanings:

i. His/her or their father;

ii. One who bears the same clan name (*isiɓongo*) as his/her father

---

[1]) Callaway, 121.
[2]) Doke and Vilakazi, 278.
[3]) Callaway, 121.
[4]) Wanger, 379.
[5]) Ibid.
[6]) cf. W. M. Eiselen–I. Schapera, "Religious Beliefs and Practices" in Schapera (ed.)
The Bantu-speaking tribes of South Africa, London, George Routledge and Sons,
1937, 263. See also Krige, 282.

namely his/her father's brother, the son of his/her *father's father's* brother
i.e. their guardian.

   iii. Term used out of respect for somebody of the age of his/her father;
   iv. Any sister or half-sister of father i.e. paternal aunt.

This term is not a specific Zulu designation for the Supreme Being and
where it does carry the meaning of "Father" in the Izl. it is a much broader
term than the Christian designation "Father", e.g., as used in the Apostolicum.[1]) When he states in his *Isifundo* that a person should honour
(*hlonipha:*) his/her *uyise*[2]) this should be taken into account.

Only Shembe I uses it. He utilises it in both instances where he gives
their confession of faith namely Izl. 73[1] and 154[1]

73	154
1. *Ngiyakholwa ku Yise*	1. *Ngiyakholwa Kuyise*
Onamandla onke,	*Nakumoya oyingcwele.*
Kumdali wezulu nomhlaɓa	
Nakumoya oyingcwele.	
1. I believe in the Father	1. I believe in the Father
who is with all power,	and in the holy *umoya.*
in the Creator of heaven and earth	
And in the holy *umoya.*	

The circumscription of *Yise* in Isl. 73 as almighty and as Creator of heaven and earth is not found in Isl. 154 of which Sundkler maintains that it
gives the *summa fidei* and *credo* of the Nazarites.[3]) In Isl. 19[1-4] he speaks
about *uyise wamakholwa* (Father of the believers) referring to *Thixo
uMkhululi. Yise* is thus Creator and Father of the believers; the head of
the Nazarite family, a term which emphasizes blood relationship and
which Shembe I again uses to describe also himself. Those which come
to *iNkosi*, small and big remember him and then he adds in Isl. 64[4]:

Weyise wezintandane	Oh! Father of the orphans
Siseɓusweni ɓakho	We are before your face.
Sikhumbule usesule	Remember us and wipe us now
Lezo zinyembezi.	Those tears.

---

   [1]) The term "Father" does not refer to one family only but to a cluster of families.
This "Father" is not *exclusive* but *inclusive*: Shembe continually states that the
Supreme Being at *Ekuphakameni* is not selective.
   [2]) cf. Prayers for the Sabbath, Sections 34–36, 20, 21.
   [3]) Sundkler, Bantu Prophets, 283.

8. *uBaba*

Ur. B. *Vava* meaning to *protect*.

i. My or our father used without the possessive pronoun;

ii. One who bears the same *isibongo* as my father i.e. my father's brother, the son of my father's brother, the son of my *father's father's* brother;

iii. One of the same relative age as my father;

iv. My paternal aunt;

v. Used out of respect to a chief or a person of consequence; also by a servant to his master; or by a woman when courteously (in *hlonipha* language, i.e., in reverence and respect) addressing a man or a person who is so kind to another as to be like a father;

vi. The sense of protection is part of the significance of this word. The Zulu often uses it with regard to his superiors and to those he thanks.[1]

vii. It is used with differentiating adjectives: *uBaba omkhulu* a. my father's eldest brother; b. my grandfather (paternal and maternal) i.e. *Babamkhulu*. This term is also applied to the brothers of my grandfathers and grandmothers.

When Shembe I uses the word *Baba* it has, as *Yise*, a much broader connotation than "my father" in the western sense. Shembe uses it in two senses: 1. For earthly people; 2. For the Supreme Being as in the Zulu Bible translations. (cf. John 17[5].)

When he refers to the Zulu royal house he speaks of *uBaba bethu* ("our fathers" cf. Prayers for the Sabbath, Section 21, 19). In Isl. 1 *uBaba* may also refer to Shembe who wandered about and had no place of refuge until he discovered *Nhlangakazi*. (Izl. 1[1-7], cf. 3[3]). In Isl. 68 Jehova, *Baba* and the *amakhosi* (royal ancestor spirits) are mentioned together. Jehova has saved the Nazarites from their enemies (verse 2); through the powerful *amakhosi* (verse 3); they wandered in the wilderness (verse 4), they have been payed for on the mountain of *Nhlangakazi* (verse 6) who has changed their slavery (*bugqili*) to a lordly state (*ubukhosi*, verse 8).[2] *Baba* stands here for the Zulu ancestry and its supernatural authorities. Izl. 1 and 68 should be read in conjunction with one another.

Baba is the one who takes a deep interest *in his own*. They approach him with their tears and depart with satisfaction (Isl. 15[4]); he stands with all his sin before *Baba* of heaven (*baba osezulwini*, Isl. 26[3]); the singer

---

[1] The younger diviners and novices call the diviner who initiated them, whether man or woman, *uBaba. Sundkler*, Bantu Prophets, 352.

[2] The text incorrectly has *uKukhosi*.

states he is not like *Baba* i.e. in holiness (Isl. 32¹). Gradually Shembe I applies this designation to himself when he describes *Baba* as "our *uNkulunkulu*" (*Nkulunkulu wethu*, Isl. 32³.). Just as each tribe had its own name for God, so the Nazarites have their own. To be like *Baba*, "our *uNkulunkulu*", is a Christian and not a Zulu influence.

It is again difficult to discern whether Shembe refers to himself or to *Baba* as the Supreme Being. His intimate association with the super-natural world has *not only changed himself but also the image of the Supreme Being*. Because Shembe I is the only effective mediator and in intimate contact with the supernatural world, God has become his God and he himself the *image* of God, but this image is God himself. When he speaks of "Our *Baba* who is in heaven" (*Baba wethu osezulwini*, Isl. 35¹)¹) one is not sure whether he addresses Shembe in *Ekuphakameni* or *Baba* in heaven. *Ekuphakameni* is heaven. One has always to take into considera-tion his theological position based on realized eschatology and when he maintains that *Baba's* heaven is not in need of the sun (Isl. 27²), the moon (verse 3) nor of light (verse 4), he has *Ekuphakameni* and himself in mind. The theme of this Isl. is that of the Nazarite theological position namely (cf. 47¹):

Ezulwini lakho Baba	In thy heaven *Baba*
kuya khanya impela.	it is light indeed.

Shembe is the true light of this city and thus of the world (cf. John 1⁹); he is the *Baba* who is requested to give a love for him that is complete (Isl. 47⁴). The Supreme Being is no more loaded with mystery, far away and unpredictable. He has come near and Shembe is his manifestation. The secrets of heaven are theirs. They have now a deeper understanding of their own past which has been put into the framework of salvation history. It has become dynamic. This world is no more hidden and obscure but every thing has fallen into place. *Baba* reigns and Jesus him-self went to him as he stated: "Now I go to *Baba*" (*Sengiya kubaba*, Isl. 61³). But Shembe is here. *Baba* saves and gives courage (Isl. 67⁵).

In a large number of Izl. that follow, the designation *Baba* does not appear. iNkosi is now in the forefront with the occasional appearance of *Thixo* and Jehova. In Isl. 96 chorus *Nkosi Baba* is asked to pity his *umoya*, his name is beautiful in the face of the holy *Baba* (Isl. 125⁵). These Izl. are composed to be sung by his followers and through the sacred hymns they address the one who has become for them a supernatural being. With

¹) cf. Matth. 6⁹.

him are "the fruits of righteousness" (*Izithelo zokulunga*, Isl. 179⁴).
Shembe I as *Baba* is nowhere so clearly revealed as in Isl. 201 where he is
pictured as being in charge of the *Book of Life*. cf. verse 4.

Ngigeze wena Baba,	Wash me, you *Baba,*
Ngihlandzeke ngokwenene;	may I be cleansed truly;
Lime ngawe igama lami	that my name stand through you
*Encwadini yokuphila.*¹)	in the Book of Life.

Shembe II uses the term *Baba* only in connection with his father.
cf. 221¹¹.

Baba wami ongithandayo	My *Baba* who loves me
Uze ungikhumbule,	May you remember me
Mina ngane yakho encane	Me your small child
Ngisasele emhlabeni.	I am *still* remaining on earth.
Ngiyathanda Baba wami	I would like my *Baba*
Ukuba ngibe nawe.	That I be with you.

¹) This total dependence is also expressed in Isl. 228¹ where he complains that his
father (Baba) is concealed and does not appear to him in a vision: (Awubonakali kimi).

In Isl. 226⁵ he asks *Baba* to decorate his *umoya* with festive attire which
is not bought with gold—"it comes from thee *Baba*" (*Evela kuwe Baba*).
He is totally dependent on his father. For the Zulu man is dependent
upon those nearest to him and for this reason Shembe II has completely
discarded *uNkulunkulu* and used the designation *Baba*. It says so much
more. He depends on *Baba* for his resurrection who himself is resurrected
(Isl. 233⁶) and being anxious about his future he asks: "Give me hope,
Baba" (*Ngiphe Baba ithemba*, Ibid. verse 3). As sinners they look to *Baba*
alone and he states "you alone are holy" (*wena wedwa uyingcwele*, 239³);
their hearts ask for him who is the living *uThixo* (*Thixo ophilayo*, Ibid.
verse 2); and *Baba* is asked for ears which are opened to hear his word
(Isl. 240¹). Their total dependence as a movement from Shembe I as well as
their sense of community is most clearly expressed in Isl. 239⁶. They come
to their *father* of whom they alone are inheritors.

Namhla sibuyela kuwe,	Today we return to thee,
Thina nabantwana bethu,	We and our children,
Siyilifa lakho wedwa.	We are your inheritors alone.
Singakhonzi izitha zethu.	May we not serve our enemies.

In Isl. 219 the term *Baßamkhulu*[1]) is used for Shembe I. He is to them as a community *Grand-father*, and to his son *father*. The intimate relationship with, and dependence upon, Shembe I is expressed in this Isl. This is seen in verse 4.

Sihleli osizini	We stay in trouble
We Baßamkhulu,	Oh *Baßamkhulu,*
Kuleli lizwe	in this world
We Baßamkhulu,	Oh *Baßamkhulu,*
Zinyembezi zodwa	it is tears only
We Baßamkhulu,	Oh! *Baßamkhulu,*
Kuleso sigodi sosizi.	With that dale of trouble.

The inspiration of Shembe's father is greatly missed. To him he is a divine being. He states it as follows "Who Shembe was I do not know. I am his son, but I do not know who he was. Shembe was not born as you and I. He was born of Spirit and was Spirit. He was the one sent (*uThunyiweyo*), sent to the Bantu and to all nations".[2]) It is clear that for Isaiah Shembe the term *Baßa* emphasized the ancestor aspect of the Zulu religion,[3]) and not *uNkulunkulu*. *Baßa* expressed the nearness of the Supreme Being as well as his concern for his people. Through *Baßa* the *amakhosi* and the ancestor spirits in general found their way into the movement. Law as ritual prohibition, which means law in its magical aspect and associated with the community and its continuation, is directly related to the ancestors with the result that with *Baßa* the name Jehova also becomes prominent. Moses is in their eyes the greatest ancestor. Shembe I is the new Moses who opened up the old wells which give their water in a most refreshing manner. He is truly the father of their community.

9. *umenzi* (*aßenzi, pl.*). It should be written *umenzi*

i. Maker, doer; ii. Creator.
<*enza* i. Do, perform, behave; ii. Bring about; iii. Come to pass; iv. Defraud. This verb is used in Ex. 20[11].

---

[1]) Shembe I is addressed as the "great" father, the grandfather. The hierarchy of age is strong in Zulu society. The "great" father has authority even over one's own father and must be shown the greatest respect. "He orders about and must be implicitly obeyed". Krige, 27.

[2]) Sundkler, Bantu Prophets, 330.

[3]) Sundkler relates how a preacher stated that Shembe "was sent by the God of Sendzangakhona and Shaka and Dingaan". Ibid., 330.

Shembe uses *umendzi* more than *umDali* (Creator) which is also more
commonly used amongst the Zulus in general. *umEnzi* and *umDali* are
interchangeable. These words are also in the creeds in this sense, e.g.,
Creator (*umDali*) is used in the Apostels' creed and Factor (*umEnzi*) in the
Nicene creed. *umEnzi* (Maker) is often used without any addition but not
in Shembe's case. In the prayers he speaks of "the Maker of heaven and
earth" (*umendzi wezulu nomhlaɓa*, Prayers for the Sabbath, Section 1, 16
and Section 15, 18) while in the Izl. he uses only *umEndzi* e.g. "Our
Maker rested on the Sabbath" (*Waphumula umendzi wethu*, Isl. 200⁴.) and
in Isl. 212², in which he maintains that the Sabbath is the key, he states:
"We have been called by our Maker" ("Simenyeziwe ngumendzi wethu").
In the *few* instances he used the name *umEndzi* he either used it in connection with the community (*iɓandla*) or with the Sabbath, as his interest is
not directed to the creation of the universe, but man's salvation through
his message.

It is nevertheless interesting that Shembe uses this word which had
been overlooked by missionaries, because of the constant use of *umDali*
or *uNkulunkulu*. No Zulu, who has not been under christian influence,
will use *uNkulunkulu* and *umEndzi* interchangeably.

10. *Jehova*

Like *uMvelingqangi* and *umDali*, *uJehova* as a designation for God
could only be used in the singular while *uNkulunkulu* and *uThixo* could
be used in the plural to indicate pagan deities.

The designation Yahweh, in its distorted form *Jehova*, has entered the
Zulu Bible translations. In the creation story *uNkulunkulu* is used, while
the designation *Jehova* takes a prominent place in the giving of the law
on Mount Sinai.

The three Zulu translations of the Bible referred to above state in Ex.
20²: *Ngingu Jehova uNkulunkulu wakho* ("I am the Lord thy God",
Authorized (King James) version.) One should, with regard to the thunder
and lightning on Mount Sinai, keep in mind the Zulu associations of these
phenomena with *iNkosi ephezulu*, the "*iNkosi of Heaven*", whose magicians (*aɓafana* or *aɓelusi ɓezulu*: "the boys or herdsmen of heaven") are
not associated with the ancestors. He speaks through thunder and lightning and no *ukuɓuyisa*[1]) ceremony is held for a person struck by lightning
because, they maintain, the *iNkosi ephezulu* has taken him. Shembe

---

[1]) A ceremony by which a person passed away is accepted in the Zulu society and
his spirit put into office.

himself had revelations through lightning. It now plays an important part in the movement. In this Mount Sinai story the Zulu mind finds something familiar, and when the giving of the law is associated with thunder and lightning after the mountain had been sanctified (cf. Ex. 19[23]), not only the name of the Supreme Being associated with this event will be of significance but also the law itself.

Of importance is the word used for the Supreme Being in connection with this central event for the Nazarites, a community in which a name is of great significance. All three Zulu Bibles referred to state in Ex. 19[20] that *uJehova* "came down upon Mount Sinai". (*wehlela phezu kwentaba yaseSinayi.*) In Ex. 20[3] "other gods" is translated with *onkulunkulu*, in all three translations; in Ex. 20[7] about not taking "The name of the Lord God in vain" all three translations have *Jehova uNkulunkulu*. With regard to the most important commandment for the Nazarites namely on the Sabbath (Ex. 20[10]) two have *Jehova uNkulunkulu* and one *Nkosi uNkulunkulu*. In the summary of the law in Matthew 22[37-39] all three translations have *iNkosi uNkulunkulu*. *Jehova* used in the Old Testament has been omitted in the New Testament. In Ex. 20[11] with regard to the resting on the Sabbath and its blessing, the translations use only *Jehova*.

Three designations for the Supreme Being are used here, namely *Jehova*, *uNkulunkulu* and *iNkosi*. *Jehova* is the most prominent with regard to Mount Sinai and the giving of the law and *Jehova* is the most prominent designation for the Supreme Being in the *Izihlabelelo*. But it should be remembered that the three designations *uJehova*, *uThixo* and *uNkulunkulu* do not appear at all in at least a hundred and forty Izl. where *iNkosi* takes precedence. While *uNkulunkulu* appears about a dozen times in Shembe's Izl., *uThixo* about twice as many times, *uJehova* is mentioned over sixty times, twenty times in four Izl.

In what sense did Shembe use the designation Jehova? This makes an analysis necessary. He often uses it in the *Prayers*—sometimes in conjunction with *uNkulunkulu* as in the Mount Sinai event in Exodus (cf. Morning Prayers, Section 9, 2; Evening Prayers, Section 12, 10; Section 25, 12; Prayers for the Sabbath, Section 11, 17) and with *iNkosi* (cf. Morning Prayers, Section 7, 2; Sections 18 and 19, 3; Section 20, 4; Evening Prayers, Sections 10 and 11, 10; Prayers for the Sabbath, Section 20, 18). Shembe, who brought two worlds together, uses *iNkosi* and *uNkulunkulu* together with *Jehova* for this specific reason and was greatly helped by the Zulu Bible translations. It is only later under the influence of the strong legalistic approach and the nationalistic element that he pushed *uNkulunkulu* into the background. In the beginning *Jehova* had to be explained to his illiterate followers, e.g., "worship *Jehova*, your *uThixo* and your *uNkulunkulu*" ("*Umkhondze uJehova uThixo wakho uNkulunkulu wakho*", Evening Prayers, Section 17, 11. See also Prayers for the Sabbath, Section 12, 17) but once *Jehova* had been naturalised *uNkulunkulu* is pushed into the background.

Jehova is the prominent name with Shembe because He is the Giver of the Law (cf. Prayers for the Sabbath, Section 3, 16) whom the genera- tions are called to praise. (Izl. 22[1,4]; 37[1]; 60[1]). In the Isl. on the Sabbath (188) only *Jehova* is used as a designation for God. The name of *Jehova* is mentioned in the Prayers for the Sabbath not less than nineteen times, *uNkulunkulu* about six times, *Thixo* only once and *Jehova Thixo* once.[1]) The designation *uThixo* is not associated with the law and commandments in general. It is *Jehova* and *uNkulunkulu*—the last being associated with the ritual prohibitions of the Zulu society. *Jehova* eventually became deep- ly associated with the Zulu supernatural world (Isl. 1[4]) and he stays at *Ekuphakameni* (Isl. 6[5]).

In a society in which power is appreciated, *Jehova* is now hailed as the Supreme Being of power as evidenced at Sinai. This is stated in Isl. 10[2]:

uJehova ukuphela	*Jehova* alone is
Inkosi enamandla.	*Inkosi* with power.

In Isl. 15 *Simakade*, *Jehova* and *Baba* are associated and *Jehova* is monopolised for Africa as his law is being rejected by his enemies. It is now the *Jehova* of the law that distinguish them from the *uNkulunkulu* of the missionaries. cf. Isl. 17[3]:

Izitha zika Jehova[1])	The enemies of *Jehova*
Zivukela wena,	rise up against thee,
Phaphamani phaphamani	Wake up, wake up
Nina maAfrica.	Ye Africans.

They are now the *defenders* of *Jehova*. *Jehova* is not limited to nation- alistic aspirations but satisfies through the law the deepest spiritual needs of the people to the exclusion of the Cross. He states in Isl. 39[1]:

Mbonge uJehova	Praise thou *Jehova*
*Mphefumulo wami usenethuba**	My soul while you still have a chance.

* -thuba, (intuba, izintuba): i. opening, passage, pass; ii. small side entrance to a kraal. Jehova has opened a way for the soul; given it a pass as it were together with a passage.

---

[1]) cf. *Izihlabelelo* pp. 15–23.
[2]) cf. Isl. 120[3].

Jehova is also asked to loosen *his umoya* (Isl. 44, chorus)[1]); parting from *Jehova* spells trouble for the heart (Isl. 65, chorus)[2]) and not only here but also with regard to the resurrection is *Jesus* excluded and *Jehova* substituted (cf. Isl. 51[1]). With the consciousness of death being strong he calls on *iNkosi Jehova* (Isl. 67[1-6]); he goes alone to the grave and calls on *Jehova* (Isl. 184[2]); recovery from illness is from *Jehova* (Isl. 119[2,3,4]); *Jehova* has brought on them the decoration of his word which they have to receive with white hearts (Isl. 69; cf. Rev. 3[18]); they are not with war-shields and weapons but have the name of *Jehova* (Isl. 119[5,6]); the hosts and angels and saints praise *Jehova* (cf. Isl. 106[6]). The name of Jehova has become superior magic.

Izizukulwane zonke zase zulwini	All the generations of heaven
Zojabula ngawe Kuphakama,	They will rejoice through you at Ekuphakameni
Uma zingena ngamasango	When they enter through the gates
Zize kudumisa uJehova.[3])	may they come to praise *Jehova.*

The question could be asked: Who is *Jehova* in this case? Is it the Supreme Being or is it Shembe? Shembe is a manifestation of *Jehova*! In Isl. 116[2] he states:

Udumo luka Jehova	The fame of *Jehova*
Lus' Ekuphakameni.	Is in *Ekuphakameni.*

Twice Shembe makes reference in this Isl. to Paramount chief Solomon Ka Dinuzulu to whom he gave one of his daughters Zondi and this adds to the "fame of *Jehova*" (cf. verses 1 and 5). He now calls the different tribes to *Ekuphakameni*. Thiose who do not respond to the injunctions of *Jehova* will land in fire (Isl. 146) or cf. Isl. 149[2]:

Nizo lahlwa nguJehova.	You will be thrown away by *Jehova.*

Jehova is the one who judges. In Isl. 186 (see appendix) one again asks *Who* is *Jehova*? In old Zulu religion the Supreme Being manifested himself throught the light of the sun and moon and now, speaking about *Ekuphakameni*, Shembe states in Isl. 186[4]:

uJehova yena yedwa	It is *Jehova* he alone
Ulilanga kwanenyanga.	he is the sun and the moon.

---

[1]) See also Isl. 52[1]; 184[1-5].

[2]) See also Isl. 146[2].

[3]) Sundkler refers to widows of a chief who, with reference to Shembe I, exclaimed: "There is Jehova dressed in white", Bantu Prophets, 313.

In the hymns ascribed to Shembe after his death the name of *Jehova* does not appear and Shembe II uses it only in Isl. 225[1] where he states that *Jehova* has created him.

Jehova is the Supreme Being who gave the law and Shembe is a manifestation of *Jehova*, who, as his representative, reveals his divine qualities. As Christ was man and God, so is Shembe. Through Shembe *Jehova* has become their very own in the sense that they possess him—a form of henotheism. As *Yahweh* was localized in the temple in *Jerusalem* and the *torah* the mediator, so *Jehova* has been localized in *Ekuphakameni* but with Shembe as His manifestation and the law as the key to enter the holy city.

Conclusion: Shembe's concept of the Supreme Being

Shembe is not interested in the Creation of the universe but in man's destiny. He thus hardly refers to *uMvelingqangi* and *umDali*. The Supreme Being is in his theology not a *deus otiosus* or a *deus incertus*. Shembe I, the Christ of the Zulu nation, has revealed *Jehova* in all His glory at *Ekuphakameni*. He is His representative but more—he is also a Supreme Being. *Ekuphakameni* is heaven and heaven, for Shembe cannot be without a God. The Shaka myth which started to work on his person[1]) was violently destroyed by the whites and it may be possible that the myth was transferred to the Black Christ of the *iBandla lamaNazaretha* in particular. He is the one who revealed to them the *Jehova* of the law with whom he eventually became essentially *one*. In his Trinity there is room for the inborn Zulu concept of hierarchy. As the hosts of heaven are at *Ekuphakameni* so the Supreme Being is present in all his glory in his sanctuary. Shembe is the supernatural personified. As the royal ancestors, and through them *uNkulunkulu*, could only be approached by the king, in the same way could Shembe's God only be approached.

Jehova has been naturalised amongst the Nazarites. He is explained as *their uThixo*, a loan word which was accepted in the course of time. *uBaɓa*, and not *uNkulunkulu*, is the designation together with *iNkosi*, which was instrumental in maintaining the contact with the ancestral world. The utilising of Zulu terminology for the Supreme Being, without a clear explanation in preaching and teaching, of the many roots with which it is associated, may have contributed to the theological confusion that prevails. The Zulu did not have a cult with regard to *uNkulunkulu* the designation used in Genesis 1 and the Supreme Being naturalised by

---

[1]) cf. *Asmus*, 17–18.

the missionaries is the one distantly removed in the Zulu mind. Shembe took it seriously that God came in Christ to the world. Jehova who spoke to Moses on Mount Sinai and gave the law is this Supreme Being and, as history could be repeated, Shembe is His representative and thus the Christ of the Zulu nation. Jesus Christ was a form of God's revelation but has returned to the Father.

The nearness and farness of God have been much discussed with regard to the religions of Africa. *uNkulunkulu* was not merely far away, so far away that it is pointless to make any contact with him. The Zulu hierarchical system puts him far away as one could not approach a superior without taking meticulous consideration of the paternal hierarchy. *uMvelingqangi*, the name omitted by the missionaries and given to Shembe, could be approached directly. The Nazarite is more interested in *divine involvement* as the pre-christian Zulu always had been via his ancestors. The Biblical concept of God, as expressed by empirical Christianity, has so often been that of a *deus otiosus*, a God floating in the air, without really having contact with man. But the hunger for revelation and divine involvement has always been strong with the Zulu. The intense desire for being has ever been present. This could be seen in the Zulu notion that an important ancestor could appear in the form of a snake which, even though dangerous, should not be disturbed. This is the concretization of the inner desire to have contact with the supernatural. It is this same attitude that prevails when spirits are actually "seen" by the pre-christian Zulu. Christ fulfilled in his time, and for his people, this hunger for revelation most efficiently. Such a revelation must be repeated. God could again be seen as He was seen in Christ and for unhistorical clical thinking, the whole salvation history could repeat itself in the Zulu context. To state that Shembe I is merely a reaction against a pale white Christ, as Sundkler did, is an oversimplification, in spite of the element of truth it carries.

God's mediate presence is to man unbearable and even more so to a society in which men kept themselves busy with their ancestors. Man always puts between the Supreme Being and himself intermediaries whether it is his religion, his liturgy and ritual, human beings or saints. This happens in spite of man's hunger for revelation. The most universally known God of the Zulu, as with most other people in Africa, is of human origin. Shembe has usurped the place of God as a result of his mediatorship and his followers have accepted him as God. The ancestors (these "semi-divine" beings) and the community belonged together for the Zulu and so did the Supreme Being as the final authority over the ritual prohibitions. The true Biblical understanding of *koinonia* suffered as a result of the fact that many Zulus were taken out of their homes, were isolated on mission stations and became foreigners to themselves and to their own! In a this-worldly pragmatic religion, as the Zulu religion was to a great extent, the concern is intimately connected with man, human relations, political, social, economic and agricultural concern. In such circumstances there is the continuous *presence* of the supernatural from where everything is controlled. This desire was met in the King or Chief who had intimate contact with the supernatural forces through the royal ancestors and it was met in the kraalheads through their contact with the ancestors and in the *isangoma* or diviner. Pushing all this indiscriminately into the background, has naturally established a *vacuum* which was filled for Shembe himself by a syncretism of the old and the new in which the old remained basic. The breaking up of Zulu society has seen in Shembe its Saviour. In preaching, teaching and practical living the Christ of the missionaries remained distant and Shembe succeeded in satisfying the need for this *divine involvement*. God has become near and Shembe is a manifestation of Him. The divine beings were for the Zulu with the cattle, the lands, and although unapproachable, *uNkulunkulu* was behind it all. This gap had been filled by Shembe and now as a result of specific Biblical influence, he is a God who loves and who has tears over them. They did however not receive this deep sympathetic approach from the God many of the missionaries preached.

CHAPTER TWO

THE MESSIAH

The Messiah in the *Izihlaɓelelo* is not Jesus Christ. Shembe I is the mediator of the *iBandla lamaNazaretha*. In order to establish who the messianic figure actually is, one has to analyse the context in which certain concepts are being used.

1. *Jesus Christ*

The name of Jesus Christ is mentioned only in a few Izl.[1] The omission of the name of Jesus is obvious and Shembe clarifies this in his Izl. He himself has usurped the place of Jesus. Only once does he mention *uMkhululi* (Liberator) in conjunction with the name of Jesus. This is in the very beginning of the *Izihlaɓelelo*. namely Isl. 2[4]:

Namaɓandla namaɓandla asezulwini	And the hosts and the hosts of heaven
NgoJesu uMkhululi	through Jesus the uMkhululi
Ongafiyo.	who does not die (is eternal).
Amen, Amen, Nkosi yami.	Amen, Amen, my Nkosi.

In Isl. 5 the way of Jesus is pictured as hard and difficult (verse 1); that the gate is narrow (verse 2); that He had no place to rest (verse 3) and that they have to take up the Cross (verse 5). All these are specific scriptural reminiscences. This is also the case in Isl. 23[4] where Shembe states that Jesus said if they love Him they will stay with Him. (cf. John 15, 17). Only "the brave ones are of Jesus" ("*amaqhawe ngaka Jesu*" Isl. 50[2]) and in this same Isl. Jesus is still pictured as the judge (verse 6).

Sukani kukhulume uJesu	Give way, that Jesus may speak
Niyokusha emlilweni.	You will burn in the fire.

---

[1] Schlosser however incorrectly states that the name of Jesus is mentioned only as the one who promised to send the Spirit. Eingeborenenkirchen, 240. Schlosser further refers to the necessity in the Zulu social system of a mediator between God and man and then translates (or had it translated) "*Singena ngaɓanye*" Isl. 164[1] "We enter with the help of others". It should literally read "We enter by ones" ("One by one").

Two other references are made where he has only Jesus in mind. He speaks in Isl. 66[6] of the Father of Jesus, the Rewarder of love and in Isl. 109[2] he refers to the words of Jesus expressed over against Judas with regard to his betrayal.

Shembe gradually *excluded* Jesus, firstly, by stating that his time has come and that he goes to the Father; secondly, the promise of the Holy Spirit when he leaves and, thirdly, Shembe himself has usurped the position of Jesus Christ. This development is clear from the following.

In Isl. 61[3] he states:

Isikhathi sami sifikile	My time has come
Sengiyanishiya lusapho,	I am now leaving you my children/ family
Salanini kanjalo	Stay ye so (then)
Sengiya kuƁaƁa.	I am now going to the Father.

Jesus has himself said that He leaves and this is interpreted in a most literal sense. In Isl. 58[3] he already referred to Jesus' promise about the sending of the Holy Spirit:

Lowo owasethembisa wona	That which you promised us
Ngo Jesu Krestu Inkosi	Through Jesus Christ the iNkosi
Wathi auyikusishiya sodwa	You said: You will not leave us alone
Uyosithumela umoya oyingcwele.	You will send us the Holy Spirit.[1])

Jesus Christ's significance in the theology of Shembe is due to the fact that He promised the Holy Spirit whose coming is requested in the *chorus* of Isl. 58: "May thy Spirit come, Nkosi" ("*Umoya wakho mauze Nkosi*"!). Jesus Christ is often interpreted as *Spirit* and His *leaving* the earth means that a substitute or successor has to be found.

The way is open for Shembe to accept fully the position of Jesus Christ. cf. Isl. 84 with its 3 *Amens* after *each verse*.

1. Yinhle kangaka Inkosi yethu	So good is our iNkosi
Muhle kangaka uSimakade.	So good is Simakade.
Kantike yinhle kangaka	After all, just as good
Inkosi ya MaNazaretha.	The iNkosi of the Nazarites.

---

[1]) Reference has already been made to Shembe I as born of the spirit and who was spirit. Gelfand, M. (Shona Ritual, Cape Town, Juta and Co., 1959, 2) states: "Some Mashona, would classify Jesus Christ, the Great Spirit of the white man, as another *mhondoro*, like *chaminuka* and the other rain makers... ...He is thus able to adapt his religion, merely tagging on Jesus as another *mhondoro*."

6. Umuhle wenangwe[1]) yethu   Beautiful are you leopard of us
    Umuhle wena Krestu* wethu,   Beautiful are you our Christ,
    Sukuma wena Nkosi yethu   Stand up you iNkosi of us
    Uchoɓoze izitha zethu.   That you may crush our enemies.

* -Krestu (umKrestu, aɓaKrestu) means: saint, saintly man, one who leads a Christian life.

Shembe has now projected all attention on himself which was not difficult in a system where the mediator between God and man is indispensable. The Zulu semi-deified kingship and the christian Messiah has given the further impetus for the establishment of a "divine" Mediator within the Zulu society.

2. iNkosi[2]) (pl. amakhosi)

This term is used in the Zulu Bible translations for *Lord* or King. It is however for the Zulu a word with deep-seated connotations e.g. when Shembe speaks in the *Izihlaɓelelo* about *Nkosi yamakhosi* (the king of kings, The Evening Prayers, Section 24, 12). Sundkler states that the kingship pattern is imprinted on all the independent movements so that the leader, whether he is a "Bishop", "Overseer", or "President", is the *iNkosi* (king) and the movement is the tribe.[3])

(i) *Names for the Supreme Being and iNkosi used together or interchangeably*

The Supreme Being is referred to as *"Nkulunkulu Nkosi"* (Evening Prayers, Section 23, 12) *"Nkosi yethu Simakade"* ("Our *iNkosi Simakade*", Isl. 15[1]). Jehova is referred to as *iNkosi* (cf. Isl. 6[5]). Shembe's direct relationship to the Supreme Being has also been instrumental with regard to his exclusion of Jesus Christ. From the very beginning the designation *iNkosi* refers rather to Jehova than to Jesus Christ. (cf. Isl. 1). In Isl. 10[2] this emphasis is obvious:

Umkhokheli wakhona   The payer of debts of there
Munye kuphela;   is one only;

---

[1]) The Zulu king has been called by such praise names as "father leopard", "noble elephant".

[2]) It has the following meanings: i. King, paramount chief; ii. Term of respect for royalty or a person in high governmental authority, lord, sir; iii. Magistrate; iv. (pl. only) Spirits of the departed; v. Lord (New Testament usage).

[3]) Sundkler, Bantu Prophets, 102.

UJehova ukuphela   it is Jehova alone
Inkosi enamandla.   the iNkosi with power.

The exclusion of Jesus is also due to Shembe's emphasis on the law
which is the very source of their redemption—the Sabbath is according to
Shembe, the very core of the law. cf. Isl. 21[2].

Ngaphandle kwakho asina mkhululi   Apart from thee we have no
                                                        umkhululi
We Thixo ka Adam;   Oh Thixo of Adam;
Woza usikhulule   Come that you may loosen us
We Nkosi yeSabatha usishiyelani.   Oh Nkosi of the Sabbath why do
                                               you leave us?

Shembe restored the Sabbath so that "the road which goes home to
Jehova our *iNkosi*" ("*indlela yokuya ekhaya Inkosi yethu*", Isl. 57[1]; see
also Isl. 86[1,2]) leads to "the inhabitant of Zion" ("Kumhlali ne Zion",
Isl. 57[2]). It is no longer the way of Christ but of the messianic Shembe and
his Jehova. In Isl. 60[4] Jehova has to be praised for sending "Isaiah his
Servant". It is a natural development that Shembe should be on the side
of the lawgiver. The worshippers of Jesus are the breakers of the law;
they worship the Sunday-God not Jehova.

Other reasons could be mentioned for pushing Jesus into the background. Jesus' emphasis on His being "the way, the truth, and the life:
no man cometh unto the Father, but by me" (John 14[6]) has excluded the
possibility of accepting the saints of the pre-christian Zulu world into the
fold of the Biblical God. This is unacceptable to a society in which the
emphasis is so strong on the communion of the saints—and to them all
those who were of significance are holy ones. At the gate is no more Jesus
and the Cross but Jehova, Shembe and the law.

After his confession of faith in Isl. 73 the emphasis is on the Supreme
Being and in the last approximately hundred Izl. the name of Jesus is
totally omitted and *iNkosi* either refers here to Shembe himself or to
Jehova, Thixo, uNkulunkulu, Simakade or Baɓa. It is easier to bring
Jehova and Baɓa together than Jesus Christ and Baɓa with whom the
whole Zulu history is associated.

Shembe II has only his father in mind when he uses the word *iNkosi*.
He does not use it in conjunction with the names for the Supreme Being
even though he speaks about "*Nkosi yethu Simakade*" ("Our Nkosi
Simakade", Isl. 243[1]).

(ii) *Jesus as iNkosi*

One comes to the conclusion, after having read the *Izihlaɓelelo* over and over again, that Shembe has deliberately projected this designation on himself and not on Jesus Christ. There are however instances in which the designation *iNkosi* does refer to Jesus Christ e.g. Isl. 140[4].

Wozani weɓathengwa	Come ye that have been bought
Enathengwa ngegazi leNkosi...	Bought with the blood of the *iNkosi*

In the centre of the Holy Communion stands Shembe so that *iNkosi* here is again an ambiguous designation.

(iii) *iNkosi as the term for a paramount chief*

Shembe refers to Solomon ka Dinuzulu, the Paramount Chief or king, to whom he gave one of his daughters. He repeats the following verse twice in Isl 116 (cf. verses 1 and 5):

Uyaɓizwa Nkosi Solomoni	You are being called *Nkosi* Solomon
Mntaka Dinuzulu.	the Son of *Dinuzulu.*
Naludumo luka Jehova	Here is the fame of Jehova
Lus' Ekuphakameni.	it is in *Ekuphakameni.*

(iv) *Shembe as iNkosi*

Shembe is the beautiful *iNkosi* of the Nazarites (Isl. 84), the one who came on the clouds. (cf. Isl. 7[4]).

Beza neNkosi yaɓo	They came with their *iNkosi*
Yembethe amafu.	Who was enveloped in clouds.

He has come to call *all* people. cf. Isl. 24[1].

Bonani uza ngamafu	Look ye, he comes with the clouds
Uzoɓiza aɓantu ɓonke.	He comes to call all people.

In Isl. 7[5] he states that the saints go out to meet their *iNkosi* and in Isl. 24[2] that they came with the *iNkosi*. Shembe as Mediator is pictured as the *iNkosi* who is in the centre of the heavenly and earthly hosts. He is the one in whom the history of Bethlehem has been repeated. He is the *iNkosi* of the Judeans (Isl. 34[1]) whose star[1]) is seen over Ekuphakameni (Isl.

---

[1]) The stars are praising Shembe, they also bow their knees before him. cf. Isl. 110[2].

Izinkanyezi zezulu	The stars of heaven
Zidumisa wena	They praise you
Ziya guqa ngamadolo	They are kneeling with knees
Zidumisa wena.	They praise you.

94³)¹). In Isl. 197² Shembe states that he was *called* in his mother's womb:

Wangiɓiza Nkosi ngezwi lakho	You called me iNkosi through
	your voice
Ngise siswini sikamame.	I was still in my mother's womb.

The *iNkosi*, in this case the Supreme Being, has sent Shembe—the only one he has sent. cf. Isl. 77².

Kodwa mina ngedwa	But I alone
Ngivela kude;	I come from afar
Ngithunyelwe iNkosi	I am sent by the *iNkosi*
Phakathi* kwenu.	In your midst.

 * *Phakathi.* Adv. (Ur.B. -ti, kati: midst) i. In the midst, inside; ii. Between. Shembe does not claim to "possess" anybody, i.e., his spirit does not enter anybody as the *isangoma* is possessed. He has however the spirit at his disposal. cf. Superscription to Isl. 162.

Shembe's supernatural call has given him supernatural power. He is now the one who removes *curses*—the most feared condition in pre-christian society is that of being under a curse. cf. Isl. 215³.

Azisuswe nguwe weNkosi	Let them be removed by you, *Nkosi*
Lezo ziqalekiso,	those curses,
Lezo owakhuluma ngazo	those which you spoke of
Kuɓaphuli ɓemithetho.	to the breakers of the laws.

In Isl. 216 the nationalist Shembe is the *iNkosi* of the Zulus; in Isl. 217 they are pictured as standing before their *iNkosi* and in Isl. 218 the Zulu nation is addressed stating in verse 1:

Yizani wema Zulu	Come ye Zulus
Siyiɓonile Inkosi yethu	We have seen our *iNkosi*
Sivela thina kwelizayo	We come from the world that is to
	come
Siyiɓonile Inkosi yethu.	We have seen our *iNkosi*.

Coming from the other world is not strange to the Zulu mind as one could enter it through dreams. But here Shembe has his own supernatural coming in mind. The superscription to this Isl. simply states *eGospel* written a few months before his death, most probably the second last he wrote. In the superscription to Isl. 220, which he has supposedly written after his resurrection, he is referred to as "nkosi Isaiah Shembe".

---

¹) He is described as Lord of Ekuphakameni by a preacher who states: "The God who spoke in Eden is here today!" Sundkler, Bantu Prophets, 334.

In Isl. 221[3] Shembe II refers to him as the "Nkosi yamakhosi" (the king of kings). The stars wept and the earth quaked when *iNkosi* left (Isl. 221[2]). Shembe II continuously refers to his father as *iNkosi* (cf. Isl. 228[6]). Now that his father is himself in the world beyond, Shembe II comes to him with the following request in Isl. 229[2]:

Bakhumbule wena Nkosi	Remember them you *Nkosi*
Aɓokhokho ɓethu:	Our great grandparents:
Badlulile emhlaɓeni	they have passed through the earth
Bese ɓumnyameni.	Being in darkness.

Shembe I is in a better position to understand the needs of the Zulu ancestors. The christian influence is still evident with the educated Shembe II who cannot accept that the ancestors are *per se* sanctified. Whether he here has purgatory in mind is not clear.

3. *uMkhululi.* (pl. aɓakhululi)

khulula: 1. Set free, deliver; ii. Unloose; iii. Getting somebody out of difficulty by speaking on his behalf.

For Redeemer in Job 19[25] two Zulu translations have *umhlengi* (i. Helper; ii. Escort.) while one uses *uMsindisi*, but in Is. 44[6] this translation also uses *umhlengi*[1]). The term *uMkhululi* has more to do with liberation from bonds and is used more freely by Shembe than is the case in the Zulu Bibles. He uses it only once directly in connection with Jesus (Isl. 2[4]), a few times with *Thixo* and once with *uNkulunkulu.* (cf. Isl. 163[1]). The word is often used by Shembe I also in the sense of the liberation of the African nations from subjection. The word has been utilised to describe the loosening of *umoya* from the bonds of negative forces. Among a people who consider themselves to be in political, economic and social bonds, the term will also have a wider than religious significance. When bound by negative forces within and without, the free spirit is limited and unable to rule the circumstances. Loosening does not mean inner change but getting rid of, to be released from.

In Isl. 21 he has excluded Jesus as the *uMkhululi* (Liberator) and describes *Thixo ka Adam* as the only *uMkhululi*; *Thixo* is here referred to as the *iNkosi* of the Sabbath. It is the *Thixo* of Abraham, the patriarch, who is being asked to free them. (Isl. 21[3]). The observance of laws, ritual prohi-

---

[1]) In Isl. 188[4] the verb is used in the sense of being sifted.
Wasihlenga wena Nkosi.   You have sifted us *iNkosi*.

bitions, guarantees their freedom. In the pre-christian Zulu society sacrifices and *isangoma* practices liberated the weakened *umoya* in bonds. In
this activity of liberation Jesus is completely excluded. cf. Isl. 35[4].

Ngize kuwe Mkhululi	I have come to the *uMkhululi*
Ngikhulule kuzo zonke,	Loosen me from them all,
Nginamathele sengigeziwe	That I cling, having been washed already,
Esifu6eni sika Abraham.	To the breast of Abraham.

In Isl. 40[3] he speaks of the Liberator of the bound (*Mkhululi wezi6oshwa*)
and when the word is again used in Isl. 66[4] one is not certain to whom it
refers. In Isl. 108 Shembe may have himself or Jesus in mind—it is doubtful
that it is Jesus. In Isl. 128[3] Jehova is pictured as the *uMkhululi*. The reference to Shembe becomes more expressed from Isl. 142 onwards where it
often sounds as a refrain that the *uMkhululi* "has come" (*ufikile*) and Mary
and Joseph are also called upon to rejoice. This again should not mislead
the reader to think it refers to Jesus. Shembe is only concerned to give his
coming supernatural and historical status. (cf. Isl. 142[4]).

In Isl. 150 the *uMkhululi* is for the first time brought into association
with the soul (*umphefumulo*, verse 2) and *umoya* (verse 5) after he stated
that *uMkhululi* has *now* arrived (*usefikile*). He is pictured as being with
love (verse 1), with power (*amandla*) and thus saves (verse 2), gives courage,
is a refuge and frees from bonds. Shembe is now the powerful one, the
Liberator of the nation. He is not merely an earthly liberator but is the
Supreme Being. cf. Isl. 163[1].

Sondelani 6antu nonke	Come nigh all ye people
KuNkulunkulu	To *uNkulunkulu*
Uyanithanda uMkhululi	He loves you, *uMkhululi*
Bantu nonke.	All ye people.

All heavens praise him and any reference here to Jesus is misplaced. It
is a Zulu redemption through a Zulu liberator, a grand theocracy in which
the personified *uNkulunkulu* of the Zulu nation is active. cf. Isl. 214[1].

uMkhululi wethu—	Our Liberator
Thina ndzalo ka Dingana	We the progeny of Dingaan
Simzwile ufikile.	We have heard he has arrived
uMkhululi ufikile	The Liberator has arrived!
uMkhululi usefikile!	The Liberator has now arrived!
Wema Zulu sesimzwile.	Ye Zulus we have already heard about him.

This Isl. should be seen in connection with such nationalistic songs as Isl. 17 where the Africans are called upon to stand up for what is their own. Here is now the Liberator who comes with the authority of a Divine King and Messiah. For Shembe II the *uMkhululi* has returned to the holy city after his death which reminds of the *ukuɓuyisa*. Shembe I is now again active even though he has passed away. cf. Isl. 229⁴.

Ufikile umkhululi	He has come, the uMkhululi
Bayavuka ɓonke,	They wake up all,
Nawe zulu nawe Mhlaɓa!	And you heaven and you earth
Muphakamiseni.	Elevate him.

4. *uMsindisi*. (pl. aɓasindisi)

<sindisa: Rescuer, Saviour, Redeemer, Healer.

This word is used in the Zulu Bibles in the sense of Saviour, Rescuer or Redeemer. The designation is used by Shembe in the sense of Saviour, Healer and Political Liberator. In Isl. 41⁴ *uMsindisi* is used in the sense of spiritual Saviour. In Isl. 80 the history of Bethlehem is transferred to *Ekuphakameni* with Shembe the *uMsindisi* and in Isl. 188, the Isl. on the Sabbath, with its 15 Amens, the peoples are admonished to come to *uMsindisi*. Shembe is the rescuer through the Sabbath. The *uMsindisi* is related to the community. All nations are invited to this *uMsindisi* and here the meaning of political liberator is obvious. cf. Isl. 103⁵.

Sihambise izwi lakho	That we may send your word
Ezizweni zonke,	to all nations
Zivuke zikulandele	that they awake and follow you
WeMsindisi wazo.	Oh! their *uMsindisi*.

Salvation is from the Zulu nation which receives preference. cf. Isl. 45¹⁻⁴.

Zizwe lalani uzulu¹) ezwakale	Nations go ye to sleep that the Zulu nation may be audible
Phambi ko Msindisi.	before the *uMsindisi*.

In Isl. 46 he repeats in each of the five verses:

Phakama Africa	Rise up Africa
Funa uMsindisi.	Seek the *uMsindisi*.

---

¹) Uzulu could also refer to a chief or all those subject to a king. In the loc. poss. KwaZulu means in, from Zululand (cf. verse 2).

This is addressed to all the sons and daughters, men and women who are in slavery. *uMsindisi* is thus more a political designation.

5. *uMkhokheli.* (pl. aƃakhokheli.)[1])

i. One who pays, paymaster; one who pays another's debts.
ii. Leader in woman's church society.
< khokhela: i. Exhibit for, pay for, repay for; ii. Retaliate, requite; iii. Pay off, pay wages.

The word is used in Zulu Bible translations. Jesus Christ is the payer of debts. Shembe however states it is Jehova. cf. Isl. 10[2].

Umkhokheli wakhona	The Payer of debts of there
Munye kuphela;	is only one;
U Jehova ukuphela	it is only Jehova
Inkosi enamandla.	the *iNkosi* who is with power.

In Isl. 104[3] *Nkulunkulu Nkosi* is called the "holy payer of debts". ("Mkhokheli oyingcwele".).

6. *iNceku.* (pl. izinceku)

An official in a chief's kraal who transacted important business for the chief or king, who looked after his food, a steward.
< ncekuza: seek favour with a superior, act servilely.

(i) *The Bible and iNceku*

This designation, indicating a person of important rank or position, has been used in Bible translations. Moses is called "my servant Moses" ("*Inceku yami uMose*", Numbers 12[7]) after reference has been made to the *umoya* which is on him. The *Inceku* is associated with the highest authority in the nation and the further association here where Moses is pictured as giving *umoya* will appeal to the non-christian Zulu. (cf. Numbers 11[17].).

In Isaiah Israel is called God's servant ("*wena-Israyeli, nceku yami*", uIs. 41[8]). The designation *iNceku* is used in Acts 3[13] in connection with Jesus. The New Testament Greek reads *paida*, translated in the English Bibles *as son* while in the Zulu it is translated as *servant*. Paul calls

---

[1]) The chief's wives enjoy special status as church stewards (aƃakhokheli) ex officio. Sundkler, Bantu Prophets, 99.

himself a servant (*iNceku*) of Jesus Christ (Rom. 1[1]). John speaks in Revelation about God's servants, the prophets. (*izinceku zakhe aбaprofethi*, Rev. 10[7]).

Shembe's call as iNceku

Shembe looked at this term *iNceku* with the Bible and his own Zulu world as the background. It was a term held in the same high regard as the others he applied to himself. *He was called* in the same way as Jacob and states "I was called by your Voice" (*Mina ngaбizwa izwi lakho*, Isl. 136[1]). Calling by the *Voice* plays a significant role in Zionist movements; it is a channel of revelation. Shembe as the *iNceku* is surrounded by the messengers of heaven. cf. Isl. 136[5].

Endaweni ethile	In a certain place
Wayihlangaбeza iNceku yakho,	You went out to meet your *iNceku*;
Ngezithunywa zasezulwini,	through the messengers of heaven
Yesuka yaku landela.	he stood up and followed you.

The hosts of heaven have gone out together with Jehova to meet this *iNceku* who is divinely called, who has left "mother and sister" (verse 6).

(iii) The iNceku and preaching

Shembe as the *iNceku* is the preacher and his ordination and strengthening comes from *iNkosi*. cf. Isl. 113[1].

Nkosi yelula isandla sakho	*Nkosi* stretch out your hand
Phezu kwe Nceku yakho.	Above your servant.
Igcwalise ngomoya wakho,	Fill him with your *umoya*
Ishumayele izwi lakho.	that he may preach your word.

Special blessing is asked on the preaching of the *iNceku* in Isl. 134.

(iv) Shembe, the iNceku, as the Moses of Africa

Africa must rejoice because Jehova remembered Africa cf. Isl. 60[4].

Waбakhumbula aбantu бakhe	He remembered his people
Aбanqulu zisoбala,	whose hips are naked
Waбathumela uIsiah* Inceku yakhe	You sent them Isaiah your *iNceku*
Ngoбa elungile.	because he is righteous.

    * should be uIsaiah or uIsaya.

Isaiah Shembe is here the Moses not only of the Zulu nation but of Africa and he intercedes for them. In him, as the only righteous one, the

hopes of Senzangakhona and Dingaan have been fulfilled. Here is the
serious deep concern of a human for his fellow human beings nowhere
more intensely expressed than in the above Isl. and in Isl. 42[4] where he
states:

Ekukhaleni kwe Nceku yakho	In the weeping of your *iNceku*
Awuzangu6ali6ale a6antu 6akho.	You never forgot your people.

Although Shembe refers only once to Moses, not in the Izl. but in the
"Prayers for the Sabbath", Section 3, 16, where he states that Jehova has
written the law through Moses, his *iNceku*, Shembe has also usurped his
position.

(v) *The iNceku as forgiver of sins*

Shembe has added this function to the *iNceku*. cf. Isl. 217[1].

Ayinhlanhla ya6o	Oh the good fortune of them
A6athethelelwa izono za6o,	Whose sins have been forgiven
Bese lapha emhla6eni	while here in the world
Phambi kway' Inceku yakhe.	in front of his *iNceku*.

(vi) *The iNceku resurrects*

Shembe II does not refer to his father as *iNceku* but as *iNkosi*. He states
that the *iNkosi* and *iNceku* (he and his father) resemble one another in
the grave, namely, their flesh is destroyed. In Isl. 242[3] he refers to himself
as the little servant (*iNcekwana*). He now asks eternal life from his father
in Isl. 233:

4. Wathuma Inceku yakhe	He sent his *iNceku*
Iza na6angcwele	*who* came with the saints
Ngayo ingu6o yokuphila	with the blanket of life
Bangem6esa mina.	they clothed me[1]).
6. Mangi6heke kuwe Nkosi	Let me look unto you, *iNkosi*,
Ngisinde ekufeni	that I may be saved from death
Mangi6am6e isandla sakho	or let me hold your hand
Ngiphume emgodini.	that I come out of the pit.

iNceku has received a much wider meaning than is the case in the Zulu

---

[1]) Vilakazi states that the essence of the old Shembe is in the new flesh, his mantle
of power is cast upon his son. This the Zulus understand because with them "the son
is the extension of the father's personality". The Zulu expresses this idea as follows:
"*ukuzala ukuzelula amathambo*." Isonto Lamanazaretha, 57.

Bible translations. It describes Shembe as the political leader and forgiver of sins. To Shembe II his father is *iNkosi* and he now the *iNceku*.

7. *iDwala* (i(li)dwala, amadwala. pl.)

i. Large, flat, exposed rock; ii. very hard soil; iii. Species of grass; iv. A woman unable to deliver at childbirth as a result of malformation.

This word is used by Shembe figuratively in the first sense. It may refer to Matth. 16[18] where Peter and the rock (*idwala*) are associated or to Ps. 61[8] which reads "lead me to the rock that is higher than I" (*ngiholele edwaleni eliphakeme kunami*) or to 1 Peter 2[6] "Behold I lay in Sion a chief corner stone, elect, precious" (*Bhekani, ngibeka eSiyoni itshe legumbi elikhethekile, liyigugu*). But most probably it bears reference to a popular revival hymn with the following words in the first verse:

> "Rock of Ages cleft for me
> Let me hide myself in thee."

In Isl. 101[1] he speaks about the eagle under whose wings they may hide themselves as the rock of old (*dwala laɓadala*).

In both Izl., in which his confession of faith appears, reference is made to the rock (*idwala*). It is the third person in Shembe's trinity although one could hardly speak of a trinity in his theology. After confessing his faith in the Father, the Holy Spirit, the holy congregation of the Nazarites, the fellowship of the holy *at* Nazareth, Shembe adds: cf. Isl. 73[3]

Idwala elihle	The beautiful rock
Lama Nazaretha	of the Nazarites
Owazi*khethela lona uJehova	which you selected for yourself
	Jehova
Ngokulithanda kwakhe.	because of his loving it.

* zi = reflexive.

In Isl. 154[4] he expresses himself as follows:

Uyidwala lokuphephela	You are the rock of refuge
Uyisihlangu sama kholwa;	You are the shield of believers;
Ngosizwa nguwe kuphela	I will be helped by you alone
Wedwala lokuphumula	You rock of rest
Ngoɓa ngiyathanda ukuliɓona	Because I would love to see it
Lelo lizwe elizayo.	That world which is to come.

Again Isl. 73 is much clearer than Isl. 154 and thus much more adequate as a confession of faith—not that clarity is a characteristic of creeds! In Isl. 73 Shembe clearly refers to himself and is intimately associated with the Father and the Holy Spirit which may be associated with Jesus Christ, as the Zulu has difficulties in picturing a holy spirit without reference to a person. Shembe is the rock dressed up with Nazarethness (verse 4), washed with hyssop and shining in brightness before *Yise* (the Father). Here the rock (*idwala*) and the Holy Spirit is not co-equal with the Father.

In Isl. 154 the rock and *uMkhululi* are associated and identified (cf. verses 4 and 5) as is the case in Isl. 168[3] where he states:

Ulidwala lethu yena	He is our rock
Siyophumula ngaye	we shall rest by him
Ungu mthundzi wokuphephela	He is the shadow of refuge
UMkhululi wethu.	our *uMkhululi*.

Ekuphakameni has become a "rock of ages" because the resurrected Shembe I dwells there. Shembe II states in Isl. 221[10]:

Kuphakama ulidwala	*Kuphakama*, you are a rock
Umi ngunaphakade;	you stand forever;
Amathambo ayingcwele	the holy bones
Uwalondoloze wena.	You look after them.

He has turned it into a place of refuge and when Shembe II feels that he has lost the contact with his father he feels completely abandoned. cf. Isl. 234[1].

Thixo wami Dwala lami	My *Thixo*, my Rock,
Wena ungikhohlwa ngani;	Why do you forget me;
Ngiyalila imihla yonke	I cry daily
Ngokuhlushwa isitha sami.	because I am troubled by my enemies.

8. *uThumekile*. (The one sent). <thuma: send, send on an errand.

It has been indicated that Jesus Christ's significance for Shembe is due to the fact that he promised to send the Holy Spirit. Shembe himself was considered to be born of the Spirit and to be Spirit and was the one Sent (*uThunyiweyo*). In Isl. 139[3] he states that he already arrived. cf. Isl. 139.

1. Ufikile olandelwa izizwe	He has arrived who is followed by nations

Ufikile simzwile.	He has arrived, we have heard him.
Baɓazani wemadoda,	Spread (the news) ye men
Baɓazani zizwe nonke.	Spread (the news) all ye nations.
5. Kwathiwa asiyukushiwa sisodwa,	It was said we shall not be left alone
Ufikile simzwile.	He has come we have heard him.
Mlandeleni ɓantu nonke	Follow him all ye people
Ufikile simzwile.	He has arrived, we have heard him.

Shembe describes himself here as the holy spirit promised, and verse 5 reminds of the words of Jesus in John 14[18],[20]. So often Shembe is pictured as the Comforter, the one who wipes away all tears. In his theology he is thus also the manifestation of the Holy Spirit.

In the superscription to Isl. 134 Shembe states that he, "the suffering servant called uThumekile", received this prayer in which the blessing on the *iNceku's* preaching is asked. In Isl. 221 in which Shembe II keeps himself busy with his father's death he states in verse 1:

Zafika izithunywa	There came the messengers
Zilande uThumekile.	in order to fetch *uThumekile*.

That Shembe is the promised one, the holy spirit who came, is a further reason for the obscure position of Jesus Christ in the movement.

9. *Ingelosi*

Shembe further describes himself as Michael. In Isl. 20[5] the Nazarites are admonished to wake up as Michael already stands before them, and in Isl. 55[4] the soldiers (*impis*) are made to sing "I have now seen the angel of heaven". In Isl. 125[3] he states that his name is "beautiful before the face of the angels" and in Isl. 201 the reference to Daniel 12 is applied to himself —he is the angel of Israel. He has a special position amongst the angels as is already stated in Isl. 7[2].

Nansi enye ingelosi	Here is another angel
Iphuma empumalanga.	He coming from the east.

10. *Isikhonzi*

Shembe refers to himself as the suffering servant, *isikhondzi senhlupheko*[1]). *Isikhonzi* is a word used for messenger, voluntary servant, worshipper

---

[1]) inhlupheko (pl. izinhlupheko): Trouble, worry, grief, suffering.

as well as choir boy or altar attendant. Shembe uses it in the sense of messenger and servant. In the superscriptions to quite a number of the Izl. Shembe states that the "suffering servant" has received it at this or that place. In this case also it is Jehova and Shembe, not Shembe and Jesus Christ. In the superscription to Isl. 144 he states: "The prayer of the suffering servant Shembe on June 7, 1927. Within the gates of *Ekuphakameni* he had quietened his *umoya* on that day for Jehovah. His *umoya* was caused to wander until it came to the joy of the chosen ones."[1])

The *isikhonzi* is not a lesser designation than *iNceku*. Shembe is the suffering servant for his people and in not less than twenty-seven of his last ninety-one Izl. does he use this designation in the superscriptions. With *isikhondzi* he expresses his humanity as Shembe has both a human and divine nature. He expresses with this designation also his expiation for his people.

B. There are still a number of other names through which Shembe I refers to himself. A brief reference to them is necessary.

1. *Mthandi* (umthandi, aбathandi. pl.): One who likes, loves.

He is the "lover of sinners" (*mthandi wezoni*, Isl. 189[4] cf. also Izl. 31[3]; 40[3].). He is the "lover of the Samaritans" (cf. *chorus* Isl. 40), having here in mind most probably all those who worship God without observing the Sabbath. Shembe II also uses the designation *mthandi wezoni* in Isl. 241[5] and in this case it also refers to his father. Shembe I pictured himself continuously as the lover of *all* sinners.

2. *Mniki wamandla* (Giver of power). cf. Isl. 189[4].

Shembe I was indeed considered to be the one who has and who gave *numinous* power.

3. *Mesuli wezinyemбezi* (Wiper or Eraser of Tears).

This is what Shembe II calls his father (cf. Isl. 241[5]). Shembe I often stated that he wipes away tears, e.g. Isl. 134[5].

4. *Mhawukeli wezinyemбezi* (Pitier of Tears).

In the Izl. the request is repeated "pity my *umoya*" and now in Isl. 31[3] Shembe I is referred to as the "one who pities tears".

5. *Msizi* (Helper). <siza: Help, aid, assist, succour. cf. Isl. 76[3].

---

[1]) Umthandazo wesikhondzi senhlupheko uShembe ngoJune 7, 1927, ngaphakathikwamasango aseKuphakameni wayethulele umoya wakhe uJehova ngalolosuku wazuliswa umoya wakhe waze wafika entokozweni yaбakhethiweyo.

Umthwali akazethuli	The carrier does not unload himself
we msizi wami.	Oh! my helper.

6. *Mondli wezintandane* (pl. aɓondli)

Mondli: Nourisher, one who rears an orphan, foster parent.

Shembe I is the *Nourisher* of *orphans* (*izintandane*) who is asked to nourish the heart. (*Yondla inhliziyo yami*, Isl. 76 chorus.). In Isl. 104[4] the request is to nourish his *umoya*.

7. *uMthetheleli* < thethelela: Forgive, let off.

Shembe I is the forgiver, the one who lets off from death or punishment. (cf. Isl. 145[5].).

8. *Malusi:* Shepherd.

He is the *malusi olithemba*, "the shepherd of hope". Isl. 104[2].

9. *Umqondisi:* Enlightener, instructor.

Shembe II, obviously referring to his father, asks in Isl. 236[4] for the Enlightener to be sent.

10. *Bongekile:* < ɓonga: Praise, give thanks, be offered in sacrifice, worship, sacrifice to. *Bongekile* is actually difficult to translate. cf. Isl. 190[2].

Lelo lizwe alidingi lutho,	That land is not in want of anything;
Siyohlala ngokwenama	we will stay in happiness
Siyohlala no Bongekile.	we will stay with Bongekile. (The One Praised.)

11. *Umthokozisi:* < thokoza: 1. Be grateful, happy; ii. Enjoy good health; iii. Praise, give thanks; iv. Enjoy. cf. Isl. 139[4].

Ufikile uMthokozisi	He has arrived the one who makes happy
Mlandeleni zizwe nonke.	follow ye him all ye nations.

In Isl. 100[5] the passive form is used and Shembe refers to himself as *uThokozwayo*.

12. *Sokhanyiso:* < khanya (caus. khanyisa): i. Be light; ii. Glisten, be polished; iii. Be transparent; iv. Be light-coloured; v. Be clear, intelligible.

Sokhanyiso: Father of Light. cf. Isl. 179[2].

13. *uBatshazwayo:* < ɓatshazwa: Be admired, praised, be popular. cf. Isl. 94[1].

Thina simzwile	We have heard him
uBatshazwayo	The one who is praised
Ufikile Ekuphakameni.	He has arrived at *Ekuphakameni*.

14. *Shembe ndodana kaMayekisa:* indodana (pl. amadodana): i. son; ii. son- in-law.

He uses his surname only once in an Isl. namely Isl. 213[1] where he speaks of himself as "*Shembe indodana kaMayekisa*". ("Shembe, son of Mayekisa...")

15. *Nkosi ndodana ka Thixo.*

In the Zulu Bible "Son of Man" is translated as *iNdodana* (cf. Matth. 25[31]) and "only begotten son" (John 1[18]) also. Shembe II describes his father as "*Nkosi*, son of *Thixo*" (Isl. 241[1]). Shembe II has here in mind scriptural references in which Jesus is described as Son of God. Shembe is in this sense son of *Thixo* but as His manifestation he is also *Thixo*. He is human and divine, man and God.

Conclusion: Shembe, the eschatological King or Black Christ

In Shembe the kingship type of leadership is combined with the office of the *isangoma* (diviner or doctor). What is said of both could be said of him. In the *isangoma* lies the future which he *sees* and creates, being in this sense a Messiah. Without the *isangoma* the whole life will be a continuous threat without any hope. The *isangoma* profession is not by choice but he/she is chosen, elected by a spirit, while the office of kingship among the Zulu is institutional.

The king or chief forms an important link with the supernatural world. The position of mediator is thus indispensable in the Zulu religious-social system. He never becomes a medium of the royal ancestors or shades which he addresses only in the plural as *amakhosi*. He is the highest symbol of what is powerful, of *numinous* power. He is the richest man in the nation and the increase of his prestige means the increase of that of the whole nation. He is also the centre of ritual. Treason against the king is treason against the whole people because he is the symbol of the unity of the whole tribe and as such sacred.[1]) The king is in a sense sacral, and, ruling over the life and death of his subjects, although not autocratically but delegating some of his functions to the chiefs and the *amakhosi* (senate), had also to act and speak according to the supposed injunctions from the Supreme Being and the royal ancestors. This happened not mechanically but took place in the sense of receiving advice. The king had a cosmic meaning and was the author of all zestful living, the personification of the tribe, the only channel through which the highest authorities in the

---

[1]) cf. *Krige*, 224.

"continued tribe" could be approached. It is never said of him that he dies but that he is *brooding* (*uyadunguzela*). As earthly representative of divine powers he held in the Zulu society a semi-divine position. The destiny of the country is equated with his life. On him they depended for rain, weather and fertility, and to him as representative of the shades the first fruits of the earth were sacrificed.

After the death of the king he maintained his authoritative position which is equal to that of the Supreme Being who is too far removed for purposes of worship. The royal ancestor spirits thus become ruling spirits. The *Nhlangakazi* events should be seen in the light of the royal ancestor cult. During the *Great Umkhosi* the graveyard of the royal ancestors are visited as that of Shembe is visited today. To Shembe also these royal ancestors had metaphysical power with the result that he continuously makes reference to Sendzangakhona, Shaka and Dingaan in the *Izihlaɓelelo*.

In Shembe the restoration of '*uzuluness*' is once again realized in its full glory. After referring to the fountain of Sendzangakhona from which they drank long ago, he refers to the contemporary position of the Zulus as seen in the light of *Ekuphakameni*. cf. Isl. 216[6].

Wathi uTshaka kasishayeki nakho	Shaka said we are not beatable,
	that also
Kuwena Mhlangana nino Dingana!	to you Mhlangana and Dingaan!
Kanti namhla sekunjalo	and yet today it is so
Kuwena Mhlangana nino Dingana	to you Mhlangana and Dingaan
We Nkosi.	Oh! *Nkosi*.

The hereditary kings or chiefs are referred to as *amakhosi ihlanga*, king of the reed, a reference to the Zulu myth about the origin of things and people.[1] Shembe fully accepted this position of mediator. He referred to himself with different praise names in the same way as the king was referred to with these *iziɓongo*. The king was approached with such praise names as noble elephant, leopard, "thou who art as high as mountains", "the black one".[2] This last praise name did not come into existence as a result of reaction against the whites. Black has always been to the Zulu the colour of strength and the *isiɓongo*, "the black one" means "the strong beloved one". Black beasts called *umzimu* were sacrificed to the royal ancestors during droughts.[3] The king received powerful so-called black

---

[1] cf. *Lugg*, Agricultural ceremonies in Natal and Zululand, Bantu Studies, Vol. III, No. V, 359.

[2] *Gardiner*, A journey to the Zoolu country, 91.

[3] cf. *Stuart*, ukutumetule, 224.

medicines—others were supposed to die if they took it—which included parts of a black bull in order to strengthen him. This fortification is known as *ukuqunga*, a process which the king goes through annually during the *Great Umkhosi* when he purified himself in the river into which ashes from the royal vessel were thrown. The Black Christ need not merely be a reaction against a so-called racialistic pale white Christ.

The psychological and religious disposition for the re-establishment of the Zulu kingship through a messianic figure such as Shembe is strong.[1] The office of kingship had specific mystical values with a "divinity" of its own. Since the time of Cetshwayo the Zulu kings were installed with christian rites but Zulu traditional customs were maintained. Much in Shembe I reminds of the Zulu kingship and a parallel could be drawn on many other points. The king's regalia were sacred as that of Shembe is kept sacred. They are considered to be the very entity of the community. These articles of the kings are shown during many ritual occasions while those of Shembe are only taken during the January procession to Nhlangakazi. The king's regalia are kept in the royal kraal (*indlukulu*) while that of Shembe is kept in his house at Ekuphakameni. The staff of Shembe, which is a magical instrument, has its prototype in the chief's sacred stick or *induku yomuzi* which, together with the sacred assegai, plays a role in the First-fruit ceremonies. Shembe's holy vessels remind of the king's sacred vessel and together with the secret scriptures (to which he refers in Isl. 34[3]) and the holy drum syncretism has been effectively construed on this level. The vessel of the king was the most powerful instrument to overcome enemies and find lost cattle.[2]

Those of Shembe are carried to Nhlangakazi not without purpose. At Ekuphakameni a type of memorial is seen which reminds of the *inkáta* or sacred coil, the most sacred article of the tribe, symbolising tribal unity, the circular form of which is "believed that it has the power of collecting up all traitors and disaffected subjects and joining them together with the rest of the nation in affection for the king".[3] All these objects have symbolic value in the Zulu sense—so also the key-like structure along the path, the holy stones in "*Paradisi*", the star, the clothing and so on.

Shembe himself is the Messiah and the office of diviner has become a

---

[1] In Scripture the royal Psalms e.g. Ps 2, 72, 110 are not Messianic but form a bridge to the Messianic faith. The whole religious-political idea complex which was connected with the king, what is expected from him, how he was approached, what miracles ascribed to him, this was the strongest basis, the feeding ground for Messianic expectations.

[2] *Callaway*, Religious System, 345.

[3] *Krige*, 243. The inkáta used by Shaka was kept until Cetshwayo's reign when it was burned by the British in 1879.

constituent part of his Messianic call. The belief in the eternally active life principle, *numinous* power or vital force, finds its effective expression in the *isangoma*. To this office however no political power is attached. The *isangoma* is a medicine man whose medicine has magical rather than pharmateutical value. The diviners are the only people who regularly pray to the spirits and sing hymns to them.[1] He/she maintains the link between the shades and the living. Bryant states that he does this "by means of a special concentration of power within him, which enables him to understand things which are beyond conception of ordinary mortals. This power in the case of the diviner is derived from the ancestors themselves".[2] The prophetic office of the *isangoma* is stimulated and inspired by the inspiring agency of the ancestors. The spiritual life of the tribe is his concern. The continuous threat of the community by visible, negative and destructive forces of life makes the function of the *isangoma* an essential one. The magical world is his/her *spiritual mother earth* whose main function is to heal the sick. The contact of the *isangoma* with the spirits through dreams and trance situations is a religious-magical contact. Shembe emphasized this relationship in Isl. 218[1,2] where he states "*sivela thina kwelizayo*" ("we come from the world that is to come".). The *isangoma*, through healing, opens up the way to a brighter future and fights his way through the magical world and its dangers counteracting it right at the centre. He *is* in this sense a Messiah. The office of king and *isangoma* is the background of Isaiah Shembe who describes himself as the diviner in Isl. 157[2]. Here we find a centrifugal *self* with centripetal attraction.

But he has made contact with a legalistic-moralistic type of interpretation of Christianity which suited the religious climate of a society in which ritual prohibitions played a central role. Through them the ancestors are influenced so that they have to do with positive magic. This has established the basis for syncretism. Isaiah Shembe has re-established the significance of these ritual prohibitions and made the Sabbath the very basis of Salvation. Jehovah, the God of the Sabbath, and Shembe were now intimately associated. Shembe is the Saviour of the law and through the Law. Most probably he took his name from Isaiah who stated in 61[1] "The Spirit of the Lord is upon me because the Lord has anointed me". The eschatological king of Isaiah became Shembe himself and in him the kingdom of God is realized. The fallen house of Israel, in this case of Sendzangakhona, will be built up again. Shembe had no eschatological message in his Izl. in the sense of Yahweh intervening in history and making

---

[1] Bryant, A. T., "The Zulu cult of the dead", in Man, No. 95, 1917, 145.

[2] Ibid., 143.

all things new—this has been realized already. The new Sinai Covenant has been fulfilled and Micah's promise of a new Zion has been realized. Isaiah Shembe is the child born (cf. Is. 8^{23}–9^7 and Isl. 136^1) he is the Immanuel of Is. 7^{2-17} (cf. Isl. 93^5); he is the *ebed-Yahweh*, in Shembe's language the *iNceku* of Jehova; he is a Messiah and the hope of religious and political restoration through the law of Moses. The Supreme Being is present in his mighty works. Messianism in the Bible is inseparably linked up with Jesus Christ while it is in the *iBandla lamaNazaretha* inseparably linked up with Isaiah Shembe. He is more than the promised prophet of Deut. 18^{15} which is a basic text in the Zionist movements—he is truly a Messiah to his followers, a god in whom the divine and human are inseparably associated; he is to them truly Christ, the holy one who has risen and continues to live at Ekuphakameni. The corner-stone of this movement is thus not Jesus Christ but *Isaiah Shembe*. He wished to be the political, social and religious Saviour of the Zulu nation in the first instance but also of all other nations.

CHAPTER THREE

MAN AND THE SUPERNATURAL WORLD

A. *uMoya* or ummoya (sing.): imimoya or immoya (pl.). The word belongs to the umu-imi or magical class and bears the following meanings: i. Wind; air, breath; ii. Substantialness, fullness of matter, solidity; iii. Spirit, soul, life; iv. Rumour; v. Nonsense; vi. (mod.) Climate, climatic conditions.

This section is mainly concerned with the first three types of the meaning of *uMoya*. The second type of meaning, though idiomatic, is also important with regard to this study.

The Old Testament *ruach* has been translated into Zulu as *umoya* (cf. 1 Kings 22²¹) as well as the New Testament *pneuma* (cf. 1 Cor. 15⁴⁵). Callaway maintains that the untaught Zulu will not use *umoya* in the sense of *spirit* or soul but only apply it to the air breathed.[1] Even though the word has been used in a wider context than mentioned by Callaway, his statement is nevertheless significant.

In the *Izihlaɓelelo umoya* is used with three different meanings: i. Impersonal power, force or energy; ii. Personal Being; iii. Simply as a metaphor.

1. *Impersonal power*

i. Shembe has ritualized work, and his theology in this connection is significant. Work was to him of the new social order and he made it a mark of a true Nazarite.[2] The word *umoya* is used only once in the *Prayers* and refers to work. He approaches *Nkosi Jehova* with the request to give *umoya*, in this case physical strength, to cultivate, weed, plough, and herd the cattle.

ii. The fundamental meaning of *umoya* is that it constitutes the vital force of the body. It is more than mere physical strength. An analysis of Isl. 13 will give some clarification. Shembe states in verse 2 the following:

---

[1] *Callaway*, The religious system, 10, (footnote).
[2] cf. *Izihlaɓelelo*, pp. 2–7; cf. *Vilakazi*, Isonto Lamanazaretha, 50.

Ukunxanela komoya wakho	The ardent desire of your *umoya*)[1]
Makungifune kungithole;	Let it search for me, let it find me;
E6umpofwini 6omoya wami	In the poverty of my *umoya*
Mangithokoze namhla weNkosi.	let me be happy today, Oh, *Nkosi*.

What could be received is elaborated in the following verses in which the well of Jacob is not merely called to mind but described as existing in their midst. The water in this well is not merely symbolic in the Zwinglian sense but gives *power*. Thus the invitation in verse 3:

Yizanini 6antu nonke	Come all ye people
Sondelani ngase mthonjeni;	Come ye near to the spring
Lowo mthombo ka Jakobe	That well of Jacob
Lapha* kwasinda khona*	Right here recovered the
amaSamaria	Samaritans.

* *Lapha* (Adv. here) and *khona* (not indicative of any place but indicates location or presence which may be here, there or elsewhere) used together give problems with regard to translation. The idea of continuity however is here being expressed. *Khona - lapha* = right here.

After referring to talents and gifts (*amathalenta neziphiwo* verse 1) which are *necessary* for *umoya*, its 'poverty' is further erased by the *holy water*. This history for unhistorical cyclical thinking is repeatable in time and transferable in space. *Umoya* is fed and strengthened at the Jacob's well of the Zulus, the Samaritans in this case. And so the people came to Eku-phakameni as the woman came in Samaria to Jesus (cf. John 4[5–30]): cf. verse 6:

Emveni kwaloko 6amncenga 6athi	After it they begged him saying,
Hlala nathi izinsuku ezintathu*,	Stay with us three days,
Usiphuzise nathi sonke	And also make all of us drink
Njengalo mfazi omphuzisile.	Just as in the case of the woman to whom you gave to drink.

* The three days may refer to Christ's death and resurrection. In this case it will mean that the water gives everlasting life.[2])

Material things are in direct relationship to a person's *umoya*. In Isl. 14[1] he states that *hope* (*amathemba*: although in *plural*, is more often used in

---

[1] This word is most difficult to translate and without circumscription will be retained in the translations.

[2]) cf. Sundkler, Bantu Prophets, 151 ff. for the Bethesda type of movement which concentrate on purification rites excercised at a sacred pool related to the Bethesda pool described in John 5[4–7].

the singular) and *gifts* (*neziphiwo*) are disappointed (*kudanile*) and comes with the request: cf. verse 4.

Uthokozise umoya wami	You may make my *umoya* happy
Ngokuthandwa nguwe.	through its being loved by you.

As an impersonal power *umoya* may be strong or weak.[1]) In Isl. 23[2], after stating that good faith has been *poured* into him "which", he states, "is thy *umoya*", Shembe complains about the strength of the *amandiki namandawu* (evil spirits associated with magic, which is said to have entered from the north[2]) and then he asks for strength stating that he is sick in his body and in his *umoya*, which does not merely refer to physical sickness but to a general condition of weakness as a result of "sin". The *umoya* can also be sick as is clear in Isl. 23[5].

Namhla ngiyakuthanda Nkosi	Today I am loving thee *Nkosi*,
Khipha konke ukufa kwami;	take out all my sickness from me;
Okuse mzimbeni wami	that which is in my body
Nokuse moyeni wami.	and which is in my *umoya*.

A Zionist will not say that a person's *umphefumulo* (soul) is weak or strong but he will maintain that a person has a strong or weak *umoya*. *uMoya* is thought of as power. The average christian theologian interprets, for example, the Pentecost event in personal terms. The Holy Spirit gives light and spiritual power in a non-physical sense. Shembe's approach is different. The Pentecost event signifies to him spiritual and physical completeness, strength and power which is basic to inner security. The *umoya* is thought of as something substantial which could be poured in. cf. Isl. 135[3].

Thela* kimi umoya wamandla	Pour into me the *umoya* of power,
Ngiya kwedlula esigodini sosizi.	I shall pass by the valley of destruction.

* thela: i. Pour out, pour into; ii. Sprinkle, scatter over, etc.

In Isl. 113[1] Shembe does not merely speak of "pouring out" but "filling up" with *umoya*. He states:

Nkosi yelula isandla sakho	*Nkosi*, strech out thy hand
Phezu kwe Nceku yakho.	over thy servant.

---

[1]) The *Izihlaɓelelo* do not speak of *bad* or *evil umoya* or he is with a good *umoya* (*unomoya omuhle*).

[2]) -Ndawu: Member of the Ndau tribe of Southern Rhodesia and Portuguese East Africa which the Zulu consider to have a special ability in magic.

Igcwalise ngomoya wakho,	Fill him with thy *umoya*
Ishumayele izwi lakho.	that he may preach thy word.

Here the *umoya* is bound to office and ritual. In early Christian history the prophets went out from Jerusalem where the laying on of hands took place. God's history started here and went back there. This kind of Jerusalem caliphate exists at Ekuphakameni. Through Shembe the transference of supernatural *numinous* power is the most effective. The January and July festivals are great occasions for "filling up" with such power. cf. Isl. 103[4].

Sithumele wedwa Nkosi	Send him alone, *Nkosi*
Leso sichaka sakho,	that servant of yours
siɓuthele sigcwalise*	that we may gather and we may fill up
Ngalowo moya wakho.	with that *umoya* of thee.

* gcwala. (caus. gcwalisa): Become full; to fill, supplement.

uMoya is thought of as a condition. Shembe had been taught in the church that one receives power through the Holy Spirit but to this he gave the interpretation of his own world view. For the pre-christian Zulu everything is filled with vital force or *energy* as Asmus calls it.[1]) The *umoya* of a person can be in his hair, his blood, his regalia, his sacred dress and his possessions give it to him. In the analysis of the *umoya* concept one should not be limited to its immediate meaning. When Shembe speaks about *umoya* it will be far from reality and truth to translate it simply by *spirit*. When he uses the term, not only is a person's personality involved or the idea of completeness or fullness or *spirit* but also man's ability to get beyond himself in order to receive the benefits of supernatural power. This *numinous* power could be transferred by a stick, stone or staff. In 1899 Marett[2]) coined the term *animatism* in order to give a more adequate, precise and refined description of Tylor's animism which he considered to be "a bare and meagre definition of religion".[3]) Animatism wishes to circumscribe the personal spiritual power, the vital force, that pervades everything. Animism and dynamism are two terms which could be applied to the Zulu religion. Marett's animatism, which he anomalously circumscribes as impersonal spiritual power, is the hidden, mysterious, pervading energy or vital force[4]), the cosmic universal power. Conversion to Chris-

---

[1]) cf. Asmus, 31.
[2]) Marett, R. R., Threshold of Religions, London, 1909.
[3]) Tylor, E. B., Primitive Culture, London, John Murray, Vol. I, 1873[2], 426.
[4]) cf. Tempels, P., Bantu Philosophy, 1959.

tianity is often hampered as a result of the conviction that to discard what is traditional will lead to destruction as one is cut off from the very source which gives *numinous* power.

The pre-christian Zulus were not mere animatists thinking of unco-ordinated energies. With them this force is found in the deity, the ancestors, spirits, animals, medicines and things; it is the very essence of being. All things have hidden inner power.[1]) Whether this power comes from personal or impersonal forces, souls, spirits, gods or material things does not matter; the fact remains that religion which does not give *numinous* power, is of no consequence. The clear-cut distinctions some anthropologists wished to make between magic and religion is so much nonsense. Shembe I is revered because of this power he possesses. His return to the ways of his ancestors has a double meaning, namely, it is a return to the ancestor cult as potent forces in human life but also to the forces of nature which are the powers behind the rivers, streams, pools, rocks, wells, hills, and both the power and the personality are worshipped. It is with this background that the *umoya* concept receives its significance.

The Zulu mind, as expressed in the *Izihlaɓelelo*, does not distinguish between physical and spiritual power. The sense of security evident in the Nazarites finds its origin in their *knowledge* of having acquired *umoya* and of having contact with its source. It is at Ekuphakameni (cf. Isl. 49³). There the condition of completeness is reached. cf. Isl. 49².

Lapho sengiɓona	When I see
Ngikushiya Ukuphakama,	I leaving Ukuphakama,
Mawuhloɓe* umoya wami	let my *umoya* be decorated,
Ungadingi lutho.	So that it is not in want of anything.

* hloba: Put on finery, dress up, decorate oneself.

Perfection or completeness is a much wider concept than pietistic salvation. The whole being in the here and now is included and it includes both the spiritual and physical existence. The doctrine of perfection has given Shembe a theological basis for the Zulu concept of *numinous* power. Completeness means to be free from sickness, sin, embarrasments of different kinds. Dr. Berglund states "Salvation to the Zulu is not a matter of salvation from sin, death and hell as it is with the Christian, but it is redemption from sickness and ill-health, financial and political embarras-ments, and here the *umoya* conception finds an implanted field in which it labours freely and without any opposition at all".[2])

---

[1]) cf. Asmus, 45, 46.
[2]) *Berglund, A-I*, Letter dated 14.XII. 64.

uMoya could also be *inhaled*. In Isl. 165 Shembe has the two-weeks festival on the Nhlangakazi mountain in mind where *inter alia* the *impepho* plant is burned and inhaled in a symbolic act. He states in verse 4:

Holani umoya	Inhale *umoya*,
Hlabani Ngamandla,	Fight bravely,
Niphathe izikhali ngalo ukholo.	So that you may carry the weapons through this faith.

Shembe II described the feasts at Ekuphakameni as good *umoya*: cf. Isl. 240³.

Amadili akho Thixo	Thy feasts, *Thixo*
Angumoya omuhle.	they are good *umoya*.

Although only certain individuals have *umoya*, as only certain people had *isithunzi* (personality) which gives them authority, the whole community shares in it. The king, the chief, the kraal head had special *isithunzi* and *umoya* but all could have a share in it. Although *umoya* seems to be highly individualistc its effects are not individualistic. The chosen one is fully mediator in the Zulu sense of the word—he is the sum and substance of the community. They share in what he has obtained.

2. *Personal Being*

Before discussing the above-mentioned meaning of *umoya* a brief reference to the Zulu concept of "spirit" is necessary. The different names for soul and spirit indicate the Zulu attempts to circumscribe man's whole being. One could speak about a free spirit and a corporeal soul. The free spirit could leave the body while the corporeal soul is bounded to it. The free spirit is the shadow soul. The corporal soul is the life-principle while the free spirit is the wandering entity which cannot stay away too long from the body. After the *Rites de Passage* the free soul becomes part of the ancestor community, taking up its function as a guardian spirit after the *ukubuyisa* ceremony. Although the free spirit is somewhat passive to life itself it has nevertheless a definite function in man's life. Man is helpless when the free spirit leaves him. The shadow (*isithunzi*) is seen as the lengthening of the free soul to the outside. Callaway states about the Zulu, that the shadow of a person grows shorter as he grows older and that this short shadow is buried with the corpse but the long shadow has "gone on".[1] The long shadow becomes an ancestral spirit. The free spirit has

---

[1] *Callaway*, Religious System, 91, 126.

an extra bodily activity and has a definite part to play in the conscious activity of the person. It is related to a person's authority.

The *isithunzi* or free spirit is not mentioned in the *Izihlaбelelo* but this pre-christian concept still bears influence on the *umoya*. The *isithunzi*, which eventually became the ancestral spirit, could be removed by medicines and kept in captivity. This is known as *thweбula*, which is a medicinal charm used for *killing* or hypnotizing. Only the *isithunzi* of a man could be *thweбulad*. A man's *isithunzi* has a physical likeness to his person, e.g., as is the case in photography. This is the reason why the photograph of Shembe I in the *Izihlaбelelo* is thought to have magical power. A person's *isithunzi* goes *aбaphansi* (to those underneath) as the *umoya* goes to "those underneath", because "these two cannot be separated".[1] Vilakazi states that when the *umoya* is taken away from the *isithunzi* "then we have disintegrated that of man which remains to make him live on after death".[2] The *isithunzi* however is dangerous for the period, usually a year, before the *ukuбuyisa* ceremony takes place.[3] These shades could be seen as the late Shembe had been seen.

Although *isithunzi* is not mentioned by Shembe its influence on the *umoya* concept is still present. The *umoya* is to him a free spirit. Both Shembes are true to the Zulu interpretation. They do not maintain that a person's *umphefumulo* (soul) disappears because then it will mean that a person is dead. *uMoya* has to do with a person's authority and well being. When Shembe states that he has lost his *umoya*, he means that he has lost his authority, his personality, his *numinous* power. It is of great significance for the whole community that Shembe's *umoya* be strong as was the case with regard to the king in the tribe. This is evident in Isl. 150[5].

Zinqamukile namhla iziбopho
Eбezi бophe umoya wami.
Madili okwenama wozani
Uyajaбula umoya wami.

The bonds are today broken apart
which had bound my *umoya*.
Large happy gatherings, come ye,
My *umoya* rejoices.

These gatherings are dependent upon Shembe as the source of *numinous* power and are proofs of the greatness of his *umoya*. Shembe is in the fortunate position that his name is in the book of life and his *umoya*, which is in intimate association with his *name* (or *isithunzi* in pre-christian terminology), is now protected. cf. Isl. 201[1].

---

[1] cf. *Vilakazi*, Zulu Transformations, 88.
[2] Ibid., 89.
[3] *Krige*, Social system, 284.

Anginazikhali, anginazihlangu	I am not with weapons, I am not with war shields
Zokuvikela umoya wami,	with which to defend my *umoya*,
Nanti igama lami seliyahlangulwa	Here is my name now protected
Encwadini yokuphila.	in the book of life.

The *umoya* could be *bound* as is evident in Isl. 19[1].

Thixo Mkhululi khulula umoya wami	*Thixo*, Liberator, liberate my *umoya*
Ngakhe phakathi kwezizwe,	I have built amongst the nations,
Ezizonda umoya wami	which are jealous of my *umoya*,
Weyise wamakholwa	Oh, Father of the believers,
Khulula umoya wami.	liberate my *umoya*.

The last two lines are repeated in each of the four verses of this Isl. Sin means that one's *umoya* is caught by negative forces. This is clear in Isl. 236[4] where Shembe II states:

Zonke izono maziphele	Let all sin come to an end
Ukhululwe umoya wami.	and my *umoya* be freed.

Shembe I does not refer to Jesus Christ as the Liberator of the *umoya* but approaches *Thixo* and *Yise* (Father, the word used in both creeds where Jesus Christ is excluded). It is rather the God of strength, of *umoya*, than the Jesus Christ of the Cross, who is called upon. Later in Isl. **44** *chorus* his request is directed to Jehova, the God of Sinai and the law.[1])

Ngisize Jehova	Help me, Jehova,
Ukhulule umoya wami.	that you may free my *umoya*.

In Isl. 29[3] the *umoya* is described as an entity which could die:

Uphephise umoya wami	May you protect my *umoya*
Usinde ekufeni.	that it may escape from death.

The *umoya* will be *resurrected* according to Shembe II as stated in Isl. 221[8].

Umoya wami uzovuka	My spirit will rise
Wembath' inyama entsha.	and be clothed in new flesh.
Kwaphakade 6engizelwe,	From old I was born
Nanini ngiya ku6akhona.	forever I will be there.

---

[1]) cf. also Isl. 52.

Shembe I often described *umoya* as being in bonds, and many approach him to loosen their *umoya*. In Isl. 31[2,3] he states with an obvious reference to himself:

Mhawukeli wezinyembezi	Sympathiser with tears
Hawukelumoya wami.	pity my *umoya*.

and adds in verse 2

Umzimba usuphelile	The body is now finished
Akubube okwenyama,	May that which is of flesh be destroyed
Ukuze umoya usinde	So that the *umoya* may be saved
Ngosuku lweNkosi.	On the day of the *iNkosi*.

This same idea is expressed by Shembe II in Isl. 242[4] although he puts the flesh and *umoya* in opposition to one another. The *umoya* is pictured as appearing in the day of Judgement—this is not said of *umphefumulo*.

3. *As metaphor*

Shembe states in Isl. 49 *chorus*:[1])

Hayi wenhliziyo yami	Lo! you my heart,
Mawunikele umoya wami	may you give my *umoya*
Iminduze* yasendle	lilies of the field
Uhlo6e uphelele.	that it may be decorated and be complete.

* -Nduze: Name of three species of lilies which grow in damp places in Natal.

The reference is obviously to Matth. 6[28-30]. The close connection between the heart and *umoya* is also found with the non-christian Zulu who refers to a person's *umoya* as the *second* heart, which signifies a person's conscience.[2]) The heart is thought to be the seat of *umoya* and *umphefumulo*. Shembe has most probably in the above-mentioned Isl. also Matth. 12[35] in mind. *uMoya* in this Isl. refers to his personality, his outward appearance, his spiritual and physical authority and dignity. These rare lilies with which he has to be decorated figuratively refer to everything that elevate his being, his very "I", his whole person.

---

[1]) Shembe II asks also for the decoration of his *umoya* with unperishable attire, not bought with gold but coming from his Father (Ba6a). Not a change of heart but a decoration is asked for.

[2]) cf. *Vilakazi*, Zulu Transformations, 87.

The close relationship between *umoya* and *inhliziyo* (heart) is expressed in Isl. 65 chorus.

Umoya wami unosizi	My *umoya* is in trouble,
Inhliziyo yami ihluɓukile.	my heart is forsaken.

Here again the Zulu mind of Shembe is at work. His *umoya* (which in this case may also refer to his spirit) is not bound by time or space. It could be caught by evil forces with the result that the heart is forsaken. One could interpret this section in the sense that his *umoya*, his person, has allowed evil forces to get power over it so that the heart has no authority over his being and over others. When the *umoya* experiences trouble the heart is forsaken or in distress.[1] The heart and the *umoya* (spirit) could be distinguished but not separated. *uMoya* experiences mental pain, grief, and misery and is used interchangeably for the whole person.

As the *umoya* can be the cause of the heart's distress so it could be the cause of the heart's refreshing. cf. Isl. 145².

Thela amazolo omoya wakho	Pour out the dew of your *umoya*
Enhlizyweni enosizi.	in the distressed heart.

He asks for newness in his *umoya*, i.e., in his innermost being and in his outward appearence. cf. Isl. 109 chorus:

Mangethwase Nkosi yami	Let me change, my *iNkosi*[2]
Ngiɓemusha emoyeni,	That I may become new in *umoya*
Ngiɓafuze aɓangcwele	so that I resemble the saints
Aɓaseɓusweni ɓakho.	who are before thy face.

This is a typical revival hymn. Newness in his *umoya* is requested but this does not mean conversion in the scriptural sense. The word *ethwasa*, translated as *change*, actually means to come out anew. Shembe has however most probably the obvious religious meaning of the word in mind, namely, to show signs of change when a person becomes spirit-possessed. The Zulu says: *uyethwasa lomuntu* ("This person is possessed"). The word is also used in connection with initiation; change means for Shembe to receive something, an addition, to receive *numinous* power and thus obtain security and completeness. Change does not mean a renewal of the heart, a breaking down of the "I" but an addition to it after something dirty (because that is what sin signifies) has been removed. This chorus evokes

---

[1] cf. Isl. 145³.

[2] *Vilakazi, Isonto Lamanazaretha*, 94, translates this line: "Let the spirit descend upon me, my Lord".

many pre-christian associations in the mind of a syncretistic-oriented Zulu. Jesus Christ is here also completely *excluded* from any association with the *umoya*. Shembe expects *numinous* power which is not to be obtained from a Cross. cf. Isl. 184[1,3,5].

| Woza Jehova woza Nkosi, | Come Jehova, come *Nkosi*, |
| Uwembese umoya wami. | that you may clothe my *umoya*. |

The *uMoya* must be saved (cf. Izl. 104[3]; 231[1]) and in Isl. 121[3]. Shembe I speaks about the fire which burns his *umoya*, obviously referring to the day of judgement. *uMoya* thus refers to his innermost being.

What does the *Izihlaɓelelo* understand by *umoya*?

1. i. As an *impersonal power* it is what is generally described as *numinous* power or vital force which could be conveyed through different media such as places, things, supernatural beings and persons. It could even be inhaled. It is most effective during the festivals at Ekuphakameni and Nhlangakazi with its dancing, singing, praying, baptisms and holy communion.

ii. It gives a sense of security, inner conviction and strength, and assures supernatural contact;

iii. It could be weak or strong—weak when a person is in trouble and strong when a person's personality is strong and can act undisturbedly. Its weakness is often described in personal terms, e.g., sickness. It is never used in the sense of being evil.

iv. *uMoya* is explained in terms of substance, something with which the heart of a person is "filled up". Purification and *umoya* go together. This is not just a Baptist reminiscence but the Zulu religion knew this "filling up" with *numinous* power, e.g., the king during the Great *Umkhosi* had to be strengthened through ritual washing and medicines.

v. It has only once been used in the sense of physical strength[1]), unless Isl. 165[4] is also given this interpretation.

2. i. As a *personal being* it is related to Jehova, Thixo or Baɓa—not to the Cross which is rather a sign of the weakness of *umoya*.

ii. The *umoya* could leave the body and reminds of the *isithunzi* or free spirit in the Zulu religion.

iii. *Umoya* gets into trouble, becomes distressed, saddened and grieved.

---

[1]) *Sundkler's* definition of *umoya* as related to piety, good christian behaviour, and the sum of supernatural gifts such as speaking with tongues, is limited, as it has a wider meaning. cf. Bantu Prophets, 244.

iv. It needs to be continuously strengthened and refreshed.

v. It is in close relationship with the heart, its seat.

vi. The *umoya* continues to live after death and will be judged.

3. i. Used *metaphorically* it signifies the whole person.

ii. It signifies also a person's conscience.

iii. It stands for authority and personal dignity.

iv. The active part in the human being is described as *umoya*; not as *umphefumulo*. Shembe does not use *umoya* in the sense of instinct as the Zulus often do.

v. It could be decorated, which means the strengthening of the personality through gifts or through possessions by which a general sense of security is established. As the king's *umoya* beamed through his regalia so also that of Shembe I and II and their followers: they are clothed, as it were, with it.

B. *Umphefumulo (pl. imiphefumulo)*

i. Breath; ii. Life; iii. Soul.

This study is mainly concerned with the second and third meanings. Soul is in the Old Testament designated as *nephesh* and in the New Testament as *psyche*.

In the four Zulu Bibles used the translations for soul (*umphefumulo*) and spirit (*umoya*) were the same with regard to 1 Cor. 15[45] "Adam was made a living soul (*umphefumulo ophilayo*); the last Adam was made a quickening spirit (*umoya ophilisayo*)".

Umphefumulo[1]) appears about eleven times in the prayers and about nine times in the Izl. ascribed to Shembe I, while *umoya* is mentioned over forty times in his Izl., often in the choruses, and only once in the prayers.

Even when *umphefumulo* is used to circumscribe a personal being it is used metaphorically because its basic meaning is breath. The Zulus distinguish between four aspects of being a person while living, namely a. *inyama* or *umzimba*, the body which decomposes after the destruction of life; b. *umphefumulo* (or soul) namely that which makes a person live, the life-principle; c. *umoya*, vital force, that which constitutes it and which is also used to indicate "spirit"; d. *isithunzi* which literally means shadow and which becomes the shade or ancestral spirit. Apart from these the *inhliziyo* (heart, feelings) and *ingqondo* (brain, intellect, understanding,

---

[1]) Sundkler refers to it only as a designation for a woman prophetess, cf. Bantu Prophets, 120–121.

memory or mind)[1]) are of vital significance to a human being.

Most of the difficulty in coming to a true analysis of *umoya* and *umphefumulo* is due to the close relationship with regard to their basic meaning—both could mean air or breath. Prof. Vilakazi states in a letter that "the words *umoya* and *umphefumulo*, in ordinary speech, are not quite equivalent".[2]) The author of Hebrews (4[12]) states: "For the word of God is quick, and powerful, and sharper than any two-edged sword, piercing even to the dividing asunder of soul and spirit..." The Zulu Bibles have *umphefumulo nomoya* (soul and spirit), a distinction which is observed when the concepts are closely analysed.

The soul is not referred to Jesus Christ but to Jehova and the *iNceku*. cf. Isl. 39[2]

Mɓonge uJehova	Praise Jehova
Mphefumulo wami usenethuɓa.	My soul, while you still have opportunity.
Sosondela lesosikhathi	That time will come near
Akusayi kuvuma	it will not agree (i.e. it will not be possible)
Noma uye eNcekwini	even that you go to the *iNceku*
Ukuya kuyiɓona.	to go and to see him.

Here the soul is described as a personal being whose salvation lies with Jehova, the Giver of the law, the meticulous observance of which leads to salvation. The soul could take the wrong course: He states in his version of Ps. 23: "*ngiyakholwa ukhuthi uzakuwuɓuyisa umphefumulo wami ekwedukeni kwawo ngenxa yomusa wakhe.*" ("...I believe that he will cause my soul to return from its taking the wrong course through his grace." Evening Prayers, Section 6, 10).

Reference has been made to the "free" spirit and bodily soul, the last thought of in more static terms and bound to the body. In this light the soul returning from the wrong course is rather metaphorical. The bodily soul and free spirit, both concepts being related to the conscious and unconscious psyche, combine very early in a human being's life and could be used interchangeably. The *umphefumulo* is the life in a person—the Zulu states *umphefumulo upumile* (the breath has gone out) meaning death.

With Shembe I the *umphefumulo* concept had come under Christian influence. For the pre-christian Zulu, as for the Zionist, not all people had *umoya*. Thus, not all become shades or ancestor spirits but all have souls.

---

[1]) cf. Krige, 284.

[2]) Vilakazi, A., Letter to author dated 12.I.65.

Those who become shades are actually destiny ancestors set into office after the *ukuɓuyisa* ceremony while the others disappear into obscurity. The interpretation of Christianity by Shembe I has given to all souls a *destiny* and with it a sense of security so that it is not a matter of life and death whether a person has *umoya* or not. Thus, all souls could now become destiny ancestors. Not only those with *umoya*, authority, are called back to the *holy city* but all who adhere to the laws. Does this account for the role of women within the new context? He continuously emphasizes the fact that he is not selective and that nobody is excluded from Ekupha-kameni but only sin (cf. Isl. 6[1,2]). A person's soul however could be destroy-ed. He states: "*Ungakucaɓangi ukukhipha umphefumulo womunye umuntu*" ("May you not consider to take out the soul of one person" Sabbath Prayers, Section 44, 22.)

Shembe does make a distinction, even if it is indirectly, between *umoya* and *umphefumulo*. The *umphefumulo* has to do with personal salvation while *umoya* is more specifically related to *numinous* power and authority. When Shembe kept himself busy with the nation he had mainly *umoya* in mind and it is most effective at large gatherings and feasts while *umphe-fumulo* has a more personal character. The *umoya* is often described as being in bonds (cf. Isl 150[5]), that it is weak or strong while the soul needs to be saved. One has not little or much *umphefumulo* as in the case of *umoya*. In the Zulu religion *umphefumulo* took a secondary place, it went to the grave while the free spirit became the shade or ancestral spirit. Shembe did not mention *umphefumulo* once from Izl. 151 to 219. He eventually discarded the idea of souls which have to be *saved* and which after death rest at the grave until the day of judgement. He keeps himself busy with the more mobile force in his realized eschatology namely the free spirit or *umoya*. In the Izl. in which the *umphefumulo* is ignored. Shembe concentrates on his holy city, nationalistc songs, *Nhlangakazi*, the *Nkosi YamaNazaretha*, Paradise, Jerusalem, the angels, the heavenly messengers, the *umoya* concept, the pools of water, the *uMkhululi*, the *amakhosi* and so on. The whole tribe, as it were, enters his sacral community, and under such circumstances one could hardly expect any reference to personal salvation, something strange to pre-christian Zulu-thinking. Only after he started to date the revelations he received, did he make sporadic references to *umphefumulo*. But *umphefumulo* is now described in the same terms as he described *umoya*.

What did Shembe I say about *umphefumulo*?

He states with reference to uNkulunkulu: *Umkhondze ngayo yonke inhliziyo yakho nangawo wonke umphefumulo wakho* ("Serve him with your whole heart and your whole soul", Evening Prayers, 20, 12[1]). This is a Biblical reminiscence. Here the soul metaphorically used for life is called to serve—while *umoya* is used more in connection with authority.

In Isl. 53[2] Shembe states that both the flesh and the souls recover at Ekuphakameni and in Isl. 15[1] *Simakade* is described as the hope of their souls. In Isl. 64[3] he refers to the continuation of the soul:

Bakhumbule Nkosi	Remember them, *Nkosi*,
Aɓaseduze ekufeni	who are near to death,
Yamkele ngenjaɓulo	receive them with joy
Leyo mphefumulo yaɓo.	those souls of theirs.

The soul is further described as being fastened to *Nkosi* while the *umoya* again is often described as being bound by evil forces. cf. Isl. 62[2].

Zixegisa* umphefumulo wami	They (sins) loosen my soul
Eɓusweni ɓakho Nkosi;	from thy face, *Nkosi*.
Zidanisa lolo luthando	They (sins) cause that love to
	worry
Eɓengikuthanda ngalo.	with which I loved you.

  * Xegisa: become loose when intimately bound up with.

In Isl. 147 the soul is obviously referred to Shembe as its Saviour and he is not selective. He states in verse 1:

Liyaɓa ɓiza ɓonke aɓantu	It (the world) is calling all people
Alikhethi noma munye.	it does not select only one.

He describes the soul now in the same terms as *umoya*, namely that it has to be decorated, as seen in the fourth verse of Isl. 147.

Wozani weɓadingi	Come ye people who are in need
Wozani weɓasweli	come ye people in want,
Eniswele leyonguɓo	who were in want of that cloak
Yokwembesa umphefumulo	of covering the soul,
Li ya ku fika lelo langa	that day will arrive
Uzodinga lowo mphefumulo.	that soul will be in want.

This is most probably a reference to Rev. 3[5].

The redemption of the *umphefumulo* takes place by way of power from the *uMkhululi*. cf. Isl. 150[2].

---

[1]) cf. Evening Prayers, Section 25, 12; Section 29, 13; Prayers for the Sabbath, Section 13, 18.

Unamandla uMkhululi	He has power, *uMkhululi,*
Okusisindisa	of redeeming us.
Uyakufuna uMkhululi	The *uMkhululi* seeks you,
Wena mphefumulo wami.	you my soul.

If one accepts that the prayers were written early and that the Izl. are more or less in chronological order, one must conclude that *umphefumulo* (whose redemption was for him related in his church to the Cross and baptism,) played a more significant role in the first years of his life when his ecclesiastical background had still a strong influence. When the Zulu religion took precedence *umoya* became prominent because of its association with *numinous* power, personal authority, well-being and strength in magical acts. In Zulu religion man can do nothing to his *umphefumulo,* only to his *umoya* and *isithunzi,* and thus Shembe I pushed *umphefumulo* into the background. According to the Church it rests in obscurity until the day of judgement and Shembe could not think in such terms—it was difficult for him to associate a world of active ancestral spirits or shades of the Zulu nation with such a static interpretation of the soul. Salvation means zestful living and this is associated with the *umoya.* In Isl. 222[5] which could be accepted as the confession of faith of the movement about Shembe I's resurrection, not *umphefumulo* is mentioned but *umoya.*

Although the influence of Zulu religion is strong also with Shembe II, he reveals specific Christian influences in his concept of the *umphefumulo* to which he refers more than to *umoya.* In Isl. 239[2], referring to *Nkosi Thixo,* he states:

Iyafuna inhliziyo	It wants the heart
Yen'u Thixo ophilayo	you, the living *uThixo,*
Umphefumulo* wa6o 6onke	The soul of them all
Ukhumbule** ezulwini.	may it go to heaven.

* Schlosser translates as "heart" which misses the theological significance of the term in this context. The heart has no eternal destiny. Schlosser's translation of inhliziyo as "Seele" in Isl. 238[5] is justified.
** Could also mean remember.

When Shembe II asked to be saved from the second death it is again a Biblical reminiscence. cf. Isl. 227[6]. (cf. Rev. 20[14]).

Nkosi yami ngisindise	My *Nkosi* save me
Ekufeni kwesi6ili;	from the second death;
Ma uphile umphefumulo	May the soul live
Nxa kubhubha okwenyama.	when is destroyed that which
	belongs to the flesh.

In Isl. 213 he gives his version of Ps. 23 and relates the soul, as his father did, to the ways of righteousness while he relates *umoya* to the green pastures. In Isl. 234[3] he expresses surprise that his *umphefumulo* wanders away from *uThizo* (should read *uThixo!*)

Shembe II expresses a typical Zulu concept when he states in Isl. 238[1] as they consider the heart to be the seat of the soul:

Inhliziyo ayivuma*	The heart is not willing
Ukukhulula umphefumulo wami.	to free my soul.

   * The negative should read *ayivumi*.

The sinful condition of the heart affects the soul. Heart is used also by him in the sense of the flesh which carries (*phatha*) in its sinful state that which is not fitting. This has a typical magical reference. cf. Isl. 242[3].

Uku6ola kwenyama	The decaying of the flesh
Kungangeni emphefumulweni;	let it not enter the soul;
Hlezi iNcekwana yakho	lest your small servant
Ikuphathe okungafanele.	carry that which is not fitting.

For Shembe II the final destiny of the soul is Ekuphakameni. cf. Isl. 237[6],

Buya namuhla muphefumulo wami	Come back today my soul
	(Schlosser = heart)*
Ngena Ekuphakameni,	Enter into Ekuphakameni,
Kade uzula uhlupeka	Long you wandered about un-
	happy,
Ungenandawo yokuphumula.	you not having a place to rest.

   * Schlosser's indiscriminate translation of *soul* as *heart* is not clear even though the Zulu does use these terms sometimes interchangeably. This is a definite reminiscence of the *uku6uyisa*.

Shembe II, with his higher education and stronger influence of the Christian tradition is not as clear with regard to the distinction between *umphefumulo* and *umoya*.

C. *Inhliziyo*

i. Heart (physical organ); ii. The seat of the emotions; courage, hope, desire, appetite; iii. The seat of the soul; iv. Conscience (good or bad), mind, will, patience; v. The seat of nausea.

The Zulu Bible translations have *inhliziyo* for the Old Testament and the New Testament words for heart. The pre-christian Zulu uses heart also for soul while *umoya* is called the second heart referring to one's conscience.

In the *Izihlaƃelelo inhliziyo* is used in two different senses: i. Physiological; ii. Metaphorical.

1. *Physiological*

To the heart, as the central organ of the body and the seat of physical strength, there is hardly any reference in the *Izihlaƃelelo*. This however, is also the case in the Old and New Testaments. Shembe I uses it in this sense only in the *Prayers* (cf. Morning Prayers, Section 10, 2). Shembe II uses it both in the physiological and metaphorical sense in Isl. 225[5].

2. *Metaphorical*

The heart in its metaphorical use circumscribes the innermost of a person; the basis of a person's spiritual life. Shembe I uses the designation heart over sixty times in the Prayers and Izl.

When he states that Jehova has to be served with the whole heart and whole soul, a Biblical reminiscence (cf. Morning Prayers, Section 10, 2), he does not identify the two concepts but both together could exercise the ideal service of Jehova which includes the physical and spiritual sides of a person. The merits of the heart and soul build up the *umoya*. Jehova has to be served with "good fruits in the heart" (*izithelo zoƃuhle ƃenhliziyo*... Evening Prayers, Section 29, 13.). These are *inter alia* observance of the laws. His request is: "Give us hearts to keep thy laws" ("*Usinike izinhliziyo zokugcina imithetho yakho*", Evening Prayers, Section 16, 11). Man serves Jehova with the heart.

Hearts could be hardened, a typical Biblical reminiscence (cf. Is. 46[12]). He admonishes them not to harden their hearts as their fathers Dingaan and Sendzangakhona did (*aƃazendza lukhuni*, Prayers for the Sabbath, Section 21, 19). In Isl. 29[2] Shembe refers to the guilt of his own heart (*amacala enhliziyo yami*) which has a negative effect on his *umoya*. The heart has to be filled with hope, faith and trust. When the *umoya* or free spirit is under the power of evil forces the heart suffers (cf. Isl. 76[1]), as is also seen in the *chorus* of Isl. 65.

Umoya wami unosizi	My *umoya* is in trouble
Inhliziyo yami ihluƃukile.	my heart is deserted.

But the heart in its turn, as the seat of the *umoya*, could be the cause of the *umoya's* suffering: cf. Isl. 96[1]

Inhliziyo iyangedusa	My heart misleads me
Ngiyancipha e6usweni 6akho*.	I am diminishing in thy face.
Chorus: Siza siza Nkosi Ba6a	Help, help, *Nkosi Ba6a*
Uhawukele umoya wami.	Pity my *umoya*.
He then adds in verse 2:	
Khuluma wena Nkosi yami	Speak ye, my *Nkosi*
Khuluma wena nenhliziyo yami...	Speak ye to my heart...

   * It actually means: *I am a fool.*

Shembe I pictures the heart as the very seat of all his trouble and even declares in Isl. 121[3] *Inhliziyo iyisitha sami* ("the heart is my enemy"). The heart, as in Scripture, is to Shembe the very seat of a person's inner life. Interesting however is the fact that Shembe can stand objectively over against his heart as seen above and repeated in Isl. 105[2].

Inhliziyo yami yangiphikisa	My heart contradicted me
Ngaphakathi kwami.	in my innermost being.

It is as if his heart is under evil forces which control it and over which he has no say. This is actually expressed in Isl. 108[4].

Amaketango* asenhliziyweni yami	The chains which are in my heart
Angakhululwa nguwe.	Can be loosened by thee.

   * Loan word from Afrikaans: ketting.

Shembe does not state that his heart has to be loosened but chains in his heart. It is his *umoya* which has to be unbound. This is also the case with Shembe II (cf. Isl. 238[1]). The heart causes it to be in chains. In the Prayers Shembe I started off to mention the heart and *umphefumulo* together but now it is the heart and *umoya*.

(i) *The heart and the word*

Only by opening their hearts can they receive the word of the *iNkosi*. (cf. Isl. 130[2]). The entering of the word is prevented by the heart (Izl. 130[3]; 169[3]). His heart is compared with an animal, it does not want to follow. (Isl. 154[2]). He adds in Isl. 204[4]:

Lisa khathele izwi lakho	Your word is still tired
Enhliziyweni za6aningi.	in the hearts of many.

Here he wishes to express the fact that the word is not yet fully accepted by many and asks that it should be increased (*yanda*). In Isl. 223[1] Shembe II repeats:

Yipha Nkosi i'nhliziyo zethu	Give *Nkosi*, to our hearts
Ukulizwa izwi lakho.	to hear thy word.

(iii) *The cleansing of the heart*

This takes place by way of ritual washing. In this case also no reference is made to Jesus Christ. The removal of the negative magical substance through ritual washing makes the Cross superfluous. When he states in Isl. 157 that the soap of generations could not remove even one (sin) (verse 5), that he washed from the rising till the setting of the sun (verse 6), it is not a rejection of ritual washing[1] but an emphasis on the fact that ritual purity could only be achieved through him as their *uMkhululi*. Shembe II asks for the fountain where he could wash away the dirt (sin) and be complete (cf. Isl. 228[2]); they are those whose hearts are white (*aɓanhliziyo zimhlophe*, Isl. 217[5]). For Shembe II it is not merely ritual washing but he speaks in typical Biblical language about a heart which is contrite. cf. Isl. 235[3].

Ngenhliziyo ethoɓekileyo	With a heart which is contrite
Uyaɓemukela wena.	You accept them.

The one however who accepts them is his father. Shembe II states further in Isl. 240[2], referring to Baɓa

Uyagcina inhliziyo	He preserves the heart
Eqinisileyo.	which is trustworthy.

In Isl. 238[5] he maintains it is good for the heart to suffer;

Ukuze inhliziyo ikhumbule	So that the heart remembers
Ukuthi akulo ikhaya leli	that this is not home,
Kuyidokodo* lomhambi**	it is a temporary hut of a pilgrim.

   * ** Schlosser translates these words into the plural.

The *Cross* has for Shembe II also no significance. He, also, refers to ritual washing rather than purification in the Biblical sense. cf. Isl. 239[4].

Wena Nkosi unamandla	You *Nkosi* are with power
Geza* inhliziyo** yethu	Wash our hearts
Mawuqed' izono zethu.	May you bring to an end our sins.

   * Wash, bath, purify ceremoniously.
   ** Schlosser translated *inhliziyo* as Seele. Washing of *souls* is not a Zulu idea.

---

[1]) For Confessions and Purification see Sundkler, Bantu Prophets, 211 ff.

The final destiny of the heart is Ekuphakameni (cf. Isl. 232³) while that of the wicked heart is "in hell". (*esihogweni* not *esilhogweni*, Isl. 146¹). Shembe I describes the heart as having guilt, as in trouble, bound by evil forces, it is his enemy, is sinful, it refuses the word—in all these terms typical of conservative theology. Shembe II also describes the heart as sinful but speaks about it in more positive terms which shows another strain of theological influence. Both state that the final destiny of the wicked heart is hell. Shembe I nevertheless sees the heart as the vessel of God's grace.

D. *The Saints or Holy Ones*

(i) *Who are they?*

The general word for saints is *aбangcwele*—used in the *Izihlaбelelo* only in the plural. The Zulu heaven is not individualistic. It is derived from *gcwala* meaning *to get or become full* and is generally used in the perfect. The verb in the *perfect present* expresses the idea of *abounding in* and is applied to persons of extreme religious devotion who still live or who passed away and are remembered as *aбangcwele*. The term is also used with regard to the Holy Spirit namely *uMoya oNgcwele*.

Shembe I states about the *aбangcwele* in his confession of faith the following:

73.	154.
2. Nakuyo iRamente* eyingcwele	2. Nakuyo inhlangano yaбangcwele
Yama Nazaretha,	Base Nazaretha!
Noбudlelwana бaбangcwele	Ngoбa ngiyathanda ukuliбona
Base Nazaretha.	Lelo lizwe elizayo.
* iRamente = Afr. Gemeente.	

73.	154.
1. And in the holy congregation	1. And in the fellowship of the
	saints
of the Nazarites,	of the Nazarites!
and the fellowship of the saints	Because I love to see
of Nazareth.	that world which is coming.

In the first confession the holy congregation is the object of his confession—a sanctified congregation of baptized persons, a Montanist strain of theological thinking. Shembe has here in mind that holiness which is associated with the holy place of the Nazarites. Holiness is a cultic concept and although here not preconditioned by ritual purity, is closely associated with it. Again the first confession in Isl. 73 has much more to say than the one in Isl. 154. Not only does he confess his faith in the fellowship of the saints but also in the holy congregation which is a prototype of the saved humanity. For this Shembe would have Old Testament support (cf. Jer. 2[3] *uIsrayeli ungcwele kuJehova*: Israel was holiness unto the Lord...). By the "fellowship of the saints" Shembe understands much more than the established churches in their interpretation of the *Apostolicum*. It includes all those who passed away and who are accepted as holy ones. Much of the ritual emphasis is associated with the ancestor cult.

This holy congregation is constituted of *elected ones* as Shembe states in Isl. 4[2]. The saints (*aɓangcwele*) and the elected ones (naɓakhethiweyo)[1]) are called to the gates of Ekuphakameni which are now opened (*selivuliwe*). The *aɓangcwele* are all those who subscribe to the faith of the *iɓandla lamaNazaretha* as well as those of this movement who have passed on. They, together with the sanctified ancestry of the Zulu nation, form this illustrious body which *lives* in fellowship. Shembe II did not give any attention to election as he hailed from a different strain of theological thinking on this question. He stated, referring to his father (Baɓa): *wena wedwa uyingcwele* ("You alone are holy" Isl. 239[3]).

(ii) *Who are not elected?*

These are described as those who ran away from Ekuphakameni. The sin that surpasses all others is that which rejects the holy place and thus holiness. cf. Isl. 6[2].

Baɓalekile ɓakushiya	They ran away and they left you
Baxoshwa uɓungcwele;	they were repelled by holiness;
Akungeni sono kuwe	no sin enters there
Kwana sono sinye.	Not even one sin.

In the Old Testament holiness stood in close relationship to God, people, things and places. In Genesis where the cult does not play a role the word for holiness does not appear. In the Zulu religion holiness means to be magically loaded with *numinous* power, but this was limited to certain times and places. This is expressed by Shembe II in Isl. 237[5].

Bayaɓusiswa aɓakuthandayo	Prosperous are those who love thee
Umuzi we Nkosi enkulu,	the city of the Great *Nkosi*,
Banenhlanhla aɓangcwele	the saints are with good fortune
Oɓemukelayo wena.	which is poured in by thee.

---

[1]) Paul's reference to the elected ones is translated by *aɓaɓizweyo* (those called), Rom. 1[7], a term not used by Shembe. cf. also Isl. 56[3].

Cultic holiness signifies a condition rather than an act and is not related to ethics in the first instance. The word *gcwala* in the perfect present means to be full, to abound and has no reference to ethics. When spiritualization takes place, as in the *iBandla lamaNazaretha*, ethics does play a role. Holiness and sin do exclude one another for Shembe. The elected are those whose clothes had been washed (*ABanguBo zigeziwe*, Isl. 56²) i.e. ritually purified; they are made white in the blood of the Lamb (*Zendziwa mhlophe egazini Lemvana*. Isl. 56²).

The special *relationship* between the *Nkosi and the saints* is sketched in Isl. 7⁵.

Basuka aBangcwele	The saints set off
Base Nazaretha;	they of Nazareth;
BahlangaBeza Inkosi yaBo	they went out to meet their *iNkosi*
Iza ngamafu.	he comes with the clouds.

The *parousia*, witnessed by the holy ones of Nazareth, has been fulfilled. Their sense of perceiving supernatural phenomena is most highly developed. The saints here may also be those who passed on and who are keeping watch over Ekuphakameni.

(iii) *The holy ones in 'heaven'*

In Isl. 24 he pictures the saints as being gathered round the *iNkosi* of heaven at Ekuphakameni (verses 2 and 3); that those who left Ekuphakameni are disappointed while the observers of the law will be anointed (verse 5) and the breakers of the law rewarded (verse 6), to which he adds:

Bekani indleBe nizwe	Listen intently and hear
Inhlokomo* yaBangcwele.	the din of the saints.

* inhlokomo (only in sing.) < hlokoma: Din (as of many voices), a confused rumbling noise; babbling (of water).

The reference here is obviously to those who passed on and who take a keen interest in what they do. Shembe I states: "I have seen the home of the saints" (*ngiBonile ikhaya laBangcwele*, Isl. 171³), we are greeted by the saints (*siBingelelwa aBangcwele*, Isl. 164²), Jehova expresses his delight in the inhabitants of Ekuphakameni through the holy ones who come in the clouds (*ngaBangcwele aBavela emafini*, Isl. 100³), he states he has fellowship with the saints who stay, they kept watch (*ngihlanganyele naBangcwele aBehleli Belindile*, Isl. 32²), that "the gates here at this city are being opened by the saints" (*Amasango alowo muzi avulelwa aBangcwele*, Isl. 159²), and requests "May I resemble the saints who are now before thy face" (*Ngiɓa-fuze aɓangcwele aɓaseɓusweni ɓakho*. Isl. 109 chorus).

Shembe II does not refer to the activity of the saints in heaven in general —only to that of his late father.

(iv) *The influence of non-christian concepts*

The pre-christian Zulu life had no meaning apart from ancestral presence and ancestral power. The ancestral cult is not only extremely strong amongst the Zulu but has great *sociological and theological* significance. So strong are they with the Zulu that Vilakazi states they have often been described in terms of gods[1]). The dead do not merely survive but take an active part in all mundane affairs. Basically all ancestors could be worshipped but only certain ones, called *idlozi*, *ithongo* and *amakhosi*, receive attention. They go up in the hierarchy according to their social status and influence in the community. They are put into office through the *ukuɓuyisa* ceremony, a ceremony also observed in the *iBandla lama-Nazaretha* and even by Christians in the established churches, i.e., with the unveiling of a tombstone. The meaning of the *ukuɓuyisa* ceremony is explained by Samuelson as follows: "to go through the ceremony of committing the spirit of a dead relative to the care of the spirits of his ancestors and pleading that they with this new spirit may watch over them and protect the living."[2]) This function of watching over them is emphasiz-ed by Shembe I in the *Izihlaɓelelo*. The shades or ancestors are also the actual owners of the lands, kraals and animals, i.e., from them come all life and possessions.[3]) Called by the living *isithunzi zakithi* (our shades)[4]), they live with their descendants in a *symbiotic* union. This interrelationship and interaction involves a reciprocal behaviour and concern which is expressed in various ceremonies and ritual. Some maintain that they are underneath (*aɓantu aɓaphansi*) while others state they are above and watch over them from this position.[5]) It is in this last position over the gates of Ekuphakameni as guardians that Shembe I pictures them. High mountains are often sought out for special ceremonies in which the an-cestors are involved. In this light the *Nhlangakazi* events should be seen. While with the pre-christian Zulu an *ukuɓuyisa* never took place for a

---

[1]) *Vilakazi*, Zulu Transformations, 88.

[2]) *Samuelson*, Dictionary, 46.

[3]) *Asmus*, 34.

[4]) This is the real designation for those passed away. cf. Vilakazi, Zulu Transfor-mations, 89.

[5]) cf. *Nyembezi*, C. L. S., Zulu Proverbs, Johannesburg, Witwatersrand University Press, 1954, 2 ff.

woman, as only men shades were of importance[1]), with Shembe all those who believe, whether men or women, are significant, which is a specific christian influence.

All souls of the dead are active and are described as guardians over the living. They are pictured as coming on the clouds as Moses and Elijah did. The contact with the supernatural world is pictured in realistic terms, it has actually come down on Ekuphakameni. There is an intimate contact between the holy ones in heaven and on earth, although those who have passed on have a higher status. Shembe's restoration of the function of the shades is due to his concern for the well-being of the Zulu nation.

Paul also refers to the saints but in a different way than Shembe. Their holiness is not something they acquired at a place through observance of the law but is due to their dependence on God's grace as experienced in Jesus Christ (cf. Phil. 1[1]). In the centre of the saints is the sacrifice of Christ in which they share as "the elect of God, holy and beloved" (Col. 3[12]). When Jesus sanctifies himself (John 17[19]) or the Church (Eph. 5[26]) it is not only evidence of *His* divinity but also that man is dependent on him for this sanctification. The sanctification of Jesus through the Father rejects all self-sanctification. Christ's reconciliatory sacrifice is the means of sanctification (Hebr. 2[11]). To this Shembe refers in Isl. 56[2], but in the context of his theology it has lost its meaning as is evident in the holy, that is, magical water which is also used at the holy communion. Christ brings the sanctification through His sacrifice to the sanctified (Hebr. 10[10,14]) while Shembe brings it through his contact with the *numinous* power. Holiness is based on reconciliation in Christ and through the work of the Holy Spirit and not on a human being. Holiness in the *iBandla lamaNazaretha* is due to "filling up" with *numinous* power with the result that the true meaning of the Cross is obscured.

E. *Ingelosi* (Angel)

In the ancient Greek world angel signified a messenger; in the Old Testament it is the one who brings the good message, punishes enemies (cf. 2 Kings 19[35]) and leads people (Ex. 23[20]), protects Israel (Ex. 14[19]) while in the New Testament they are considered to be representatives of the heavenly world.

The indiscriminate use of *umoya* (in the sense of *spirit*) and *ingelosi* is

---

[1]) *Krige*, 169. The sense of continuity is strongly connected with birth, *i.e.*, it is that which carries on life. Children are the main cult persons in the *ukubuyisa*. Those with no children will not have an *idlozi*.

obvious in the *iBandla lamaNazaretha.*[1]) What theology does the *Izihla-belelo* maintain with regard to the Angel?

A significant statement is made by Shembe I in the *Evening Prayers, Section 35, 14* when he maintains that "because Jehova walks to all his people in their sleep you should treat well the house in which you sleep so that Jehova is not vexed to come to you through a dream (*ngephupho*)". As Biblical text here, where the only reference to a *dream* is found, he has Matth. 2[13] which is also significant and which reads "the Angel of the Lord appeareth to Joseph in a dream..." The importance of dreams in the Zionist movements as a means of revelation has been discussed by Sundkler.[2]) Shembe often maintains that he came from the world which is to come and which is possible through dreams.[3]) The above statement could be interpreted that Jehova came in the form of an Angel or Spirit. This is the only direct reference to an angel in the prayers and it could be concluded that they are not media in worship or worshipped in the movement.

(i) *The Chief Angel*

Very early in the Izl. reference is made to angels. cf. Isl. 7[2].

Ziphumile izingelosi	The angels have come out
Ukona umhlaɓa;	to destroy the world;
Nansi enye ingelosi	here is another angel
Iphuma empumalanga.	he coming out from the East.

This is an obvious reminiscence of Revelations. The problem is: Who is the angel from the East? In the Old Testament the most important angel is *the Angel of the Lord* or the *Angel of Jahweh*. This may be the angel referred to or Shembe may consider himself to be the angel. He may have the history of Jesus here in mind who was accompanied by angels especially during the time of his birth and resurrection which was a special sign of his relationship with God. (cf. John 1[51]). This is now repeated at Ekuphaka-meni. Shembe has most probably here in mind Rev. 2[1] and 3[1]. As the angel of the *iBandla lamaNazaretha* Shembe speaks to God for the members.

---

[1]) cf. *Sundkler*, Bantu Prophets, 249. Berglund, A-I. states "the dead are known as *ingelosi*". Letter dated 31.I.65. *Sibanyoni, S. D.* refers only to *idlozi* and *ithongo*. Letter dated 23.XII.64.

[2]) *Sundkler*, Bantu Prophets, 265–275. In Acts 10[22] the angel's activity as revealer is typical of the work of this being according to Scripture.

[3]) One of the main media through which the shades reveal themselves or their desires is by way of dreams. Dreams play an important role in Zionist movements where the stereotyped dreams are regarded as true and prophetic. The spirit or angel shows what robe or uniform a patient should wear in order to be cured. Sundkler, Bantu Prophets, 272; see also Krige, Social System, 286; Callaway, Religious system, 228.

In this light one is not in doubt as to whom Isl. 20[5] refers when he states:

Phaphamani maNazaretha	Wake up ye Nazarites
Naku sekusile;	here it is, it is light already;
Nangu uMikaeli	here is Michael
Emi phambi kwenu*.	standing in front of you.

* These two lines are for the sake of emphasis, a repetition from verse 3.

Michael, the Angel of Israel, has now appeared amongst them. Neither is one in doubt as to how the simple folk will interpret this Isl. The possibilities for different interpretations in exegesis are numerous; it has led to other movements being established. In Isl. 201 he emphasizes that his name "is now protected in the book of life" (*seliyahlangulwa encwadini yokuphila*) and immediately after these words Daniel 12 is referred to, which speaks about Michael the great prince who will deliver all those whose names are written in the book of life. Shembe I considered himself to be the Michael of the Old Testament. In the nationalistic songs Africa is called up and in Isl. 55[4] the *impis* (soldiers) sing: "I have now seen the angel of heaven." (*Sengiyiɓonile ingelosi yase zulwini*). The Messiah of Scripture however is not equated with an angel or angel-like being but as son of Man He has a quite different origin.

(ii) *The Angels.*

a. *They come with a message or warning.*

In Isl. 7 *ingelosi* spoke with a great *Voice* (Sundkler states that *Voice* is one of the channels of *umoya*[1]) through four angels (verse 3). They warned about judgement on sin (Isl. 7[3]) which is also a function ascribed to the angels in the New Testament. (cf. Luke 12[8f]; 2 Thess. 1[7]).

b. *They give praises to Simakade and Shembe I*

In Isl. 112[4] the angels are called upon to praise Simakade "who is fittıng to be praised" (*ofanele ukudunyiswa*) and in Isl. 125[3] Shembe states that *his* name is beautiful in the face of the angels (*Igama lami ɓelihle nase ɓusweni ɓezingelosi*), and they are called upon in Isl. 151[2] to praise his name—his name being in the Zulu context the very essence of his being.

Liɓongeni zingelosi	Praise ye angels
Leli leligama lakhe...	this name of his...

---

[1]) *Sundkler*, Bantu Prophets, 249. cf. John 12[27]. A *voice* came from heaven and the people said "An angel spoke to him". (*Ingelosi ikhulume kuye.*).

c. *Their keen interest in Ekuphakameni*

In Isl. 100[5] Shembe maintains that

Izingelosi zishaya amaphiko	The angels strike their wings
Ngokunqo6a kwethu.	because of our victory.

Shembe would agree with Acts 12[15] that a person has his angel. They are guardians at Ekuphakameni and exclude sinners (cf. Rev. 21[12] cf. Isl. 155[5]) and have in this sense, the same function as the saints from whom they are often not distinguished:

Izingelosi ziya6akhipha	The angels are expelling them,
Ezilinda emasangweni	those who watch at the gates
Ase Kuphakameni	of Kuphakameni
Ngenxa yezono za6o	on account of their sins.

The Scripture idea that the angels will be judges at the end of history has been fulfilled at Ekuphakameni. In Scripture however they are not pictured as acting independently in their capacity as judges. It is only later in the New Testament that they do independent acts (Matth. 28[2f]).

(iii) *Angels and shades*

The difficulty is to differentiate between angels and shades or ancestor spirits. Apart from *amakhosi* two other words *idlozi* and *ithongo* are used to indicate shades. Is the *ingelosi* the same as the shade? The Zionist finds enough scriptural evidence for the special position of the angel. The question has often been asked why it has become so prominent with the Zionists. Is here some point of contact in the Zulu religion for the Biblical concept angel?

The hierarchical structure of the society is maintained in the supernatural world. The father as the priest of the family approaches the *idlozi* of the family. In cases of national concern the *amakhosi* or royal ancestors of the ruling house are approached. Is there a distinction between *idlozi* and *ithongo*? Colenso found a definite distinction between *idlozi*[1]) and *ithongo* i.e., while *idlozi* is more of the household ancestral type, the *ithongo* is always a guardian spirit and mostly active in times of crisis, a position held by the angel in Scripture. The *ithongo* was a being of universal influence

---

[1]) The association of shades with the procreative principle could not be discussed here. cf. *Wilson Monica*, Divine Kings and the breath of men, Cambridge University Press, 1959, 5.

under whom all around were placed.[1]) The *ithongo* (a word hardly used in Northern Zululand while frequently used in Southern Natal) is a guardian of a certain group, the binding factor amongst the families. The *ithongo* cannot be incarnated as is the case with the *idlozi*. It is experienced as a force but not approached in the cult, while the *idlozi* is approached. Losing the *ithongo's* guardianship makes one an outcast, losing that vital something, which makes one part of the community. Berglund doubts that *ithongo* is simply the *hlonipa*, the term of honour, for *idlozi*. A clear-cut distinction is difficult because the Zulu does not keep himself busy with clear-cut distinctions and logical definitions which is the basis of our analytic scientific approach.[2]) The fact that *uMoya* and Angel are used interchangeably indicates that the Angel is also imbued with authority. For Shembe I the Angel is a messenger of high rank acting in the service of the kingdom of Ekuphakameni, while in the New Testament the Angel acts in the service of the history of Christ. The prominence of the angel in Acts and Revelation is however obvious. There is a point of contact in the Zulu religion for the function of the angel. Shembe however has also used this concept interchangeably with *aβangcwele* (saints), so that the above theory could not be categorically presented.

F. *Isithunywa* (Messenger). pl. Izithunywa. Also umthunywa (sing.) aβathunywa (pl.) <-thuma, send, as a person on an errand, send something to or by a person.

Shembe I uses the word only in class 4 of the Zulu language, i.e., the isi—izi—class and not in the personal class.

He uses the word in the sense of i. earthly and ii. supernatural messengers.

(i) *As earthly messengers*

Using it only once in the singular and obviously referring to himself, Shembe states in Isl. 103[3]:

Sivumele wena Nkosi	Allow him you *Nkosi*,
Isithunywa sakho,	thy messenger,
Sishumayele izwi lakho	to preach thy word
Ngalowo moya wakho.	through that *umoya* of yours.

(ii) *As supernatural messengers*

In Isl. 136 he relates the history of Jacob and his experimence with the

---

[1]) *Wanger, W.*, The Zulu notion of God, 663.

[2]) *Berglund, A.-I.*, Letter dated 14.XII.64.

angels, referring to them as *izithunywa zasezulwini* ("messengers from heaven", verse 5).

a. The messengers *come with the word* which comes in the clouds and this word they saw. This is a reminiscence of John 1[1] applied to Shembe I. He is now their word which became flesh. cf. Isl. 158.

2. Si6ona ngezwi	We see by the word
Livela emafini,	forthcoming from the clouds
Liza nge zithunywa	it comes through the messengers
Livela emafini.	it comes from the clouds.
3. Sili6onile lelo lizwi	We have seen that word
Livela emafini.	coming from the clouds.

It reminds of the angels who are messengers of God's events. In Isl. 159 Shembe states that "his eternal word" (*lelo lizwi laphakade*, verse 1) has been heard, that the graves of the saints rejoice because of their *uMsindisi*, that the holy ones have opened the gates and then he adds in verse 3:

Nazi izithunywa za6angcwele	Here are the messengers of the saints;
Sa6elani niya6izwa,	answer, you are being called
Nina a6alele kulomhla6a	you who are sleeping in this earth,
Izwi lakhe ohleli phakade.	his word who remains for ever.

The messengers or angels of the holy ones are ever active and with the typical "logic" of religion the saints and the messengers are guardians at the gates of Ekuphakameni. The holy ones are pictured as having messengers who bring the word to their relatives.

(iii) *Their word is a word of judgment*

They bring the word of judgement so that in this case also they resemble the angels which they are in 'fact'. The messengers went out to call many (Isl. 191, verse 2), they have to listen to their word seriously (verse 3) and the repetitions in verses 4 and 5 add to this seriousness. cf. Isl. 191[4].

Isikhathi siphelile	The time is finished
We6antu nonke,	all ye people
Ziyedlula ngokushesha	they are passing by with haste
Lezi zithunywa,	these messengers,
Uyolizwa nini izwi lakhe	when will ye listen to his word,
Wozani wezoni.	come ye sinners.

The question is here again asked: Who are these messengers? Super-natural beings or Zionist prophets? Where heaven and earth is so inter-related the same term could be used for beings in both spheres. The New Testament uses the word apostle for these earthly messengers. This word together with the word prophet hardly exists in Shembe's vocabulary. Coming from Ekuphakameni, the holy city, Shembe's messengers are in any case "celestial" beings. In Isl. 191[2] it is clear that they do come from this holy city as preachers:

Izithunywa ziphumile	The messengers came out
Ukumema aɓaningi,	to call many;
Yizwani wezoni	listen ye sinners
Hlanganani naɓa menyiweyo	gather together all ye with those who are invited
Limemeza nina lelo lizwi.	That word shouts for you.

(iv) *They give an account of Shembe I*

In Isl. 221 the late Shembe I is described as the holy father, the promised one surrounded by angels who took him away after his death cf. Isl. 221[1].

Zafika izithunywa	They arrived the messengers
Zilande* uThumekile.	they came to fetch the promised one.
Hamɓa kahle, hamɓa kahle,	farewell, farewell,
Baɓa wami oyingcwele.	my holy father.

* *Landa* could mean i. narrate, give an account; ii. follow up; iii. fetch; iv. take after, resemble; v. conform to, adhere to. One could discard the other shades of meaning in this translation. It seems that the above give the intention as this Isl. keeps itself busy with the departure of Shembe I.

F. *Amakhosi*: (inkosi, amakhosi).

–khosi

i. King; paramount chief; chief.

ii. Term of respect for royalty, one in very high governmental position.

iii. (mod.) Magistrate.

iv. Lord. (New Testament usage.)

v. In its feminine form it refers to the chief's or king's daughter. Also *Inkosazana* daughter of *uNkulunkulu* (called *Nomkhuɓulwana*) or "Princess of Heaven". She presides over the growth of corn. The Zulus used to hold dances on the hills in honour of some *Inkosikazi.*[1])

---

[1]) cf. *Krige*, 282–3.

vi. (pl. only.) Spirits of the departed kings and chiefs, thus royal shades. The *umkhosi*, the Zulu annual festival held in honour of the royal shades, was divided into two. The little *umkhosi* was held about Christmas time and the great *umkhosi* a month later when the tribe brought the first fruits to the king, as the representative of the ancestors, who blessed the crops. The effects of the *ukusula* medicines, used to enhance the growth of the crops, had to be taken away. At this feast the king is in the role of the national magician and he himself is strengthened with manifold charms. The royal shades are praised (Christmas is sometimes referred to as the *umkhosi* of the departed Christians), new laws proclaimed and others revoked. During the national *umkhosi* the burial ground of the former kings and chiefs (called *emakhosini*) is visited and the *nyathelisa* sacrifice (a present offered as tribute to a king or chief) brought. Here at the graves the regiments stand at a distance and shout "*Woza-ke, woza-lapha*": "Come therefore, come here."[1]) Which reminds of the followers of Shembe who shout at *Nhlangakazi*, "Come to us, all ye people, let the Spirit send you to us." (See also Ezekiel 37[9].)

The *amakhosi*, or royal ancestors of the ruling house, are approached through the king or Paramount chief. They were approached as a unit. The king, the only channel through which the *amakhosi could* be approached in a system in which hierarchy is of the greatest importance, had a cosmic meaning. He represents the harmonious unity between the cosmic powers and this is what Shembe I attempted to restore. The very destiny of the country was equated with the king's life. On him they depend for rain, weather, fertility. Krige states "the kings said heaven belonged to the royal house".[2]) Heaven belongs to the kings and the royal clan name *iZulu* became the name for 'heaven'.[3])

The *spirits* of kings became the ruling spirits in 'heaven' and are served by their subjects through the king, as *uNkulunkulu* is too far away to be worshipped. The tribe as a whole acknowledges "the Chief's ancestors as a source of communal well-being and prosperity".[4])

The *amakhosi* play a definite role in the theology of the *iBandla lama-Nazaretha*. In this light the events on Nhlangakazi should be seen. cf. Isl. 37.

---

[1]) cf. *Lugg*, Agricultural ceremonies in Natal and Zululand, Bantu Studies, Vol. III, No. IV, 373–8.
[2]) Krige, 247.
[3]) Callaway, Religious System, 120.
[4]) Eiselen, M. W.–Schapera, I., "Religious Beliefs and Practices" in Schapera (ed.) The Bantu-speaking tribes of South Africa, London, Routledge and Sons, 1937, 251.

3. Waɓavikela ezitheni zaɓo

Ngamakhosi anamandla

. . . .

4. Waɓakhuphula ngengalo
enamandla
Entaɓeni yas' Enhlangakazi.

He protected them from their
enemies
through the powerful *amakhosi*.

He brought them out with the
arm which is powerful
on the mountain of Nhlangakazi.

The *numinous* power of the *amakhosi* is associated with the most solemn and secretive religious ceremony of the Nazarites, namely the *umkhosi wamadokodo*[1]) or "Festival of the Tabernacles".[2]) Here the Black Moses meets Jehova and the *amakhosi*, an interesting combination. The fourteen days of healing, sacrifice and praying is the occasion for filling up with inner vital force or *numinous* power.

In Isl. 68 the relationship of Jehova and the *amakhosi* is clearly stated after he has referred in Isl. 67 to *Baɓa* and to *Nkosi Jehova* as the *Nkosi yamakhosi*, mentioning the names of the great royal house of the Zulu nation namely Sendzangakhona, Dingaan, Shaka, Mpande, Cetshwayo and Dinuzulu. In this Isl. they are described as sinners[3]) but he and Jehova has not left them, i.e., they are not better than their fathers. cf. Isl. 67[3].

Ukuɓa ungangivumi Nkosi
yamakhosi,
Inyama yami ngoɓa ayizange
ikwendze
Nkosi Jehova okulungileyo;
Kodwa ukhumbule umoya wami,
Nkosi yami.

If you do not accept me, *Nkosi* of
the *amakhosi*,
my flesh, because it has never done,

Nkosi Jehova, what is right,
but remember my *umoya*, my
Nkosi.

The term *amakhosi* is a very suggestive one to the Zulu, and Shembe deliberately uses it to express the meaning it conveys to the pre-christian Zulu. He states in Isl. 68 that Jehova saved the Nazarites from their enemies (verse 2), that he protected them "with the *amakhosi* who have power" (verse 3), that Jehova put them on the palm of his hand (verse 5), and adds:

---

[1]) -dokodo: i. Roughly made hut of branches and grass; ii. Booth, tabernacle. -dlangala is also used to indicate a temporary shelter erected by travellers. cf. Vilakazi, Isonto Lamanazaretha, 78.

[2]) cf. Sundkler, Bantu Prophets, 199.

[3]) In the *Prayers for the Sabbath*, Section 21, 19 he warns them that they should not be like their fathers who hardened their hearts, that they carry their sins.

6. Waɓakhokhela entaɓeni	He led them at the mountain
Yas' Enhlangakazi.	of Nhlangakazi.
. . . .	
7. Wachitha iceɓo	He scattered the device
Laɓa cebɓ* ɓaɓo	of their schemers
8. Waphendula uɓugqili ɓaɓo	He changed their slavery
Baɓa ukukhosi**.	It became kingly authority.

  * Misprint: should read *ceɓi*.
  ** Misprint: should read *uɓukhosi*.

With all the degenerating phenomena he observes around him, e.g., the breaking up of the Zulu social system, the political situation of his people, he naturally turns to his fathers as is already clear in the very first Isl. He has also the glorious era of the Zulu nation in mind and blames indirectly the whites for destroying this. The *amakhosi* is primarily related to this aspect. cf. Isl. 106. He is concerned about Africa and that Jehova's enemies have already despised the eternal kingly authority (cf. Isl. 17[5]) after having destroyed that of the Zulu nation. It is for the restoration of this authority that he pleads and this they receive on Nhlangakazi. This is undubiously stated in Isl. 17[4].

Aɓe mukeliswa uɓukhosi	Those who are given kingly
	authority
Phezu kwentaɓa,	on the mountain,
Phaphamani phaphamani	rise up, rise up,
Nina maAfrica.	Ye Africans.

The mount Sinai of the Nazarites is not only related to Jehova but also to the sanctified royal ancestry of the Zulu nation. It is indeed a mountain of political and religious liberation, concepts later not separated in Shembe's mind. They drink both from the fountain of Sendzangakhona (Isl. 216[5]) and from the rock of mount Sinai (*kulelotshe lasentaɓeni yaseSinayi*, Isl. 83[5]). Shembe has become indeed the Mediator of the Zulu nation.

H. *Umoya Oyingcwele*[1])

Both Shembe I and II have surprisingly very little to say about the Holy Spirit in the *Izihlaɓelelo*. The pre-christian Zulu does not accept only one

---

  [1]) *Bryant, A. T.*, Dictionary, states that it should be *uMoya ocweɓileyo* as "the word *ngcwele* is Xhosa, not Zulu". *Cweɓileyo* is the perf. tense of *cweɓa*: i. Become clear, pure, fresh; ii. Quiet; iii. Blue, green; iv. Be holy. Vilakazi and Doke, Dictionary, states that *ocweɓileyo* means a saint.

holy spirit—all the *amadlozi, amathongo* and *amakhosi* are "holy" in the
Zulu sense of the word, i.e., loaded with *numinous* power. When Shembe I
speaks about the Holy Spirit it is only once related to Jesus which is different
from the New Testament approach where the Holy Spirit is first revealed
in Jesus and then comes through Him to the congregation.

The only instance where he brings the Holy Spirit in relation to Jesus
Christ is in Isl. 58[3] where he states:

Lowo owasethembisa wona	That which you promised us
Ngo Jesu Krestu Inkosi,	through Jesus Christ the *Nkosi*,
Wathi auyikusishiya sodwa	you said you will not leave us alone,
Uyosithumela umoya oyingcwele.	You will send us the holy *umoya*.

Then comes the following request in the *chorus* relating the Holy Spirit
to healing. The spirit of the *isangoma* was mainly related to healing:

Umoya wakho mauze Nkosi	Let your *umoya* come, *Nkosi*
Uɓaphilise aɓantu ɓakho.	that it may heal your people.

Shembe leaves here the impression that the promise of the Holy Spirit
has not yet been fulfilled; that Jesus has withdrawn into the background
and that well-being and good health are dependent on the *umoya* of the
iNkosi. Shembe never states that the Holy Spirit leads men in the truth and
that He glorifies Christ. In both confessions of faith (cf. Izl. 73 and 154)
he confesses his faith in the Holy Spirit (*Nakumoya oyingcwele*) without
any reference to Jesus Christ. The trinity consists for Shembe in the
Supreme Being, the Holy Spirit and Shembe; and the Holy Spirit is not
co-equal with God. On a few occasions he refers *umoya* to *iNkosi* who
could be Jehova or Jesus Christ but more probably Jehova. The essence
of the trinity of which Shembe is the manifestation reveals itself in only
one mode of existence. As the son is the manifestation of the father, so
Shembe is of the trinity. In Isl. 13[2] he speaks about "the thirst for your
umoya"; in Isl. 23[1] that "your *umoya*" (*umoya wakho*) is good hope and
in the superscription to Isl. 144, which he received on June 7, 1927, he
states that it was from the *umoya* of Jehova that he received this Isl. as
Jehova caused his *umoya* to wander about on that day while Shembe
quietened his[1]). The typical pre-christian Zulu concept of the wandering
umoya, the free spirit, is here obvious. The *umoya* is rather discussed in

---

[1]) See also superscription to Isl. 162. Here he states that he *kept* his *umoya*. It seems
as if each being in authority has its *uMoya*. In Shembe's case his is not the same as
that of Jehova. Jesus Christ had his *uMoya*, which He promised to send, and in the
same manner Shembe has his *uMoya*.

terms of an ancestor spirit or shade than in terms of the ever-present Holy Spirit of Scripture, even though it may be referred to preaching as is the case in the New Testament. To this he refers in Isl. 113[1]..

| Igcwalise ngomoya wakho, | Fill him (*iNceku*) with your *umoya* |
| Ishumayele izwi lakho. | so that he may preach your word. |

Preaching in the New Testament centres on the work of the Holy Spirit. For Luke the Spirit was a Spirit of prophecy. To this Shembe would also subcribe: cf. Isl. 103[3].

| Sishumayele izwi lakho | That we may preach the word of thee |
| Ngalowo moya wakho. | through thy *umoya*. |

The emphasis will naturally be on the pouring in of numinous power when the *umoya* is mentioned. In Isl. 145[2] he requests that the dew of the *umoya* of the *iNkosi* may be poured into his heart, in Isl. 135[3] "pour into me the *umoya* of power" (*thela kimi umoya wamandla*) and in Isl. 103[4] he states that they gather and fill up "with that *uMoya* of yours." (*ngalowo moya wakho*). The Pentecost event has been explained in the light of the *numinous* power of the Zulu religion. For Shembe the power of the Holy Spirit is not associated with the glorified Christ. Paul saw it as a Gift and Power of the end times, while Shembe sees it as the power of a new era which has already been introduced through him. Although *pneuma* (spirit) is with Paul often described in impersonal terms (cf. 1 Cor. 12[13]; 1 Thess. 5[19]) it is not an unknown power. Paul is convinced that its source is the glorified Christ which leads to an openness to God and the neighbour, while for Shembe it directly referred to his own Messiahship and is granted to those in the fellowship of the *iBandla lamaNazaretha*. The *umoya* is to him the *uMoya* of power. This it was for Luke also (cf. Acts 1[8]) but other than with Luke, it is for Shembe not Christ's power; it is *umoya* for the self and for one's group. The Spirit emphasized for Luke the lordship of Jesus while for Shembe it emphasizes his own lordship. In Acts all members of the new congregation have the Spirit—with Shembe some may not have it. The Holy Spirit is not a spirit of authority as in the Nazarite sense but of *service*; not of human decoration but of renewal and rededication to the Person and Work of Jesus Christ. It is not the spirit of salvation, this is only through Christ, but it gives conviction of sin, i.e., of man's alienation from the redemptive work of Christ. For Shembe it is the Spirit of *numinous* power which does not refer to the Cross.

An important function of the *umoya* for Shembe is *healing* from sickness, and as sickness and sin are related it has thus a significant task to fulfil. cf. Isl. 215[1].

Izwe selifile	The nation is now dead
WeNkosi yamaNazaretha	oh, *Nkosi* of the Nazarites
Beka indleɓe yakho,	put your ear (i.e. listen!)
Yamkela isililo salo	receive its lamentation;
Umoya wakho uze	may your *umoya* come
Kwaɓagulayo,	to the sick
Ungaɓafulatheli	do not turn your back upon them
Ushilo ngezwi lakho.	you have spoken through your word.

Through his uMoya Shembe, the great healer of the nation, makes them well (*ɓaphile aɓagulayo*, verse 3.). The association of *umoya* with power is continuously repeated—he never states that it convinces of sin or the work of the Cross.

Shembe II, with reference to his father, maintains in Isl. 223[1].

| Ngingu mlandeli wakho | I am your follower |
| Nowo moya oyingcwele. | and that of the holy *umoya*. |

In Isl. 243[2] the question is asked: Who is the holy spirit in this case, keeping in mind that Shembe II considered his father to be such a spirit. He states:

| Yehla Moya oyingcwele | Come down holy *uMoya* |
| Ngena wena kithi. | enter into us. |

Both Shembe I and II have surprisingly few references to the Holy Spirit. This is unexpected as Shembe I hails from a church in which the emphasis was rather pneumatological than christological. To both Shembes however all ancestors are holy spirits as is the case in the Zulu religion. It is difficult for them not to associate the holy spirit with a person. Shembe I rather speaks of "your spirit", the spirit of the *Nkosi* or of Jehova, even though it is mentioned as an independent being in his confession. Their emphasis is rather on holy *spirits* than the Holy Spirit, although in the case of Shembe II the holy spirit, referring to his father, is of special significance. It is interesting that Shembe, who took the name of *Nazir* for his movement, had not more to say about them, e.g., Samson on whom the spirit "leapt". (cf. Judges 13[25]; 14[10,19]; 15[14].) In the early days of Israel the ecstatic state into which a person entered was considered to be the safe test of spirit possession. (cf. 1 Sam. 10[6,10]; 11[6].) Some of Shembe's hymns could easily lead to ecstacy but Shembe did not reveal in the *Izihlabelelo* such a tendency. The emphasis on himself as Mediator and Liberator, that the activity of the *uMoya* is experienced in purification, healing and in a person's general spiritual condition, has made Shembe much more sober in his religious activity. Shembe, the Divine King, has overruled Shembe, the spirit-possessed *isangoma*. As the king and Messiah he is not possessed.

CHAPTER FOUR

THE COMMUNITY

A. *The Congregation*

1. *iBandla lamaNazaretha*

Different terms are used in the *Izihlaɓelelo* to designate the concept *congregation*, namely:

a. *iBandla*[1]) which could have the following meanings:

i. An assembly of men to hear a trial or announcement of the chief; social gathering; ii. Congregation, company of believers, church, denomination. In the plural as *amaɓandla* it is used in the *Izihlaɓelelo* in the sense of hosts.

b. iRamente: derived from the Afrikaans word *gemeente* meaning congregation. This designation appears only once (cf. Isl. 73[2]).

In both confessions of faith (Izl. 73, 154) Shembe refers to the fellowship of the saints but only in Isl. 73 to the holy congregation (*iRamente*). In Isl. 102[1] reference is also made to the holy congregation (*iɓandla eliyingcwele*) of Nazareth gathered at Ekuphakameni. The designation Nazarites or Nazareth is repeated four times in three different forms in Isl. 73, namely "the holy congregation of the Nazarites", (*iRamente eyingcwele yama Nazaretha*); "the fellowship of the saints of Nazareth" (*Base Nazaretha*); "the beautiful rock of the Nazarites" (*Lama Nazaretha*); Nazarethness (*ɓuNazaretha*) and once in Isl. 154[1] namely "of Nazareth" (*Base Nazaretha*)[2]). The unity of the Nazarites is to Shembe a major concern as is evident in Isl. 199 and also Isl. 203 which consists only of the following words:

Wonke amaNazaretha	All the Nazarites
Makaɓe munye	let them be one
Njenge ɓumɓa	like a lump
Lika semende.	of cement.

---

[1]) In Zulu society the *iɓandla* is mainly used to indicate the council consisting of adult men who are the advisers to the headman. The spot where they generally sit is also called *iɓandla* which is immediately in front of the cattle kraal or just outside the main entrance to the village. Krige, 51.

[2]) The long white robe worn by the preachers is called the *umNazaretha*.

Jesus is only once brought in connection with the hosts (*amaɓandla*) of heaven (cf. Isl. 4²); the interest of these hosts in those on earth is expressed in Isl. 12¹ where he asks "weep for us" and in Isl. 165⁶ in which Nhlangakazi is called to mind, he states:

Jaɓulahi kanye nathi	Rejoice fully with us
Maɓandla ezulu.	hosts of heaven.

These hosts of heaven are also called upon to proclaim the word of the great iNkosi (Isl. 165⁵). Here again the relationship between the hosts in heaven and those on earth is so intimate that it is difficult to establish which are actually referred to. (cf. Isl. 89⁴). The strong sense of community with those in heaven is often expressed in the *Izihlaɓelelo* even by Shembe II (cf. Isl. 229⁶). Nothing is more firmly believed in than the communion of the saints. Shembe I especially, does not think *analytically* but *synthetically*, i.e., all his experiences are reproduced in one great totality. This totality is the object of his thinking and there are no "gaps". There is no divorce between heaven and earth. Man, Nature and the Unseen are inseparably involved in one another. Shembe has defined his world in non-christo-centric categories giving tribal assurances, types of assurances which the pilgrim Church cannot give. In the tribe man was shielded in all his relationships if he observed the ritual prohibitions. In this way he influenced the supernatural world which is magic in its positive form and which reveals itself as moralism in the christian community. Shembe, influenced by this approach, stated: "The congregation which is humble and respectful the Maker of heaven and earth, the Maker must agree to bless our kneeling and the humbling of ourselves."[1]) In the ethnic 'church' man has supernatural power in his own hands and such a 'church' eventually stands alongside Christ and His sufficient work on the Cross.

2. *Amakholwa*

This word for *believers* is actually the passive form of *khola*. The verb *kholwa* could have the following meanings:

i. Be satisfied; be contented. To have had enough of anything, e.g., food, gratification, evidence, trouble.

ii. To be satisfied with a person's word, or with the person himself. Thus, have confidence in, rely on, trust in.

---

[1]) Bandla elihle elithoɓekileyo nelihloniphekayo lika mendzi wezulu nomhlaɓa, umendzi makavume ukuɓusisa ukuguqa kwethu nokuzithoɓa kwethu. Prayers for the Sabbath, Section 15, 18.

iii. Believe in (with locative).

-kholwa (i(li)kholwa, amakholwa pl.). Shembe uses also the word *aбakholwa* for believers. (cf. Isl. 100[1]). Samuelson states: "This word is used because there is not another exactly applicable to mean to believe."[1]) The Zulu simply adhered to the activities and ritual prohibitions of the tribe into which he was born. It is thus difficult to find a synonym for the christian concept "to believe". Bryant refers to this difficulty as follows: *ngikoliwe ku 'Nkulunkulu,*—a term in common use among missionaries and supposed to mean "I believe in God" (whereas really seeming to say, if anything, that "I am in God's estimation, convinced or satisfied", or possibly "I am a satisfactory person to God") is a manner of speech quite foreign to the Zulu idiom."[2]) Bryant is of the opinion that whenever "believe" would seem to infer hope, trust or confidence in, the Zulu word *themba* is more adequate, as the word *kholiwe* would, according to him, always mean a passive state of satisfaction in the mind of the Zulu devoid of any active hoping or confidence reposed in God. This scepticism of Bryant is overstated but experience has testified that the statement bears some truth as membership is often considered to be a passive state of reception.

Faith is described by Shembe as something *concrete*, associated with *numinous* power which may come to an end when their faith stops. This relationship is expressed in Isl. 28[2]:

Hhayi aбaphelamandla	Oh! those whose power has ended
Ekukholweni kwaбo,	in their faith,
Bayogijima бekufuna	them will run looking for it,
Ukukholwa kwaбo.	their faith.

This passive state of reception, obtained through ritual washing and confessions, finds its greatest satisfaction at Ekuphakameni. cf. Isl. 207[2].

Sizwa ngendaбa	We hear through the account
Besitshela бethi	they telling us, saying:
ENazaretha	at Nazareth
Sokholwa sichichime.	we will believe and we will overflow.

In this Isl. he uses the word Nazarethness (*uбuNazaretha*) for Nazarite faith. He does not use the word *uбukholwa* which means christian character, christian belief, Christianity. The request is that this Nazarethness may increase (*thuthuka*, Isl. 207[1]) i.e., increase in size, wealth and in importance,

---

[1]) *Samuelson*, Dictionary, 225.
[2]) *Bryant*, Dictionary, 312.

that it grows and becomes influential. In Isl. 73[4] he maintains that he has
already dressed up beautifully with Nazarethness before the Zulus. In the
Izihlaβelelo Shembe does not claim the designation christian for his movement.[1]) Passive reception of spiritual power is associated with Nazarethness: cf. Isl. 208[1]:

Thaβani, thaβani,	Be satisfied, be satisfied,
Bufikile uβuNazaretha.	Nazarethness has arrived.

Repeating in verse 4 his request that Nazarethness increase, he adds:

Zifuna ukuphuza kuwe,	They want to drink from you
Zikholwe zichichime[2])	that they believe, they overflow
Ngezwi lakho.	with thy word.

"Believe" (*kholwa*) has for Shembe the same connotations as *gcwala*.
This is now associated with Nazarism or Nazarethness i.e. to become
filled up to satisfaction with that which Nazareth or Ekuphakameni has
to give. The *amakholwa*[3]) receive these benefits; their faith has to be
rewarded. cf. Isl. 189[4].

Ngilandele amakholwa ngokholo.*	I followed the believers with faith.
Ngiyokuβonga ngokuβonga,	I will praise with praise,
Mniki wamandla.	Giver of power.
Ngingadingi ngingesweli	I must not be in want, I must not lack
We mthandi wezoni.	You lover of sinners.

* -kholo: faith, belief, creed. See also Isl. 165[4], 169[2].

The faith of the Zulus is directed to Shembe I who states in his second
last Isl. namely 218[5]:

Kholwani wemazulu	Believe, ye Zulus,
Ngathi thina sodwa.	through us alone.

'Faith' is not satisfied unless it has seen, and here at Ekuphakameni is
the *iNkosi* of the Zulus who came from the future world. Through him
alone the benefits of this world are at their disposal.

---

[1]) *Sundkler* states that in Zululand they are a separate community, a *tertium genus*,
over against both the non-christian and christian communities. See Bantu Prophets, 95.

[1]) See also Isl. 16[3]. For *ukukholwa*: to believe, see Izl. 41[3], 105[4], 169[2-4]. -kholwa
is also used to express belief in the world of the iNkosi.

[2]) For *amakholwa* see also Isl. 165[112]. In Isl. 19[1-4] he speaks of the "Father of believers" (*Yise wamakholwa*).

3. aɓangcwele

This term used for the living Nazarites and their holy ones who passed away, and always used in the plural as Shembe could not think in individualistic terms in this connection, has already been discussed in chapter III.

4. Isithunywa[1])

This term, nearly always used in the plural, and used for earthly and heavenly messengers, has also been discussed in chapter III.

5. Isikhonzi. (Worshipper or servant)

This word is derived from *khonza* which means:
i. Make oneself servile to another; to live in a state of voluntary servitude.
ii. Pay homage, pay respects to.
iii. Worship.

The noun *isikhonzi* (pl. *izikhonzi*, Shembe I uses also *aɓakhonzi*) means a voluntary servant, a messenger, worshipper, choir boy or altar attendant. *Inkonzo* (pl. *izinkonzo*) means service, subjection to a chief (*umkhonzo* is a present sent with greetings as an expression of loyalty), a church service, worship.

In Isl. 205[2] Shembe uses *isikhonzi* in the sense of voluntary workers which is a reminiscence of Joel 4[13], Matth. 9[37,38], Mark 4[29] and John 4[35,36].[2]) The word *labourers* in Matth. 9[37] is translated in the Zulu Bibles with *izisebenzi* while Shembe uses *isikhonzi*. cf. Isl. 205[2].

Amaɓuya ezwi lakho	The fields of your word
Avuthiwe wona;	they are ripe;
Thuma wena izikhondzi*	send ye the voluntary servants
Zezwi lakho wedwa.	of your word alone.

* isikhonzi.

In Isl. 211[3], where he uses *aɓakhonzi* (cf. also Isl. 212[2]), they are described as those who voluntarily took the yoke (*ijokwe*) on them and have accepted this task for life (Isl. 211[2]). In Isl. 212[1,2] the *aɓakhonzi* stand in the service of the Sabbath, which means for Shembe I that they are in the service of the word. In Isl. 171[3,4] the worshippers (*aɓakhonzi*) are invited

---

[1]) Ministers are chosen by 'the Spirit'.
[2]) The boys from 5 to 14 years are, in the movement, referred to as *izikhonzi*.

to the *uMkhululi* where their *umoya* is loosened from bonds before the
messengers (*izithunywa*). In Isl. 158 Shembe calls himself "the servant of
suffering of *uThixo*" or simply the "servant of suffering" or "suffering
servant" discussed in chapter II.

6. *AɓaProfithi*

As in the case of the designation *isikhonzi*, only Shembe I refers to the
prophets and only in the plural. A few references are made to the prophets
namely Izl. 7, 34, 77 and 139. His photo in the *Izihlaɓelelo* is however
underwritten in the singular, namely *Umphrofethi Isaiah Shembe* and
this is the one direct reference in the book to him as a prophet. Shembe
considered himself rather a messiah than a prophet. He states in Isl. 139:

1. Ufikile aɓakhuluma ngaye	He has arrived of whom they speak
Aɓa Profithi.	the Prophets.
. . . .	. . . .
2. Uyeza uThumekile	The Promised one comes
Uzofika emhlaɓeni	he will arrive on the earth.
. . . .	. . . .
3. Ufikile umthokozisi	He has arrived the one who makes happy,
Mlandeleni zizwe nonke.	Ye follow him all ye nations.

Shembe I has not thought of himself as merely a prophet—he is the
promised one to the nations. The title of Sundkler's book *Bantu Prophets
in South Africa* is thus misleading. Prophets are sent out in the name of the
iNkosi (Isl. 77[4]), they come from Ekuphakameni. Shembe himself, as the
angel of the East and the *iNkosi*, had been met by the prophets of Nazareth
when he came on the clouds. In Shembe's movement prophets play a role
but he *is* their Messiah.

7. *Aɓapostoli*

Only once is this designation used in the *Izihlaɓelelo*. They are associated
with and limited only to Ekuphakameni. cf. Isl. 106[7].

Imikhosi edumileyo yaɓa Postoli	The renowned armies of the Apostles,
yaɓafela izwi lakho,	those who died for thy word,
Izephakathi kwakho Kuphakama	they have come in you *Kuphakama*
Ize kudumisa uJehova.	they have come to praise Jehova.

Shembe has monopolized all the apostles and martyrs for his movement. The centre of heaven is now at Ekuphakameni.

8. *Aɓafundisi* (Teachers or Ministers, also used for missionaries)

The word appears in Isl. 34³ and is derived from *fundisa* which means to educate, train, influence. Whether it means teachers or ministers depends on the intonation, which is not given in the *Izihlaɓelelo*.

B. *The Building*

The sanctified building at Ekuphakameni is not always clearly discerned from the holy place itself. He describes it as the *indlu ka Jehova* (house of Jehova, Isl. 160⁸, cf. Isl. 86¹.) although one is not certain whether he does limit it to the building only. When he speaks about the *indlu ka Sendzanga-khona* (Isl. 111⁴) the reference is obviously to Ekuphakameni itself. The designation *ikhaya* (cf. Izl. 18³, 29¹) refers also to the city.

This holy place has to be entered *bare-footed*. cf. Isl. 60⁶.

Aɓangafaki lutho	Those who put on nothing
Ezinyaweni zaɓo,	on their feet,
Waɓalungisela ukungena	you prepared them to enter
Endaweni eyingcwele.	into a place which is holy.

This is a reminiscence of Ex. 3⁵. Shembe maintains that they turn the "house of Jehova" into a "house of play" (*indlu yomdlalo*, Isl. 60⁸) through breaking the laws. Disappointment brings him to the house of the *iNkosi* so that he could praise with the many. (Isl. 86²). Shembe II refers to Ekuphakameni as a whole as the house (*indlu*) of *uThixo*. (Isl. 232⁵).

C. *The Scriptures*

1. *Imibalo* (*umbalo*, sing.)

i. Document, writing, entry, mark. ii. (pl. only) Scriptures. iii. Large blanket.
<bala: i. Scratch marks. ii. Write, draw a picture. iii. Enter, register.

Shembe I uses this word only once in connection with Scriptures which refer most probably to the Scriptures preserved in his house. He never makes any specific reference to the Bible as such. He states in Isl. 34³ that

the teachers were gathered to investigate the writings (ɓahlole imibalo)
and then adds in verse 4:

Bafika ɓathi yeɓo	They arrived and said: yes,
Kulotshiwe kanjalo,	it is so written
Nawe *Kuphakama*	and you *Kuphakama*
Magquma as' Ohlange.	hillocks of *uHlanga.*

According to these Scriptures the history of Bethlehem is the history of
Ekuphakameni which is related to the Zulu history. The reference to
Scriptures has a vagueness about it which however is not thus interpreted
by illiterate and semi-illiterate people. Shembe uses the word which could
refer either to documents, writings or the Scriptures. The word is often
used in Scripture. cf. Luke 24[27,45]. Shembe believed in an open canon.

2. *Izwi*

Reference is often made to this word in the *Izihlaɓelelo* which could
have the following meanings:
    i. Voice; ii. Order, command, message; iii. Saying; iv. Word; v. Idiom-
atically: to give an opinion.
    Shembe uses *izwi* in different senses:

(1) *Izwi as word:*

The question is always: To whose word does the *Izihlaɓelelo* refer? Is
it the word of Shembe I or is it the Bible? and if it is the Bible, is it not
merely certain sections?

a. *The word and the Sabbath.*

Shembe with his legalistic approach, interpreted the word through the
commandments. The moralistic-legalistic interpretation of Scripture opens
up the way for such a development in a society where ritual prohibitions
are basic in the religious approach. Ritual prohibitions as positive magic,
the observance of which influence the supernatural forces, give the
disposition for regarding the Bible as a book with magically loaded texts,
the observance of which have magical effect. For Shembe I the core of
these ritual prohibitions in Scripture is the commandment on the Sabbath
and it is thus the core of the word. cf. Isl. 127 (cf. also Isl. 200).

2. Siqinise* izwi lakho	We strengthen your word,
Zosinda zonke izizwe.	all nations will be saved.
3. Zi6uthene lapha	They are gathered here
Zonke lezo zizwe	all those nations
Zifuna iqiniso lezwi lakho	they want the truth of your word
Ziligcine isa6atha.	so that they observe the Sabbath.
4. Sheshisa iSa6atha	Cause the Sabbath to come quickly
Nkosi yezulu nomhla6a,	*Nkosi* of heaven and earth,
Na6a6ili na6athathu	even two and even three
Bayalifuna iSa6atha.	are in need of the Sabbath.

* qinisa: i. Make firm, strengthen; ii. Act with determination; iii. Strengthen with medical charms; administer a tonic; iv. Confirm; v. Encourage; vi. Swear. During the first-fruit ceremonies the king, as well as the soldiers, were magically strengthened with medicines and through ritual washing. This expression has this association for the pre-christian Zulu.

b. *The carriers of the word*

The observance of the word i.e. the Sabbath and other ritual prohibitions, give *numinous* power which enables the observer to distribute such power among the nations. The word and *numinous* power are intimately related and it has concrete effects. cf. Isl. 130[4].

Sani6ona makholwa	Be greeted believers!
Nina zitsha[1]) ezinhle	you, the beautiful vessels,
Zokuphatha* leli lizwi,	for holding this word,
Zisinde zonke izizwe.	may all nations be saved.

* phata: i. Handle, feel, carry (in the hand); ii. Mention; iii. Treat, manage.

The word is something concrete, like a magically loaded entity which is carried—no wonder that in many Nativistic movements the word has become a kind of *fetish*. He speaks in Isl. 130[1] of the *izembe*[2]) *lezwi lakho* ("the medicine of this word of thee".); the blessing of the word is poured (*mpompozela*) into the hearts of those who thirst (*a6omele*) for it (Isl. 174[5]). Concerning the main carrier of this word the request is: cf. Isl. 134[4].

UJehova akwakhe* Nceku yeNkosi	Jehova should build you up Servant of the *iNkosi*

* <akha: Build up e.g. a house, erect, construct a bridge, establish. Here it means to make him strong as the king was strengthened.

---

[1]) The king's most powerful instrument was a certain "vessel" by which he could overcome personal and tribal enemies. *Krige*, 245.

[2]) It refers to a medicine used by a soldier to treat blood uncleanness after battle; also used for several types of diseases.

| Uhambise izwi lakhe Nceku | that you should spread his word |
| yeNkosi... | Servant of the *iNkosi*... |

c. *The word at Ekuphakameni*

The word is here the most effective. All are called to come quickly to Ekuphakameni to hear Shembe's word. (Isl. 63 chorus.). The *centripetal* type of missionary approach, namely that the majesty of Shembe, the *iNkosi* and Ekuphakameni, will attract all nations, is typical of the *Izihla-belelo*. The desire is to stay with the eternal word who is Shembe himself as he came from the world to come. (Isl. 218[5] cf. Isl. 77). Anyone who leaves Ekuphakameni is cut off as the twig is from the vine (Isl. 86[3]), which is a reminiscence of John 15. It is the messianic word of Shembe which comes to all nations: cf. Isl. 161[3].

Baɓizeni ngezwi lakhe	Call them through his word
Ohlala Ekuphakameni,	he who stays at Ekuphakameni,
Ophunga limnandi	whose smell is pleasant
Lokusindisa izizwe	for saving nations
Basinda ngalo aɓaningi	many got saved by it
Aɓanhlanhla yaɓo	whose good fortune
Ingaconseli phansi.	does not drop to the ground.

The christian preacher subjects himself to Scripture but Shembe has himself become the word which came on the clouds, a reminiscence of John 1. cf. Isl. 158[3].

| Siliɓonile lelo lizwi | We have seen that word |
| Livela emafini. | coming from the clouds. |

d. *Preaching of the word*

To this aspect sufficient reference has already been made in Chapter III. Shembe refers in Isl. 103[2] to the beginning of his ministry when he preached travelling through Natal and Zululand, often by ox wagon (*inqola*) and states that all nations looked to the road with great expectations. It has already been stated that his word is preached through the *umoya* of the *iNkosi*. In the beginning Shembe stood in the service of the word but later on the word stood in his service.

e. *The effects of the word*

i. It takes away *all tears* (Isl. 134[5]).

ii. It scatters their enemies (Isl. 166[1]); it is the word through which they conquer (Isl. 219[3]).

iii. It calls together *all Africans* (Isl. 17), the Shakas (i.e. Zulus) and Mabacas (Isl. 178[3,4]).

iv. It calls *all nations*—it does not select individuals.

After maintaining that this word wandered (*zule*) in the *whole, whole* world he adds in Isl. 147[1]:

Alikhethi noma munye	It does not choose even a single person
Liyaɓa ɓiza ɓonke aɓantu	it calls all people
Alikhethi noma munye[1]).	it does not choose even a single person.

The Zulu never had the idea that only some could enter the tribe. In an ethnic movement all will be welcome; there is no selection, no individualism. He calls the nations to "this word, which is above all". (*lelolizwi elophezu konke*. The individualistic approach is not appreciated.

v. This word does not merely provide in spiritual matters but gives good fortune (Isl. 202 chorus), it provides in need (Isl. 204[1]) and thus gives hope (Isl. 205[1]). The abundance it gives is expressed as follows in Isl. 205[4]:

Ziɓuthelwe eqomeni	They are gathered together in a basket
Lezwi lakho wedwa.	of your word alone.
Umhlaɓa nokugcwala kwawo,	the earth and its fullness
Kungowakho wedwa.	it is yours only.

vi. Shembe I has *manufactured* a new word as a replacement for christianity or *uɓukholwa* (which he does not use!) namely *uɓuNazaretha* (Nazarethness cf. Izl. 207, 208). *Nazarethness* arrives with the word of Shembe (Isl. 208[2]). This Nazarite mission song has put Nazareth (Ekuphakameni) in the centre of the world. Here Scripture is interpreted in the context of the tradition of Ekuphakameni or Nazarethness.

vii. The word of Shembe is heard *even by those in the graves* out of which they are called. (cf. Isl. 159.) This eternal word (*lelo lizwi laphakade*, verse 1) cannot accept the inactivity and spatial limitation of the dead. His word calls them out of the graves. (verse 4).

viii. This is a life-*giving word.* cf. Isl. 166[1].

Sinezwi lakho Nkosi	We have your word, *iNkosi,*
Sinokuphila ngalo.	we have life through it.

---

[1]) This is again repeated in Isl. 153[1,2]. He states it also invites "black and white" (aɓasundu naɓamhlophe) i.e. it does not make any racial distinction.

It could however only be received by ritually purified hearts.

Shembe II scarcely refers to the word—his major reference is to the word of his father. cf. Isl. 240[1].

In a society that hails from a scriptureless people the interpretation of scripture will raise difficulties especially in counteracting the traditional approach to religion. Practices which are in agreement with African traditional beliefs, e.g., ritual purification, sacrifices, belief in shades, polygamy are justified. Certain texts, words (for example *Amen* in the Izi-*hlaɓelelo*) and *names* are considered to be loaded with supernatural power. It is not merely a problem of *literalism* but of *magic* closely associated with Biblical literalism.

(2) *Izwi as Voice*

Sundkler refers to *ingelosi* and the *Voice* as channels through which *uMoya* makes his will known.[1]) Shembe's own call was through the *Voice*: cf. Isl. 136[2].

Wangiɓiza Nkosi ngezwi lakho	You called me *iNkosi* with your Voice
Ngali lalela izwi lakho.	I listened to your Voice.
Ngashiya indzuzo ngezwi lakho	I left gain through your Voice
Ngesuka ngaku landela.	I stood up and followed you.

He wandered in the wilderness in order to hide his sins but the voice of his sins, which in this case is his conscience, shouted at him. cf. Isl. 26[2].

Ngathi uma ngithandaza ngisehlane	And when I was praying in the wilderness
Zangimemeza ngezwi elikhulu.	They (the sins) shouted at me in a big voice.

In Matth. 17[5] the *Voice* comes as a means of *revelation*. With Shembe it comes through the messengers (*izithunywa*). cf. Isl. 158[2].

Siɓona ngezwi	We see through a voice
Livela emafini,	it comes from the clouds,
Liza nge zithunywa	it comes through the messengers
Livela emafini.	it comes from the clouds.

The voice out of the cloud in Matth. 17[5] (*izwi efwini*) is interpreted in the Zulu context. The *desire for revelation* is here again evident.

---

[1]) Sundkler, Bantu Prophets, 249.

D. *The Commandments*

a. *iSabatha*. (As a Sabbatarian observing Saturday as the day of the Lord, Shembe does not use *sonto* (Afr. Sondag) for Sunday.).

Of all the laws, commandments and ritual prohibitions the Sabbath is the most significant in this movement. It is often mentioned in the *Izihla-6elelo*. Jehova and Shembe restored the observance of the Sabbath to the Zulu nation and the world. The Sabbath is the very key to salvation. cf. Isl. 212².

iSa6atha lingu Khiye	The Sabbath is the key
Avulwe amasango.	the gates may be opened.

The "keys of the kingdom of heaven" (Matth. 16¹⁹) have become in Shembe's exegesis and theology one single key which opens the gates of heaven and of which he is the holder even after his death. As such he is the representative, not of Jesus Christ, but of Jehova who has given the Sabbath to his people.

In this light the strict Sabbath observance should be seen. The core of the Old Testament, the most significant part of Scripture for Shembe, is the Sabbath law. In the "Prayers for the Sabbath" he continually refers to its observance as the basis of their faith. (cf. Section 20, 18); it is equated with the "word of Jehova" (Section 22, 19); the sins of their fathers Dingaan and Sendzangakhona are referred to in these prayers. (Section 21, 19); it is the only commandment to which he refers in the singular (*umthetho*; cf. Section 19, 18).

The *Izl.* support the *Prayers* with regard to the Sabbath. In Isl. 21 his reference to the *iNkosi* of the Sabbath (*Nkosi yeSabatha*) deliberately excludes Jesus Christ. Shembe is on this central issue not the representative of Jesus Christ, whose attitude to the Sabbath gave him theological headaches. His request is that the Sabbath, the day itself, should come soon (Isl. 127¹) because it is the day of special power, a day in which Jehova reveals himself in a special way. Like a refrain he repeats in Isl. 98 *Isabatha namhla Nkosi* ("it is Sabbath today *Nkosi*") and adds in verse 4 *Sise6usweni 6akho* ("We are now before thy face")¹) These last words run like a refrain through the whole hymnal. In Isl. 188¹ Shembe states, adding *3 Amens*:

Simenyiwe thina sonke	We have been invited all
Simenywa Inkosi yeSabatha,	we have been invited by the *iNkosi*
	of the Sabbath,

---

¹) See also Izl. 167⁵; 193⁵; 198⁶.

Size sisindiswe	that we may be saved
Ngaleli Sabatha.	through this Sabbath.

To this he adds in verse 2:

Wasihlenga* ngeSa6atha:	You sifted us through the Sabbath.

* -hlenga: i. Sift separate; ii. Ransom, redeem; iii. Escort. The word used in the translation gives the meaning the best.

It is Shembe, the Sabbath, and Ekuphakameni where the Sabbath has heavenly power. Concrete historical revelation is taking place at this holy city at which place the Sabbath, called "the city of rest" (*iSa6atha lingu muzi wokuphumula*, Isl. 200[6]) is the most effective. It is the *mkhosi wenthethelelo* (the *umkhosi* of intercession, Isl. 188[3]); when not observed it leads to death (Isl. 200[3] cf. Ex. 31[15])[1]). The whole world outside Ekuphakameni is thus in Shembe's eyes in darkness on account of the Sabbath issue.

This day is not only "the beautiful day" (*imini enhle*, Isl. 167[5], 187[1]) or the day they have to respect (*hlonipha*, Isl. 200[7]) but the day is Shembe himself. cf. Isl. 187[1].

Imini enhle	The beautiful day,
Sa6atha nguwe	the Sabbath are you.
Phumula nathi wena,	Rest you with us
Siyakuncenga 6a6a wethu sonke	we beg you father of us all
Ngena nathi wena.	enter you with us.

This is a holy day in extremity and is personified and equated with the deity. In Isl. 188, apart from Isl. 200, the greatest Sabbath hymn in the *Izihla6elelo*, with its fifteen magically loaded Amens, all people are called to the *uMsindisi* in order to sanctify this day. Shembe as the holder of this key opens or shuts heaven.

b. *Imithetho*: (sing. umthetho)

i. Law, custom, rule, edict, statute; ii. Pronouncement, system, arrangement.

< thetha: i. Scold; ii. Try a law case; iii. Offer praises, prayer or sacrifice to the spirits; iv. Find not guilty; v. Be in sympathy with.

It is being used in the first instance as a legal term. As used in Scripture the pre-christian Zulu reader, for whom the word has a purely formalistic

---

[1]) See also Prayers for the Sabbath, Section 25, 19 and Section 28, 20. He states in this last section that where they are gathered in observance of the Sabbath Jehova looks at them as a bride looks at the groom (*u6abeka njengo makoti ehlonipha umyeni wakhe.*)

and legalistic connotation, will interpret it in this way without being aware, if not explained, that behind the law in the Old Testament stands the Gospel. The observance of the commandments, seen as ritual prohibitions, signifies for the magically oriented person *numinous* power. The moralistic or magical approach is maintained by Shembe. He admonishes the people to keep the laws (*imithetho*) of Jehova "so that your praising may be acceptable to the *uThixo* of the proclamations" (*ukuze ukudumisa kwenu kwamukeleke kuThixo wemikhosi*, Prayers for the Sabbath, Section 3, 16.)[1]). He seldom refers to "the ten commandments or laws" (*imithetho elishumi*, Morning Prayers, Section 42, 7; Isl. 85[2]) as he wishes to include all the ritual prohibitions.[2]) As the whole community was blessed by its adherence to these prohibitions, so the congregation. (Prayers for the Sabbath, Section 15, 18.).

Breakers of the laws (*baphuli bemithetho*, Isl. 145[5])[3]) are unclean (Isl. 85), and are called to Ekuphakameni where the doors are opened and the *uMkhululi* and *uMthetheleli* (Isl. 145[5] Forgiver) is. Such breakers of the law are cursed (Isl. 215[3]); their *umoya* has been grieved (*udabukile*) and their hearts are in trouble (*inosizi*, Isl. 145[3]). Individuals and nations part through the law (Isl. 178[1]); Adam was pushed out of Eden through breaking the law (Isl. 33[4]). Entering the "house of Jehova" without shoes on is considered as breaking the law (Isl. 60[8]), and so is clipping of the hair (Isl. 60[7]). The Old Testament has thus been interpreted in a most literal sense.

c. *Imikhosi* (sing. umkhosi)

This word, related to chieftainship, could mean a public announcement or proclamation or could refer to an army or hosts (cf. Isl. 106[2,7]). Shembe uses the word in the sense of proclamations only a few times e.g. in the Prayers for the Sabbath, Section 3, 16 he speaks of the *uThixo wemikhosi* (*uThixo* of the proclamations). This word is not generally used for law in the Zulu Bibles. Shembe used it to include all ritual prohibitions.

During the *Great Umkhosi* public proclamations were shouted out and obsolete laws abrogated. Shembe's statement with regard to medicine under the *Isifundo* section is such an *umkhosi*. (cf. Prayers for the Sabbath, Section 45, 22. "It is sin to handle medicine with your hand, you being a believer; you will certainly die." cf. Isl. 186[3]).

---

[1]) See also Prayers for the Sabbath, Section 4, 17. "He will never shower blessings upon you if you do not listen to his laws and keep them."

[2]) For these ritual prohibitions see *Schlosser*, Eingeborenenkirchen, 246.

[3]) See also Izl. 114[4], 215[3].

d. *Imiyalo* (sing. umyalo). <yala: i. warn; ii. Teach by painful experience.

   i. Warning, admonition, instruction, command, order.

   ii. Prohibition, negative command.

The Zulu Bible of 1961 has a heading to Ex. 20 *imiyalelo eyishumi* (the ten commandments), while the headings of practically all the other chapters use the word *umthetho* (pl. *imithetho*). Shembe uses the word *imiyalo* only in Izl. 5[4]; 75[1,2]. In Isl. 75 he states:

1. Siɓambe singayeki imiyalo yakho.	May we hold, may we not leave
. . . .	your commandments.
2. Ngokuɓa ludondolo oluhle	Because it is a beautiful staff
Imiyalo yakho.	your commandments.

   e. *Isimemezelo* (pl. izimemezelo)

Proclamation, notice.

   <memezela: i. Shout or call for; ii. Herald, proclaim.

Shembe uses the word in his superscription to Isl. 162 where he states that he kept his "*umoya* for the proclamation of the *iNkosi*."

Conclusion

The unconditional demands of the laws, proclamations and commandments is the continuous emphasis in the *Izihlaɓelelo*. With them he holds the community together, the main function of ritual prohibitions. This legalistic-moralistic approach led to the exclusion of Jesus whose attitude is not that the breaking of the law separates finally from God, in spite of the hopeless situation it establishes. Shembe did not see that Jesus established a completely different relationship to the law; that freedom from the laws is messianic i.e. christological. (cf. Matth. 17[24] ff). Shembe could not accept that the law is no more mediator between God and man as was the case in the Old Testament and that there is no righteousness through the Law.

Through the person of Jesus the Law has been removed from its key position and it is precisely this that led to Shembe's doubt with regard to the finality of Jesus and His work on the Cross. Shembe is the man of the Law and through it the Liberator of his people. He was not made a messiah by his people, he considered himself to *be* their messiah. An analysis based *only* on colour, i.e. that he merely reacted against the so-called pale white Christ, is an over-simplification of the deep-seated theological problems Shembe had to solve in his own way.

Shembe did not realize that Jesus said *yes* to the Law which He himself kept. (Mark. 10[19]). He never refers to Paul in the Izl.—for Paul the Cross is the vital issue with regard to the law. Paul's reaction against the law is a result of the Cross (cf. Gal. 2[21]), and Shembe's reaction against the Cross is a result of the law. Shembe did not understand that Paul also said *yes* to the law as the good will of God, and he who does not subject himself to it in the light of the Cross is an enemy of God. (Rom. 8[7]). For Shembe it is not the sufficiency of the Cross but the sufficiency of the law which is uppermost in his theology. cf. Isl. 24[5].

Namhla thokozani nina	Today rejoice ye
Weбagcini бemithetho,	ye keepers of the laws,
Nizogcotshwa nanele	you are going to be anointed to sufficiency
Ngokuyifeza imithetho.	for accomplishing the laws.

Shembe and the holy ones have taken now the central position with regard to the observance of the ritual prohibitions. All transgressors of the laws must bend their ears and hear the din (*inhlokomo*) of the saints. (Isl. 24[6]). In Zulu society the ancestors sanctioned the ritual prohibitions.

The position of the Old Testament in the *Izihlaбelelo* is clear. Of the limited number of texts referred to, the largest number are from the Old Testament. Shembe came from a church in which spiritual experience played its role as a result of the influence of 19th century pietism. In Shembe's case it led him via the law and ritual prohibitions to his ancestry and the Zulu religious world. Ritual prohibition in the pre-christian Zulu society was intrinsically bound up with the world of the ancestors. They are brought back in a new context. As a magical person Shembe utilises the forces and spirits of the supernatural world for his purposes. This makes man's achievements central in his theology. Israel however was not chosen because it was obedient, but to be obedient. (Deut. 7[7-11]).

The Old Testament with its intense solidarity with regard to the here and now, with Moses, Sinai and Israel the subjected people, the patriarchs, its concern with harvest, fertility and offspring, all this contributed to its popularity. In it Shembe saw the basic source for the restoration of his people not only politically but also spiritually. The faith of his fathers could find a place in it.

E. *The Festivals*

Sundkler mentions the two great festivals, the July and January festivals,

which take place at Ekuphakameni and Nhlangakazi respectively.[1]) The
2nd May, the date Shembe died, is a day of memory. Isl. 221 has a superscription that "it should be sung on the day of memory only". Shembe II
wrote it on Nhlangakazi in Jan. 1938. Vilakazi maintains that the Ark of
the Covenant is a symbol of the Covenant relationship of God with His
people, the Zulus, and that it is represented by a drum, a sacred object held
in the house of Shembe I. In October of each year the Ark of the Covenant
is taken over the Tugela River and the Nazarites meet at Judea, a Shembe
village in Zululand.[2])

Shembe does not make any specific reference to the July festival in the
Izihlaɓelelo, but many of these Izl. are composed for this occasion when for
three weeks healing services are held, dancing, preaching and the passover
take place.[3]) He also introduced the First fruit ceremonies which were
divided into two parts. The ukweshwama[4]), nyathela[5]) or umkhosi omncane
(little umkhosi) was the preliminary feast which took place about a month
before the great annual Zulu New Year Festival. The tribe then brought
their share of the first-fruits (imiliɓo). The little umkhosi has been adapted
in the movement of Shembe and is celebrated on Dec. 25. No Nazarite
could eat the first-fruits before it had been blessed (ɓusisa) by Shembe.[6])

The Zulu was rich in fixed forms, ceremonies and symbolism, and much
of it Shembe had to reject on entering the Church without receiving an
adequate explanation or its christian re-orientation. In Isl. 216[4] he maintains "we are the first-fruits of this root". (Thina siluliɓo lwaleyo mpande).
This root is that from which the Zulu nation has been derived and to which
the message of Shembe has been added. It is in this light that these festivals
should be seen.

In the superscription to Isl. 162 with its six Amens added to each of the
five verses Shembe states that he was with the umoya of the iNkosi on
Nhlangakazi and kept his own umoya for the proclamation of the iNkosi,
which reminds of the Great umkhosi when new proclamations were

---

[1]) Sundkler, Bantu Prophets, 198.

[2]) Vilakazi, Isonto Lamanazaretha, 79.

[3]) Sundkler, Bantu Prophets, 198, 228 ff; Schlosser, Eingeborenenkirchen, 279 ff.

[4]) eshwama: i. Perform the first-fruit ceremonies; ii. Treat the new crops which had
been doctored.

[5] nyathelisa: i. Cause to tread; ii. Assist king in preliminaries of the First-fruit ceremonies; iii. Give a present to the king in passing his kraal. Shembe received such gifts.

[6]) This sacrament had two roots in Zulu religion, namely to eat with the ancestors
and to eat together. Eating together means possessing together. It had also as aim to
control social behaviour. Here is a practical demonstration of the ancestors, chief,
army and headmen. It served as a means for Shembe to restore the Zulu kingship and
thus the whole hierarchical system.

announced and the royal shades approached. It is at this mountain that they drink sufficiently; it is their mount Sinai where the covenant relationship receives special significance. (cf. Isl. 83³). Nhlangakazi has for Shembe II the same significance—he received a number of his Izl. on this holy mountain of the Nazarites. In Isl. 223⁴, referring to *iNkosi*, a designation for his father (as is clear from the superscription to Isl. 220) he states:

Ekuphakameni ngiyaku kulandela,   I will follow you at Ekuphakameni
Nakhona eNhlangakazi ngiyaku   and also at Nhlangakazi I will
    kulandela.   follow you.

In Isl. 234⁴ he calls to mind Nhlangakazi the "holy place" where he spread himself before his father and asks that it should be a sweet scent (verse 5). In Isl. 228³ reference is made to the *impepho* flowers burned at Nhlangakazi, a plant burned by the *izangoma* diviners, the smoke of which they inhale to increase their divining powers. Shembe I has this in mind when he states in Isl. 165 (in which Nhlangakazi is indirectly referred to): *Holani umoya* (Inhale *umoya*, verse 4). Nhlangakazi is the restoration of the Zulu *ubukhosi* (kingly authority), the mountain of contact with the Supreme Being (for Shembe II with his father) and the royal ancestors. It is the place of "filling up" with the all-pervading power obtained through ceremony and ritual.

F. *Vital force or numinous power in the service of the Congregation*

Continuously *amandla* (power, strength) is asked for in the *Izihlabelelo*. The cry is often heard that this *amandla*, which is more than mere physical strength, is finished. *uNkulunkulu* is repeatedly referred to as "*Nkulunkulu onamandla onke*"¹) (uNkulunkulu with all power i.e. Almighty uNkulunkulu). They have been protected against the enemies through the *amandla* of the *amakhosi*, it is this power that brings them to Nhlangakazi (Isl. 37³,⁴). This power has still its effects (cf. Izl. 37, 68). *Amandla* is not static but flows like springs of water (Isl. 71³). Their dancing takes place through the *amandla* of the kingly authority (*ubukhosi*) of Shembe (Isl. 112²); he asks for the *umoya wamandla* (*umoya* of power) to be poured into him (Isl. 135³); *iNkosi* gives *amandla* (Isl. 225⁴), and Shembe II asks his father, the *iNkosi* with power, to wash their hearts (Isl. 239⁴).

When Shembe read Acts 1⁸ he had this *numinous* power in mind, and

---

¹) cf. Morning Prayers, Section 2, 1; Section 8, 2; Evening Prayers, Section 8, 10; Section 14, 11; Section 18, 11.

when Acts 2^4 states "they were all filled (*ɓegcwala*) with the Holy Ghost" he again had reason to think in substantial terms, namely that man is filled up with *umoya*, an all-pervading energy of which supernatural holy spirits are carriers or which they cause to be effective through the medium of material objects.

This power reveals itself especially in *holy water*. Shembe considers ritual washing essential with regard to purification and the restoration of *numinous* power. The king could only be strong when ritually clean. This ritual washing has made the Cross superfluous. The name of Jesus is omitted in Isl. 13 where he relates the story of the Samaritan woman at the well of Jacob. The fountain is of more importance. He continually refers to fountains (*umthombo*, pl. *imithombo*). This is the basis of the theology of ritual washing. In Isl. 79^1 the river *Mthwalume* is praised. Sundkler refers to a so-called "water church" (*iɓandla lamanzi*)[1]). In the great praise song (Isl. 93) in which the name of Jesus does not appear water receives special mention in verse 4.

Siyakuɓonga chiɓi elihle	We praise you beautiful lake
Lokugeza izono zethu.	of washing away our sins.

This way of salvation has at its disposal the mighty *numinous* power obtained by their messiah by way of his free and open and unobstructed contact with the supernatural world and its energies conveyed by way of material things, especially water. Shembe stands now in the centre of the history of redemption, the one who washes with hyssop from heaven (cf. Izl. 73^5; 192^2). Isl. 102 is devoted to the fountains at Ekuphakameni and the completeness of the blessings which this holy city can give.

It is about this completeness that Shembe II speaks when he asks for the stream where he could be purified and be complete (Isl. 228^2). With great satisfaction he repeats Ps. 23:

Uyangihola ngomusa wakhe	He leads me through his kindness
Emanzini okuphumula.	to refreshing waters.

Shembe I often stated when the *umoya* was weak: *Geza inhliziyo yami* (wash my heart, Isl. 118^2). John 3^5 will especially appeal in such a theological disposition: "Except a man be born of water and of the Spirit, he cannot enter into the kingdom of God!"

1. *Holy Communion and the Cross*

What is the theological position of this sacrament in a theology in which

---

[1]) Sundkler, Bantu Prophets, 205.

numinous power is central? Two Izl. are devoted to the holy communion, namely, Izl. 140 and 194; the last has been taken over from the Methodist hymnal. He states that he received it on the 14th Dec. 1932, less than three years before his death. The superscription to Isl. 140 states that holy communion must be served on the 14th day of the month, and adds to it the following texts: Jos. 5¹⁰, 1 Cor. 11²³, Ex. 12⁶, Matth. 26²⁰, Mark 4¹⁶,²⁷. Shembe invites all those "who have been destined to eternal life" to this "life-giving meal" (*esidlweni sokuphila*, Isl. 140 verse 1) and adds in verse 2:

Aɓasidlayo lesisidlo*	Those who partake of this meal
Banokuphila okunguna phakade;	will have eternal life;
Ngoɓavusa ngomhla wokuphela	it will resurrect them on the last day
Baɓe nami eParadise.	they may be with me in Paradise.

   * -dlo (pl. izidlo): i. Specially prepared meal or feast; ii. Holy Communion; Eucharist.

The meal is "eternal life" (*singukuphila okuphakade*, verse 4). The 14th day of the month is not without significance in the superscription. In both the Old Testament references the 14th day of the month is mentioned. In Ex. 12⁶ it is stated that the lamb shall be killed on the 14th day and in Jos. 5¹⁰ that the passover shall be kept on this day of the month. Matth. 26²⁰, one of the New Testament references, relates Jesus' eating of the passover with the disciples and the institution of the Lord's supper.

The holy communion is for Shembe rather the passover in spite of his reference to the death of Jesus. It takes place at night in *Paradisi* at Eku-phakameni at least during the great festivals. Feet-washing takes place before its celebration. Unleavened bread baked at Ekuphakameni is used and water instead of wine. The water is fetched from a source in a mountain three days by foot away from Ekuphakameni. The source, known only to three spiritual leaders of the movement, is kept secret. This secrecy reminds of that which characterizes the initiation ceremonies.

Shembe states that those who partake of this meal will have eternal life. In Isl. 194 the refrain in each verse is: "Come ye now, may ye eat, may ye live." When Shembe states in Isl. 186³ that they "drink from the tree of life, the tree in this city," he has the tree of Rev. 22², which stands on either side of the river, in mind. Here his reference is to Jehova. The holy water used at Shembe's holy communion instead of wine, has not the blood of Jesus in the Scriptural sense in mind but it has turned the sacrament into a purification rite. This is not a *nudum signum*, a mere symbolic act. The holy communion should be seen in the light of the ritual meal which took place in connection with the First-fruit ceremonies and which was an eating together with the supernatural beings.

The *Cross* in the theology of Shembe plays an insignificant role. He refers
to it in Izl. 5, 56, 87, 132 and 185, the last taken over from the Methodist
hymnal. He uses three words for the Cross namely *isiphambano*[1]) (Izl. 5[5];
132[2]); *nqamulezo*[2]) (Isl. 185) and *umuthi* (tree, Isl. 87[1]). In Isl. 132 he
mentions only the name of Jehova, and not that of Jesus, but states:

2. Bamenywa ngolenga emthini	They are invited by the one who
	hangs from the tree
Esiphambanweni:	at the Cross:
Emthini wokudelwa	on that tree that is despised
Umhlaɓa wazamazama.	the earth quaked.

About his sins he maintains:

4. Ezami zagqitshwa kanye naye	Mine were buried with him
Ethuneni, senizwile wozani.	in the grave, you have already
	heard, come.

The significance of the Cross is that the "negative" substance called sin
is buried. In verse 3 he maintains that his sins were confessed (*wayevuma:
vuma* could also mean "turning out well") on the tree of disgrace. Ritual
vomiting as a means of getting rid of the negative substance called sin or
of the evil spirits plays an important role in Nativism.[3])

Shembe understood the fact that the holy communion has more than a
mere symbolic meaning but this has been interpreted in his own terms.
Many pietistic churches attached secondary significance to this sacrament
as preference is given to baptism. Furthermore at the celebration of holy
communion the death of Christ was proclaimed as an event in the past
rather than an eschatological event. Shembe did not accept the all-suffiency
of this eschatological event. Neither did he understand that it is not the
psychological remembering of the death of Christ but it is Christ's
life and death to be remembered. 1 Cor. 11[24,25] must be understood in a
causative sense, i.e. to remember that which is mine. Shembe's holy
communion is not celebrated in this sense but its celebration at Ekuphakameni gives *numinous* power on the authority of Shembe, which is
conveyed through the medium of the elements, especially the holy water.
This remembrance is neither historically based nor eschatologically

---

[1]) It has the following meanings: i. Constant worry, lifelong burden or trouble;
ii. Cross.

[2]) *ulunqamulezo*: i. Cross; ii. Crucifixion, torture; iii. Continued trouble, persecution.
What must have appealed to him in Isl. 185 is surely verse 5 where it is stated that the
angels continually stared at this wonder on the Cross.

[3]) Sundkler, Bantu Prophets, 211–3.

directed. It is now a purification rite, through which "eternal" life is granted.

Shembe stood nearer to the passover through which the deliverance of Israel from Egypt was remembered. The passover and the holy communion cannot be identified, because the holy communion is not simply the fulfilment of the passover for the blood of the new convenant is the fulfilment of the whole sacrificial system of the Old Testament. Shembe has considered this Messianic meal not to be a meal of the joy of the forgiveness in Christ but a meal through which supernatural power could be obtained, that those who take part "will have" eternal life. This is however no hellenistic meal in remembrance of the dead or which conveys supernatural power but neither is it a mere *hinweis* (directing towards) as often proclaimed in the churches which Shembe could not accept. Christ is present in the Lord's Supper in a specific sense as mighty reality with the presence of His grace. He is personally present and where this is not accepted it is not the sacrament of Christ. Where the relation between *Word and Sacrament* has been lost, the sacrament receives its own stature and its own meaning. It could easily become an instrument in the hands of the magical person and be effective in its own right. In the holy communion it is Christ's sacrifice that is central and those who concentrate on the elements neglect the personal character of Christ in His sacrifice. Not the elements are primary but the purifying blood of Christ which cleanses of all sin (1 John 1[7]). Holy communion does mean nourishment but not in Shembe's sense, it is not magically given but in faith. Where the elements are given to the sick preferably at Ekuphakameni, he undercuts this faith in Christ's all-sufficiency.

2. *Numinous power in the service of healing*[1])

Sickness and sin are closely related in the pre-christian Zulu mind. The *Izihlaɓelelo* refers seldom in a specific sense to the recovery from sickness, but continuously people are invited to Ekuphakameni (cf. Is. 180) where all benefits for body and soul are promised. The word *sinda*, which could mean *save* or *recover from illness*, is often used in the Izl. e.g. "not only the flesh recovers but also their souls." (Isl. 53[2]). In Isl. 64[2] Shembe states:

Bakhumbule Nkosi   Remember them *iNkosi*
Laɓo aɓagulayo,   those who are sick,

---

[1]) For the importance of healing in the Zionist movements see *Sundkler*, Bantu Prophets, 220–242.

Yelula isandla sakho	stretch out thy hand
Basinde ekufeni*.	that they be saved from death.

* Here *ukufa* means death in contrast to *gulayo* (sickness). *Ukufa* could mean a serious illness, too, in contrast to umkhulanenje (a slight illness).

The magical touch of Shembe with his staff, which conveys power to the patients, is important. Holy sticks (holy in the pre-christian Zulu sense) or *izikhali* play an important part in nativistic movements. In Isl. 215[1] they are made to sing:

Umoya wakho uze	Let your *umoya* come
Kwaɓagulayo.	to those who are sick.

They are healed, not with physical medicine which spells spiritual death (this attitude prevailed in some sects) but with that which is from the tree of life which is in Ekuphakamini (Isl. 186[3]). The transference of *numinous* power leads to recovery.

inhlanhla (pl. *izinhlanhla*)

i. Luck, good fortune, prosperity.
ii. Species of medical plant.

This word, often used in the *Izihlaɓelelo*, could mean blessing (*uluɓusisi*) or enjoyment but is associated rather with good fortune. He thanks *iNkosi* Jehova (Isl. 9[3]) for the *nhlanhla* they had been given "in slavery and in bonds"; for the *nhlanhla* that they are amongst the elected (Isl. 56[3]); the angels are with *nhlanhla* which "they have poured in with happiness into the holy city" (*Ziɓemukele ngenjaɓulo emzini oyingcwele*, Isl. 81[5]); it is "good fortune" to cause the word of the *iNkosi* to spread (Isl. 117[1]); it is "good fortune" to hear the word (Isl. 191[3]); he is in want of "good fortune" given by Shembe which surpasses all those of other denominations. cf. Isl. 161[3].

Baɓizeni ngezwi lakhe	Call them with his word
Ohlala Ekuphakameni,	he who stays at Ekuphakameni
Ophunga limnandi	whose smell is pleasant
Lokusindisa izizwe.	of saving the nations.
Basinda ngalo aɓaningi	Many got saved by it
Aɓanhlanhla yaɓo	whose good fortune
Ingaconseli phansi.	does not drip to the ground.

This may be a Biblical reference referring to the cracked vessels which is unable to hold God's blessings. Shembe, the great mediator of the nations, give lasting good fortune. cf. Isl. 217[1].

Ayinhlanhla ya6o	Oh, the luck of those
A6athethelelwa izono za6o,	whose sins are forgiven
Bese lapha emhla6eni	whilst here on earth
Phambi kway' Inceku yakhe.	before his servant.

This good fortune of having sins forgiven before Shembe has a radical effect on the position of the Cross in his theology, in spite of his reference in Isl. 87[1] to "the good fortune of that sinner who hangs from the tree" (*inhlanhla yaleso soni silenga emthini*) and which "fell on him" (yasehlela). Good fortune is thus material and spiritual blessing showered onto the believer. Religion is of no avail if it does not give this good fortune: this recalls the pre-christian approach in which religion guaranteed good fortune in all spheres of life whether it was social, economic, political or religious. Basically *inhlanhla* is related to *numinous* power and is for Shembe a synonym for *ulu6usiso* (blessing) or *musa* (grace).

G. *Sin and sinners*

1. *Sin*

The word for sin is derived from *ona* which could have the following meanings:

i. Spoil, injure, damage, soil.

ii. Do what is bad, do wrong, sin.

iii. Seduce, corrupt, ravish, an immoral act.

iv. Trespass.

Isoni (pl. izoni, <ona) means sinner, criminal, habitual wrong doer. Shembe I uses also *a6oni* (sing. umoni, <ona) for sinners. cf. Isl. 41[2,4].

Shembe I and II use also other words for sin, namely:

amacala (sing. ilicala): i. Anything wrong, defect; ii. Error, fault, mistake; iii. Crime against the law, guilt, blame; iv. Charge, law suit.

insila (pl. izinsila): Dirt, body dirt.

ngcola: Be dirty, get dirty, be corrupt, immoral.

u6umnyama: Darkness, blackness.

Shembe does not use the general Zulu term for "unclean", namely *uku6a nesinyama:* "to have blackness on"[1])

Sin is described in the *Izihla6elelo* as follows:

(i) *As weight*

The metaphor of weight plays a great role in the concept of sin in Africa

---

[1]) *Krige*, 82.

and also with the Zulu. This clearly influenced Shembe's theology of sin in spite of its description in these terms in Scripture (cf. Hebrews 12[1]). cf. Isl. 157[1].

Ngehlelwe isisindo*	It has come upon me, the weight
Sezono zami,	of my sins,
Neza6azali 6ami	and of my parents
Bazishiya kimi.	they left it with me.

    * In the sing. *sindo* means weight, heaviness.

Sin is weight, and this burden is heavier because he carries the sins also of his parents (used in a wider sense) who did not observe the Sabbath. Shembe has difficulty in accepting the viewpoint that they are "lost". In the pre-christian Zulu religion all the dead were considered to be holy, and it is their position in the new context about which he concerns himself. Referring to the royal house of the Zulu nation, he maintains "today we are carrying their sins" (*namhla sesithwele izono za6o*, Prayers for the Sabbath, Section 21, 19). Through him and his faithful followers their ancestors are sanctified in the new context—they carry their sins as Christ carried those of humanity. Shembe is eventually the redeemer of the Zulu ancestry also.

Sin is actually described as *substance:* cf. Isl. 65[3].

Ngize ukuzilahla kuwe	I came to throw it (sins) away to thee
Ebusweni 6akho.	in thy face.

It is also referred to as "the rubbish heap of my heart" (*isazelo senhliziyo yami*, Isl. 129[4]), and in Isl. 162[5] Shembe maintains that Nhlangakazi could not be approached with "these burdens" (*leyo mithwalo*) which they have to leave below (*shiyaphansi*).

(ii) *As dirt*

The *Izihla6elelo* often refers to sin as something which can be washed away; a negative substance to be removed. In Isl. 125 chorus the sinner sings:

Ngizendze nga6a nensila	I made myself dirty
E6usweni 6akho Nkosi.	in thy face, *Nkosi*.

Shembe II uses *ngcola* for dirt, which refers to physical and immoral dirt. The request in Isl. 240[6] is directed to his own father:

Nkosi nami ngingowakho,	*Nkosi*, I am also yours
Anginamandla	I have no power
Okususa ukungcola	to take away the dirt
Okuphezu kwami.	which is on me.

It is something "on him" which could be removed by ritual washing. Shembe I states in Isl. 85[5] that he has sinned in taking with his hands that which is not fitting (*ngaphatha okungafanele*).

(iii) *As the works of darkness*

uThixo of power is approached for his grace (*musa*) "that we may throw away all the works of darkness" (*siyilahle yonke leyo imiseɓendzi yoɓumnyama*, Isl. 81[1]). In the pre-christian Zulu society "the works of darkness" were related to witchcraft considered to be the great curse. In Isl. 148[1,2] Shembe refers specifically to drinking as a work of darkness.

Shembe II refers to the world outside Ekuphakameni as "in darkness" (*bumnyameni*, Isl. 232[3]; *ebumnyameni*, Isl. 237[3]).

(iv) *Sin as bonds*

This aspect of Shembe's concept of sin has already been discussed under *umoya* and *inhliziyo*.

(v) *Sin as antisocial*

This is a main characteristic of sin in the African context. In Isl. 118[2] sinners are told to go or run away (*Balekani nonke zoni*); about the holy city he states that the sinners left (Isl. 6[2]). In the Zulu society breaking of ritual prohibitions was interpreted as disregard for the community and thus a sin against it.

Shembe's concept of sin could be summarized as follows: It is a negative kind of mystic quality which weakens a person's *umoya*, a burden he carries, through which evil forces overpower him; it is a material defilement which adheres physically to the unclean person until it is ritually washed away. The greatest negative effect of sin is that it puts a curse on a person.

2. *What should be done with sin?*

(i) *It should be concealed*

After referring to Baɓa (however not written with a capital letter, cf. Isl. 26[3]) he states in verse 4:

Kudingeka uzifihle* zonke izono
zakho.

It is necessary that you conceal all
your sins.

> * fihla: i. (tr.) Hide, conceal, secrete; ii. Bury.

His request to Jehova is: cf. Isl. 25²:

Uugazibeki* izono zami
Uma ngiza kuwe.

Do not look at my sins
when I come to you.

> * Should be *ungazibeki*.

(ii) *It should be buried*

The significance of the Cross is that sins have been buried in the grave.
cf. Isl. 132⁴.

Senizwile wozani

You have already heard, come.

Ezami zagqitshwa kanye naye

Mine were once and for all buried
with him

Ethuneni, senizwile wozani.

in the grave. Now you have heard,
come.

Christ's burial is interpreted as a burial of man's sins.

(iii) *It should be washed away*

Ritual washing has already been referred to. Even Shembe II looks for
the fountain where he could wash away the dirt. (Isl. 228²). This is not
ordinary washing with soap but ritual washing related to the *uMkhululi*
(cf. Isl. 157⁶).

(iv) *It should be confessed*

Ritual vomiting (*vuma*) plays an important part in the confessing of sin.
When Shembe states that his slanderers (*abahlebi*) are inside him (Isl. 105⁵),
the exegetes will easily interpret it as evil spirits which have to be vomited
out. About sins Shembe states in Isl. 87³

Ngizivuma ngizibeka kuwe
wemthetheleli wezoni.

I confess it and I put it before thee
you redeemer of sinners.

These sins are confessed to Shembe! Confession of antisocial acts
played a great role in Zulu society during initiation ceremonies, abnormal
child birth, sickness and when they had to confront the enemy.

3. *Sinners*

(i) *Forgiveness*

Although he invites sinners (*izoni*) in Isl. 87 and in Isl. 132 to come to him who hangs on a cross, and to "the meal of life", those "who have been bought with the blood of the *iNkosi*" (*Enathengwa ngegazi leNkosi*, Isl. 140⁴), it has been indicated how this has been syncretized in the pre-christian Zulu context and that the sacrament of holy communion has become a purification rite. When the sinner states to the *uMkhululi* "the buying of me is easy" (*intengo yami ilula*, Isl. 108⁴) it reveals no under-standing of what redemption means.

The Forgiver is Shembe (cf. Isl. 217¹) who is at Ekuphakameni and "he loves all sinners" (*Uyazithanda zonke izoni*, Isl. 192¹), even those who serve their own gods (*izithixo*, Isl. 188⁴). As norm he applies the Sabbath. Sin has for him a formal and ceremonial rather than ethical character. The destruction of the order of forces is due to sin. All sinners are admonished to listen to the din of the saints who play a significant role in keeping this order intact. It is with him not a question of ethical absolutes but of absolute obedience to the ritual prohibitions of which the Sabbath is central. Salvation means fitting in smoothly into the community by ad-hering to its prohibitions.

(ii) *Judgment*

Shembe states that the sinners (*aɓoni*, Isl. 214) are running away in the face of death which is part of their judgment. In such circumstances the *uMsindisi* will be "far away from them" (*esekude naɓo*, Isl. 41⁴) and "fear cuts at them". (*uvalo luyaɓasika*, Isl. 41²). The day of judgment is most realistically pictured in Isl. 28. The feeling of being abandoned, deserted, rather than a concept of guilt, is often expressed with regard to sin.

The "Book of Life" takes a prominent place in the mind of Shembe I. He states in Isl. 131².

Bonke aɓazondi ɓawo	All haters of it (i.e. Ekuphakameni)
Maɓanga lotshwa,	let them not be written
Encwadini yokuphila	in the Book of Life,
Achithwe amagama aɓo.	let their names be destroyed.

The name is his very essence and to have it written in this "Book of Life" means its eternal protection.[1] This "Book of Life" is truly a book of *Life*. He assures in Isl. 201⁵ that nobody will enter Ekuphakameni whose name is not written (*ogama lakhe lingalotshiwe*) in this book. Here is this concrete approach again at work. The "Book of Works" is also very realistically described (Isl. 70⁴,⁵), and in the *chorus* Shembe states with an obvious

---

[1] See also Isl. 59².

reference to the tombstone on which one's name is written, as the sign of eternal acceptance:

Netshe legama lami   And the stone of my name
Ngolifumana khona.[1])   I will find it there.

The erection of the tombstone is interpreted as the *ukuɓuyisa* i.e. the putting into office of the shade, which means the acceptance of its authority. These *books* mentioned in Revelation have received a new meaning in Shembe's theology—the "Book of Life" protects, shields magically, and the "Book of Works" is associated with the tombstone.

Judgment takes places also through *fire* (*umlilo*). Hell is as realistically described as was the case in pietistic preaching.

His interpretation of Jesus' words is that the sinners will burn "in the fire" (*emlilweni*) and will suffer pain (Isl. 50[6]); the story of Lazarus and the rich man is most literally described in Isl. 138. In Isl. 11[4] his request is "kindle always that fire of yours" (*Phemba futhi lowo mlilo wakho*); those who are not converted and baptized and who have not their hearts washed will land up in the "hell of fire" (*esihogweni somlilo*, Isl. 118); in hell nobody cares for another, i.e. individualism prevails (Isl. 118[3]); there is no rest but only distress (Isl. 118[5]) and their only food is trouble (Isl. 118[6]).

Shembe II has seen in fire also the pillar of fire which led Moses and the Israelites (Isl. 226[3]).

4. *Biblical reminiscences with regard to Shembe's concept of sin*

Sin is indeed described in Scripture as weight, e.g. 1 Peter 2[24], Hebr. 12[1]. There is enough in the Bible to mislead the pre-christian Zulu mind, i.e. if it is not carefully explained. With regard to the theology of sin in a society in which it is considered as a mystic magical negative substance, the churches should give adequate enlightenment. Augustine reacted in North Africa against Manicheism which made of sin a substance—*non est substantia* (Confessiones VII 8) and if it had been a substance (*si substantia esset*) it would have been good.

The Zulu Bibles generally use *isono* for sin, but also words such as *isiphambeko* (pl. *iziphambeko*) which means deception, a wrong, iniquity;

---

[1]) This may refer to the ordination of Shembe's ministers who in the process were anointed with holy oil and had to carry a heavy stone to the place on Nhlangakazi where the meetings took place. Shembe then stated: "These stones are your oath (*isi fungo*) that you have surrendered yourselves to God. These stones will be a testimony before God". *Roberts, E. L.*, Shembe – the Man and his Work, unpublished manuscript, Univ. of Witwatersrand. Quoted by *Sundkler*, Bantu Prophets, 14.

okubi, evil; *ilicala* for anything wrong. Biblical influences on Shembe's concept of sin are evident, e.g. the sinner described as a lamb lost (Isl. 16), that Jehova is a lover of sinners (Isl. 31³); Jehova even cries over a sinner i.e. He is deeply concerned (Isl. 128³); forgiveness related to a contrite heart (Isl. 179⁵); and Shembe II also refers to a repentant heart (Isl. 240²).

5. *The Biblical concept of sin misunderstood*

The relationship between God and the believer should not be seen "nomological", i.e., from law and works but from the Gospel. The revealing and discovering function of the law *is* important (cf. Rom. 3¹⁹). In Gal. 3¹⁹ Paul discusses the function of the law as a teacher. Shembe has made of the law a rigid disciplinarian whereas the law is a *usus elenchticus*, it gives knowledge of sin. Sin, for Shembe, was sin against the law.

Sin in the Old Testament is related to the impurity of the heart and violation of conscience and not in the first place to ceremonial defilement or anti-social activities. To Israel all sin was not merely a violation of the Covenant but of God himself. Shembe emphasized the antisocial aspects of sin. He further gave sin its own, independent existence as if it is a substance or even a being instead of describing it as *privatio boni*. It is described in the Old Testament as a missing of the mark, rebellion and moral wrongness. Sin is not matter, but deformation, deceit; it is disobedience and stands over against the original communion with God. It cannot be understood in itself but only in relation to God.

Shembe does not accept the fall of man. *Fall* could only be understood over against *stand* and it is only from the place where man stood that the depth of the fall could be fathomed. For Shembe the fall means that Adam had been driven out of Eden, out of a home as it were. He did not understand that fall means a fall on the stone which has become a corner stone (cf. Luke 20¹⁷⁻¹⁸). The Genesis story shows clearly what the form and structure of sin always will be, namely, that sin could only be understood from the depth and fullness in Jesus Christ. There is no possibility of a true self- knowledge without a knowledge of God and this is possible only through the Cross which is a refutation of all theories about sin.[1] Vogel states that "ungratefulness" is the most christian name for sin because of its "enmity against grace".[2] The disposition of sin is for Shembe not of vital importance, only the act. Although the Old and New Testaments do not give priority to the heart above the deed, the connection is indicated

---

[1] *Barth, K.*, Kirchliche Dogmatik, Zürich, Evangelischer Verlag Zollikon, 1953.
[2] *Vogel*, H., Die Sünde im biblischen Verständnis, Evang. Theol., 1959, 446.

and the deed is tested in its deepest motives. The whole man is put before God (cf. 1 Cor. 13$^{1-3}$). *Motivation* does not feature in the *Izihlaɓelelo*. Even in motivation sin is rebellion against God. Shembe's theology of forgiveness underestimates the reality of sin. There is not an essential relationship between repentance and forgiveness. Scripture often emphasizes humiliation before God and that forgiveness is a specific *divine* right. In the Old Testament sacrifices the reality of guilt is revealed, a debt to be taken away, which is possible through Christ's sacrifice only. It is not the curse[1]) of Shembe but the rejection of Christ's work on the Cross which is man's greatest disaster.

H. *Baptism*

Shembe refers only once to baptism itself, which is strange when one considers the fact that it plays a central role and is a purification rite, repeated. A person is baptized again when he/she feels 'unclean'. John the Baptist, who is the most important personality in most Nativistic movements, is not mentioned. In Isl. 118 it is clear that he attached great significance to adult baptism which is described as instrumentel to salvation.

1. Lalelani nanti ilizwi	Listen, here is the word.
Wezizwe nonke	All ye nations,
Phendukani nibabathizwe	be converted and be baptized,
Nize nisindiswe.	that ye may be saved.
2. Geza inhliziyo yami	Wash my heart
Iziyeke engizithandayo,	that it may leave that which I like,
Amen Hhaleluya	Amen Halelujah
Balekani nonke zoni.	run away all ye sinners.
3. Akukhalelwa muntu	Nobody is weeped for
Esihogweni somlilo;	in the hell of fire;
Akakho okhalela omunye	there is nobody who weeps for another
Esihogweni somlilo.	in the hell of fire.

Here is a typical 19th century pietistic "hell-fire" approach, with baptism as indispensable to salvation. The baptist strain often emphasized Christ *plus* baptism. Shembe's literalism, based on the teaching he received from his church, caused him to emphasize the *plus* and this became the purification rite *par excellence* with Jesus Christ pushed into the back-

---

[1]) In the Zulu society a curse meant total loss of possessions and power.

ground. There was too little sacramental confrontation with Jesus Christ, the living Lord of the sacrament, in the church from which Shembe hailed. Baptism was interpreted as a purification act even in the church. The problem is that in many churches the sacraments receive a secondary place, supplement the word, and are considered to be only appendices, while on the other hand the emphasis on them *alone* obscures the reality of Christ's work. Baptism is necessary to enter the kingdom of God but it is always based on the work of Jesus Christ on the Cross.

This sacrament is also more than a *nudum signum*, a mere symbol, by which it is not considered to be a reality of salvation. Shembe has not developed from symbolism to realism with regard to this sacrament but has brought to its logical consequences the theological disposition which regards it as a means of washing away sins through the magical effects of water. The sacrament stands in relation to Christ, a position Shembe has usurped. There is but one sacrament, namely, "the incarnated, crucified and resurrected Christ". For Shembe the sacrament does become a mystery as in the Roman Catholic Church and is, as in Protestantism, related to a mystery. The object of this relation however is different. With Shembe it is related to the *numinous* power which is in persons and things: for Christianity it is related to Christ.

The Word and the Sacraments are interrelated. The Word can be without the sacraments but the sacraments can never be without the Word. This is Shembe's problem. The elements are consecrated through the Word and not through anyone or anything else. The sacrament does not function in itself; it does not give grace but strengthens faith. Faith does not mean an independant process of growth in the human subjectivity but this strengthening refers to communion with Christ. With Shembe it is an *ex opere operato* working of the sacrament.[1]) The sacraments are not the outward signs of a supernatural giving of grace or vital force, they give no *ontic* reality but "refer" to the Word. They do not contain grace in themselves—they are not effective means of infusing grace. The *opus operatum* conflicts with the nature of the sacrament—*sola fide* gets its meaning also in the true doctrine of the sacrament. Apart from the finished work of Christ baptism loses its meaning; it is historically based and refers to Christ's reconciliatory work.

The water used in Christian baptism is a sign of purification as it was in the Old Testament (Ezek. 36^{25-26}; cf. Is. 1^{16}; Zech. 13^1; Ps. 51^7). It is

---

[1]) The analysis of E. Rudolf Lehmann is rather superficial. cf. Eine Form von Religionsmischung in Süd Afrika *in* Von Fremden Völkern und Kulturen, Herausg. Lang, Nippold und Spannaus, Düsseldorf, Droste-Verlag, 1955, 183–193.

however not purification derived from the water but from the sufficient work of Christ on the Cross. This historical event is the basis of baptism (1 Cor. 1[18]); it is Jesus Christ and Him crucified (1 Cor. 2[2]) which is the only source of man's salvation. When *numinous* power is thought to be infused the necessity of relating baptism to the cross of Christ is not accepted. John 3[5] is often used in support of the direct causality of baptism. But this "out of water" is related to the kingdom of God and the Messiah. Baptism should be a mighty witness to the efficiency of Christ's work.

I. *Miscellaneous*

1. *Decoration*

This constitutes part of one's *completeness*. *White* is the colour of priesthood;[1]) *green* of holiness.[2]) The outward whiteness of the clothes is a sign of inner whiteness. The *aɓanguɓo* (cloaks, blankets or any European dress i.e. covering in general) made white in the blood of the lamb is not metaphorical language as is the case with Rev. 3[5]. Shembe II states they are already clothed in white here on earth (cf. Isl. 236[2]). This is part of Nazarethness with which he has dressed up three times (Isl. 73[4]). The word *hloɓa* used here for "dressing up" has the meaning of adorning one-self, to decorate oneself. Shembe I had a special blackgown which is still considered to have special power, and Shembe II dresses up in a most ornate gown.

The complete and full dressing up takes place at Ekuphakameni (Isl. 49), which refers not only to the physical but also to the spiritual "dressing up" with all the benefits of this city. They are dressed up (mɓathwa: put on a covering) by those who have "a hope to be saved". (Isl. 83[2]). As in Zulu society the initiates discarded the old clothes and dressed up with the new, so they also are dressed up who are initiated into Nazarethness. The dresses (*iziqhamo* (pl.): skin blankets, coverings) are holy and brought "on us" (phezu kwethu, Isl. 69[2,4]). The city of the king's daughters, prin-cesses (*amakhosazana*) is admonished to dress up: cf. Isl. 80[5].

Yeɓo Betlehema Juda   Yes Betlehem Juda,
Muzi wamakhosazana,   city of the king's daughters,
Mawuhloɓe ngeziqhamo   be dressed up beautifully with skin
                                                                blankets
Umsinele u Jehova.   and dance for Jehova.

---

[1]) White is also the colour of Nomkhuɓulwana, the goddess of fertility.
[2]) For sacred dress see *Sundkler*, Bantu Prophets, 213–5.

Shembe II describes his *consecration* by his father and the saints as his dressing up: Isl. 233[4].

Wathuma Inceku yakhe	He sent his *iNceku*
Iza naɓangcwele	He comes with the saints,
Ngayo inguɓo yokuphila	with the blanket of life
Bangembesa mina.	they dressed me.

Completeness, washing and decorating belong together in the *Izihla-ɓelelo*. It is the perfectionism of Nazarethness. Perfectionism was part of the message of 19th century pietism. Being ritually washed, adequately decorated and anointed with *umoya*, is the essence of Nazarethness.

2. *Dancing*

The rhythm of the Izl. expresses itself in the sacred dance. For the pre-christian Zulu rhythm is the pure expression of vital force and in rhythm the *Word* finds its full expression. As the sermon concentrates on one idea until it is put across, so it is with the singing of the Izl. Spontaneity and gaiety are two significant characteristics of Zulu religion. It finds its culmination in the dance which is a form of thanksgiving and receiving. This is clear in Isl. 112:

3. Aziqiniswe	Let them be strengthened
Izinyawo zethu;	our feet;
Sisinele wena	that we dance for you
Simakade.	Simakade.
4. Nikani udumo	Give fame,
Nonke zingelosi,	all ye angels,
Kuyena yedwa	to him alone
Ofanele ukudunyiswa.	who is worthy of praise.

Receiving and giving thanks is intimately associated in the dance which is part of an *act* religion in which faith, in the christian sense, is considered to be too passive. Some of the dance songs are mere war songs, e.g. Isl. 182.

CHAPTER FIVE

ESCHATOLOGY

1. *Before thy face* (*eɓusweni ɓakho*)

Although the concept of the kingdom is implied in the *Izihlaɓelelo*, Shembe does not use the word *umɓuso* (pl. *imiɓuso*) which could mean either a kingdom, government or enjoyment of life. The locative of *umɓuso* is *embusweni*. (cf. Mark 14²⁵ in the Zulu Bibles "in the kingdom of God", *embusweni kaNkulunkulu*). Sundkler's translation of *eɓusweni* in Is. 112¹ as "in the kingdom" is not correct, neither is "*oɓukhosi bakho*" in verse 2 "of thy kingdom".¹) Shembe only speaks of "in/before thy face" (*eɓusweni ɓakho*), an expression often used and which is basic to his realized eschatology.

The city of Ekuphakameni is the kingdom of the *iNkosi* and here they stand before Jehova, Thixo and Shembe and for this reason he uses *eɓusweni*. Shembe is not concerned about a realm, a kingdom, but that all should appear before his face. It has already been indicated how it is often stated in the *Izihlaɓelelo* that "I have sinned in thy face"; "I have thrown it (the rubbish heap) away in thy face" (Isl. 129⁴). Perhaps it is necessary to give the literal translation of Isl. 112 here.

	Lit. translation.	Sundkler's translation.
1. Inkulu Nkosi	Great is *Nkosi*	Great is, O king
Inhlanhla yethu,	our good fortune	our happiness
Eɓusweni ɓakho	before your face	in Thy kingdom
Wena Nkosi yethu.	you, our Nkosi.	Thou, our king.
2. Thina Nkosi	We Nkosi	We dance before Thee
Sisinela wena,	we dance for you,	our king.
Ngalowo mandla	with that strength	By the strength
Oɓukhosi ɓakho.	of your sovereignty.	of Thy kingdom.
3. Aziqiniswe	Let them be strengthened	May our feet
Izinyawo zethu;	our feet;	be made strong:
Sisinele wena	that we may dance for you	Let us dance before Thee,

---

¹) *Sundkler*, Bantu Prophets, 197.

Simakade.	Simakade.	eternal.
4. Nikani udumo	Give ye praise	Give ye praise,
Nonke zingelosi,	all ye angels,	all Angels
Kuyena yedwa	to him alone	to Him alone
Ofanele ukudunyiswa.	who is worthy of being praised.	who is worthy of praise.

E6usweni is the locative of -so (n. *u6uso*) which could mean face, countenance or front part of anything looking in a particular direction or that part directed to one, e.g. there is darkness on the face of the earth (cf. Isl. 51[2]). Even after Shembe's death his followers are continuously aware of his presence, that they are actually still *before* his face.[1]) He repeatedly emphasized this in the Izl. e.g. Isl. 86[2].

Indumalo njalo Nkosi	Disappointment always, Nkosi,
Ngi6uyisele endlini yakho;	takes me back to your house;
Ngidumise na6aningi	that I may praise with the many
E6usweni 6akho kunjalo uyazi	before your face, it is so, you
Nkosi.	know, Nkosi.

At Ekuphakameni those in difficulty have the privilege of standing before the face of the *Nkosi*. His name is beautiful in the face of the *iNkosi* and also before the face of heaven (Isl. 125[1,3]). In Isl. 35[2] they stand before the face of Ba6a; in Isl. 181[4] he states: "We have sinned, we confess in your face" (*Sonile siyavuma e6usweni 6akho*.)

Shembe took the idea of a kingdom for granted. Ekuphakameni is its centre and before the person, who is its personification, all nations are called. Everything happens in his face, actually meaning before his face.

2. *The Resurrection*

Shembe's theology on the resurrection has a definite bearing on his eschatology. In the Zulu religion there is no coming kingdom, it is there— one could call this realized eschatology[2]), although for the cyclical type of thinking one could not use these terms. Shembe's contact with Scripture explained in terms of futuristic expectations could not satisfy his interest in the "here and now". To him this *is* taking place, it has meaning in time and space, in the "here and now". The kingdom of God has come, the

---

[1]) cf. Sundkler, Bantu Prophets, 285.

[2]) On realized eschatology see Dodd, C.H., The parables of the kingdom, London, S.C.M. 1955.

Messiah has arrived. For Shembe the dead have been resurrected. The old idea of two communities having a living contact with one another has overruled the ideas of an *endgeschichtliche Eschatologie* i.e. an eschatology which concerns itself with the end of history.

Shembe uses two words for the dead namely *aɓafileyo* (Isl. 51⁴) and *aɓaleleyo* (Isl. 51⁵)[1]); he uses both words *vuka* and *vusa* utilised in the Zulu Bibles meaning "to rise". He, however, does not use *ukuvuka* (infinitive) resurrection and *vusiwe* (passive) for a general resurrection, as is the case in the Zulu Bibles. He uses *vuka* also in a profane sense e.g. where he calls South Africa to wake up. cf. Isl. 120.

When Isl. 51⁴ is isolated from the other Izl. one could easily deduce from this verse that Shembe accepted a general resurrection at the *end* of history. He states here:

Bayovuka* aɓafileyo	The dead will rise
Bevela inxa zonke,	coming from all sides
u Jehova uThixo wethu	Jehova our *uThixo*
Uyoɓavusa** ɓonke.	he will cause them all to rise.

* *Vuka*: i. Wake up; ii. Rise (from death); iii. Get up.
** *Vusa*[2]): i. Awaken, rouse up; ii. Raise (as from the dead), resurrect, resuscitate.

This most probably refers to the ability of the Jehova of the Nazarites to give everlasting active life, because what he maintains in Isl. 148⁴ is very different. Here he states:

Mamenyeziwe* emathuneni	They have been called out of the graves
Seɓe phumile siɓaɓonile,	they are already out, we have seen them,
Bangenile emzini oyingcwele	they have entered the city that is holy,
Maka ɓongwe u Jehova.	may Jehova be praised.

* Should be *Bamenyeziwe*. This Isl. is most probably Shembe's interpretation of Ezekiel 37.

This is in line with his standpoint on Ekuphakameni as the new Jerusa-

---

[1]) See also Isl. 156³.
[2]) The *ukuvusa* custom by which a man's name is not allowed to die shows how important the continuation of a name is and its relationship to his well-being in the supernatural world. If a man has no sons his daughter has to make arrangements for the continuation of the name. The continuation of the name of Jesus Christ through Shembe is based on the concept that the son is the continuation of the father, carrying on the 'isithunzi' (dignity of the father).

lem of Rev. 21 (cf. Isl. 50). According to this Isl. however an alarm will
be heard, the dead will be called out of the graves and then he adds in
verse 7:

Shiyanini umhla6a	Leave ye the earth,
Wozanini Ekuphakameni.	Come ye to Ekuphakameni.

Shembe grants resurrection and does not accept the power of the
resurrection in Jesus Christ. In a much later Isl. he calls his "children" to
him with the assurance that he has the power to save from death, cf. Isl.
206[3].

Indlela yethuna	The way of the grave
E6eyifanele wena,	which was suited to you
Ayihanjwe yimi wemntanami	let it be travelled by me, my child,
Mawuphile wena.	that you may live.

One should remember that he is the one who came from the world that
is to come (Isl. 218[1]), which most probably refers to Ekuphakameni. In
Isl. 159 this is explained by stating that those who died have been called
(verse 1), the gates of the holy city have been opened (verse 2), that they
enter this city (verse 3); and what follows is significant:

4. Waja6ula uSimakade	Simakade was happy
Ngokuvulwa kwamathuna,	because of the opening of the graves
Lezwakala ixilongo	the trumpet sounded
Lokuvula amasango;	of opening the gates;
Ja6ulani we6athengwa	rejoice ye that are bought
Ngokungena kulowo muzi.	for getting into that city.
5. Siyaku6onga weNkosi yethu	We thank you our *Nkosi*
Thixo was' Ekuphakameni,	*Thixo* of Ekuphakameni,
Bonganini wema6andla	praise ye hosts
Awahleli kweliphezulu	who are staying up above
Nazo izixuku zalomhla6a	and the crowds of this earth
Seziyongena kweliphezulu.	they will enter up above.

Resurrection has taken place, and the resurrected and those at Ekuphakameni are in intimate contact with those who are like angels.[1]) Ekuphakameni is the visible city of the saints and above it is the invisible part of it.
This fulfilled or realized resurrection which made Simakade, the Zulu
praise name for the Supreme Being, happy is the resurrection through

---

[1]) cf. Mark 12, 25. Most probably this text had also its influence on Shembe.

Shembe who could not accept the delayed eschatology of the churches. In the superscription to Isl. 220, the only other Isl. where *vuka* (rise) is used in a profane sense, and limited to the Zulus, it is stated that it was written by "nkosi uIsaiah Shembe May, 1939 after his rising from the dead" (*Emva koku vuka kwakhe kwaɓafileyo*). Here is thus a real fellowship of the saints.

For Shembe II it is clear that his father's victory over the grave affects the life of every faithful follower of his; cf. Isl. 229[3].

Kufa namhla weyisiwe,	Death today you have been
	conquered
Awusenamandla.	you no longer have power.
Nawe liɓa unqotshiwe,	And you grave has been overcome
Nguye o Phezulu.	by him who is above.

In the pre-christian Zulu religion nothing in their sacrifices, rites, prayers and myths recalls the resurrection.[1]) It is only a question of the continuation of existence with those who had the *umoya* (*isithunzi*) put into office through the *ukuɓuyisa* ceremony. Continuity rather than immortality is assumed. This approach prevails with Shembe for whom all are "*shades*" or rather saints; all are active and all are deeply and intimately associated with what is happening at Ekuphakameni. Primitive eschatology is dynamic. Interaction takes place on a social level. The sense of community presupposes realized eschatology—the kingdom has come and Shembe is the personification of it in the same way as Jesus is described in Scripture. Here is a deep sense of *koinonia*, fellowship with Shembe, with one another on 'earth' and in heaven.

3. *The Gates*

The Zulu word *i(li)sango* (pl. *amasango*), used also in the Zulu Bible translations[2]), is used by Shembe for gate. The *i(li)sango* is the main entrance to the cattle kraal hence *gateway*.

Repeatedly the invitation goes out: cf. Isl. 4[1].

Bek'isango	See the gate
Selivuliwe.	it is now open.

---

[1]) cf. *Asmus*, 30.

[2]) cf. Matth. 7, 13; John 10, 9; Rev. 21, 12; The holy city Jerusalem with its high walls, its twelve gates (*unamasango ayishumi nambili*) and twelve angels at these gates and the names of the tribes written on the gates, appealed to Shembe's concrete thinking: to his holy city the tribes, for example Mabacas and Mapondos, are also called.

The "small gate" (*isango lincinyane*, cf. Isl. 5²) is a reminiscence of the references in the Gospels to such a small gate.¹) With Shembe however this small gate should be entered with power (*ngamandla*, Isl. 5²). The gate at Nhlangakazi is altogether small and could not be entered with burdens (*imithwalo*, Isl. 162⁵).

Ekuphakameni is not circular as the cattle kraal is, but is described as having four sides (*amacala omane*, Isl. 6⁵). This will have a bearing on the number of gates, a contentious point amongst the Zionists.

The gates of Ekuphakameni are called to "rise upwards" (*Phakamani* Isl. 6³), a reminiscence of Ps. 24⁷. Before the gates stand the hosts or armies (*imikhosi*) of angels, and the saints (cf. Isl. 106²) with the request *vula amas_ango akho* ("open your gates", Isl. 106⁴) after they have stated in verse 3.

Simi sonke phambikwakho	We stand all before you
Masango as' Ekuphakameni.	gates of Ekuphakameni.

To this he adds in verse 6:

Izizukulwane zonke zase zulwini	All the generations in heaven
Zoja6ula ngawe Kuphakama,	will rejoice by thee, Kuphakama,
Uma zingena ngamasango	when they enter by the gates
zize kudumisa uJehova.	they come to praise, Jehova.

The localized Jehova is praised only here; the city to which all nations are called in order to worship him (Isl. 79⁴). The saints of course open the gates (Isl. 159²) and the angels keep watch and actually drive sinners out (Isl. 155⁵), but who is in charge of this heavenly host?

In Isl. 42¹ uNkulunkulu is addressed as follows:

Nkulunkulu woza nami	*Nkulunkulu* come with me
Nanti isango selivuliwe.	here the gate is already opened.

Who has *uNkulunkulu* here at his disposal? In Isl. 173³ the reference is to Shembe.

Livulwe ngu6ani	Who opened it
Lelisango,	this gate,
We Mkhululi wezi6oshwa.	oh *uMkhululi* of prisoners?

In a later Isl. in which he states that he had been called in his mother's womb, Shembe himself is described as being at the gate, an important issue amongst Zionists: cf. Isl. 197⁷ (See also John 10).

---

¹) The cattle kraal also has a small gate.

Wozake mntanami	Come then my child
Mina ngisemi esangweni;	I am still standing at the gate;*
Ngingekushiye mina mntanami	I cannot leave you my child
Woza ungilandele.	come and follow me.

   * cf. Rev. 3[20].

Shembe has retained this position also after his death and remains the "holder of the key". Here is thus a complete identity between Shembe and the kingdom in whom the kingdom has become incarnate once and for all. He is the promised one who gives resurrection, life, freedom, healing, joy, a new Jerusalem, a new heaven and earth, in whom the promises of Rev. 21 and 22 are fulfilled. He is the kingdom, and standing before his face is the ultimate. This will become clearer still in the following discussion.

4. *The Holy City*

Heaven has come down on Zululand. The vision of John with regard to the new Jerusalem has been realized. Shembe's eschatology has to be seen in the light of Rev. 21 especially verses 2, 3 and 4. The earthly is elevated into the sphere of the *sacral*. Ekuphakameni is heaven—elevated out of the profane. Holy means to have supernatural contact, to be loaded with *numinous* power, and this is Ekuphakameni called by many names.

(i) *Ekuphakameni* (locative) or *Kuphakama* should first receive attention. *Phakama* (verb) (Ur. B.—pakama, be high) has the following meanings:

i. To rise upwards, as something raised by an unseen agency; to be elevated, raised high, high up, as a man on the top of a hut, as a highly situated locality, or as one hill in comparison with others around it.

ii. To become important, surpassingly large, as one kraal in comparison with other inferior ones, as one diviner is more noted than another.

iii. To raise one's voice emotionally.

Shembe uses the infinitive of the verb namely *ukuphakama* or the locative *Ekuphakameni* rather than the noun *impakama* (pl. *izimpakama*) which means an elevation, raised place; high ground, plateau, hillock. At the occasion of the burial of a deceased chief the leader will say: "*Uye kwinda-wo eziphakamileyo senzelele*" ("You have gone to higher places, intercede for us").

Shembe uses the verb mainly to give expression to his nationalistic aspirations e.g. "*rise up ye Zulus*", or his universal concern for all nations. The name however appears mainly in the *two* forms *Kuphakama* and *Ekuphakameni* at least in the following *Izihlaɓelelo*: 6, 24, 50, 63, 74, 88,

101, 102, 106, 109, 116, 124, 126, 131, 155, 159, 160, 161, 164, 174, 175, 176, 181, 192, 210, 217, 220, 221, 226, 229, 230, 232, 237. Some of these Izl. are devoted to *Ekuphakameni* only. The association of this divine place and divine presence is extremely strong. The Supreme Being is inseparably associated with this holy place just as the Canaanites had their holy place at Shechem and the Israelites had after the exile all their holy places superseded by the temple of Zion. The reality of Canaan is relived by Shembe's followers as a result of his integration of the hills, pools and mountains in Natal into the Biblical context.

In Isl. 6 Kuphakama and Judia, the Nazarite village in Zululand, are greeted (verse 1), the gates of Phakama must rise up (verse 3, a reminiscence of Ps. 24), and then the special significance of this city is expressed as follows in verse 4:

Wozani wozani	Come ye, come ye
Siye kweliphezulu;	that we go to it (land) above;
Makaɓongwe lowo ozayo	Let him that is coming be praised
Ekuphakameni.	in Ekuphakameni.

The *iNkosi* of heaven will come with the saints to Ukuphakama (Isl. 24[2]), a *parousia* which, as was indicated, has already taken place. Ekuphakameni is significant in the light of this event. From here the eternal word is preached. An invitation goes out to all to hear this word to which is added in the chorus of Isl. 63 "May ye come and hear his word" (*Nize kulizwa izwe lakhe*).[1]) Special revelation takes places at Ekuphakameni and they hasten to enter it "before the gates are closed" (*Amasango engakavalwa*, Isl. 63[3]). The preaching at Ekuphakameni has cured many (*kuɓasindisile aɓaningi*, Isl. 74[1]) and now the invitation goes out to all to come that "ye be cured" (*nisindiswe*, Ibid.).[2])

Shembe did not merely think in terms of individuals but of nations, which often occupied his mind: cf. Isl. 88[1].

Yizani nina zizwe nonke[3])	Come all ye nations
Siy' Ekuphakameni;	(that) we go to Ekuphakamnei

---

[1]) In Isl. 161[3] he states: Baɓizeni ngezwi lakhe, ohlala Ekuphakameni: he who stays in Ekuphakameni.

[2]) This is the passive form of the verb *sindisa* which could mean: i. Help a person to escape or come safely out of a danger and thus save, rescue, redeem; restore to health, cure. ii. Make heavy, over-loaded. Here one should translate it so that both redemption and restoration to health are expressed.

[3]) cf. Isl. 160[4].

Siyogcotshwa* sanele**	(that) we be anointed sufficiently
Ngamafutha*** omusa.	with the ointment of grace.

* -gcotshwa (pass.) < gcoba: i. Anoint, lubricate, smear over, rub on. ii. Flatter.

** sanele < anela: Satisfy, please; have enough of; be given sufficient of. This sufficiency is only to be obtained at the holy place.

*** -futha (Used in pl. only): Fat, (liquid or solid) oil, grease, ointment.

Anointing is intimately associated with authority, a major characteristic of umoya. The association in Scripture of anointing with authority is found in 1 Sam. 9[16]. The anointing here does not refer to that of James 5[14] i.e. the anointing of the sick, but to the anointing of the faithful (cf. 1 John 2[27]). Shembe at Ekuphakameni is the anointer par excellence. Ekuphakameni is the place where there are springs of the "water of life lasting for ever" (yamandzi okuphila okuphakade, Isl. 102[2]), and all are invited to drink from these springs (verse 4).

They are called to Ekuphakameni, that "we may glorify with the saints" (sidumise naɓangcwele, Isl. 106[4]), the place where they glorify uThixo of Ekuphakameni and where they praise Jehova. cf. Isl. 106.

5. Izulu kwanomhlaɓa wonke	The heaven and all the earth
Lidumisa wena Thixo,	it glorifies thee Thixo
Was' Ekuphakameni.	of Ekuphakameni.
6. Izizukulwane zonke zase zulwini	All generations of heaven
. . . .	. . . .
zize kudumisa u Jehova.	having come to praise Jehova.

The localized Supreme Being could only really be worshipped in this city of God. God has the right to determine where heaven and earth and all the generations should worship Him and He decided on Ekuphakameni, the city where the angels are keeping watch (Isl. 155[5]). In this house of peace (khaya lokuthula, Isl. 164[2]) the sun and the moon do not shine but only Simakade is its sun (Isl. 164[4]), which is an obvious reference to Rev. 22[5]. In Ekuphakameni stands the tree of life called "that tree which is inside that city" (Lowo muthi ophakathi kwalowo muzi, Isl. 186[3]). This again is an obvious reference to Rev. 22[2].

In this city Shembe is the life-giving factor. It is in this light that Isl. 186[3] should be read:

Uma somile ngaleligama	When we are thirsty for this name
Siyophuza emthini wokuphila.	we shall drink from the tree of life.

In Isl. 116 he calls Nkosi Solomon (verses 1 and 5)[1]), the Zulus, (verse 2),

---

[1]) cf. Sundkler, Bantu Prophets, 103, states that Shembe gave his daughter Zondi

Mabacas (verse 3) and all nations (verse 4) to Ekuphakameni repeating in every verse:

Udumo luka Jehova   The *fame* of Jehova
Lus' Ekuphakameni.   is in Ekuphakameni.

Shembe is the personified fame of Jehova, His manifestation also known as the *Nkosi* of Ekuphakameni; the only mediator between heaven and earth who has not only drawn all the generations of heaven to Ekupha-kameni but is in fact for the Nazarites the central figure of this world. He is the fame of the nations but in the first instance the fame of the Zulu, the "*Nkosi yas' Ekuphakameni*" (the *iNkosi* at Ekuphakameni, Izl. 177 chorus, 181). When he states that "we thank you our *iNkosi uThixo* of Ekupha-kameni" (*Siyakuɓonga weNkosi yethu Thixo was' Ekuphakameni*, Isl. 159[5]) who is *uThixo* here? Shembe who is in charge of the "Book of Life" has taken out of it all the names of the haters of Ekuphakameni (Isl. 131[2]); it is now defended by the nation (Isl. 131[1]). To have one's name removed from the membership roll of the church is a most serious catastrophe in the life of a member in Africa. The "Book of Life" of Rev. 5 is actually in Ekuphakameni and Shembe is in charge of it.

In Izl. 220, not written by Shembe I, the nationalistic and spiritual significance of Ekuphakameni prevail: cf. Isl. 220[2].

Khula wena Kuphakama   Become enlarged you Kuphakama
Umuzi omusha   the new city
Wadumala uZulu ezweni.   the Zulu nation bacame dejected in
                                                         the country.

In Isl. 221[10] Shembe II assures that

Kuphakama ulidwala   Kuphakama you are the rock
Umi ngunaphakade.   You stand forever.

Shembe II has received Izl. 228, 229, 230 and 232 at Ekuphakameni. Obviously referring to himself in Isl. 230 he states in the chorus:

Kunjalo namhla Ekuphakameni,   It is so today at Ekuphakameni,
Ufikile umyeni;   the bridegroom has arrived;

---

to the Paramount Chief for whom he also built a house at Ekuphakemeni. Paramount Chief Solomon-ka-Dinuzulu was friendly disposed to the African Congregational Church, founded by the Rev. C. B. Mvuyana in 1917. Their annual meeting took place in 1926 at his kraal at Mahashini. cf. Lea, A. The Native Separatist Church Movement in South Africa, Cape Town, Juta and Co, 1926, 45–46.

Wozani wezintombi   Come ye maidens
Ngenani ngamandla.   go in with power.

The parable described in Matth. 25 is applied to himself at Ekuphakameni. He continuously sings the praises of this city at which his father
stays forever. In Isl. 232 he greets the city to which they have come to stay
for a while but the time is finished (verse 1); here their hearts remain
(verse 2); in which they have hope in darkness (verse 3); he calls it the
house of *Thixo* (*indlu ka Thixo*, verse 5) which has the door to heaven and
he loves his father (verse 6). The last verse obviously emphasizes his
father's presence at Ekuphakameni. This holy city is most excellently
praised in Isl. 237, a farewell song of those who, after the feasts, leave
Ekuphakameni again; the city in which they trust "even here in darkness"
(*nakhona eɓumnyameni*, Isl. 237[3]); it is their pride and peace (verse 4).

(ii) *Ekuphakameni is also described in other terms*

    i. Eden, Izl. 33[1]; 49[3].
    ii. Paradisi, Izl. 9[5,6]; 87 chorus; 140[2].
    iii. Jerusalem, Izl. 34[3]; 101[3,6]; 152[2].
    iv. Bethlehem, Izl. 34[2]; 80[4,5]; 152[1,4,5].
    v. Nazareth, Izl. 7[4,5]; 37[2]; 45[3,4]; 73[2]; 143[1]; 149[2]; 154[1].
    vi. Zion, Isl. 57[2].
    vii. Muzi wamakhosazana, (City of the king's daughters) Isl. 80[5].
    viii. uMuzi wamaNazaretha, Izl. 10[1]; 149[1]; 218[4]; 221[6]; 224[1].
    ix. uMuzi oyingcwele, (Holy city) Izl. 148[4]; 222[5].
    x. ikhaya (home), Izl. 57[1].
    xi. Sendzangakhona, Izl. 214[5]; 216[4,5].
    xii. Lowomuzi (that city), Isl. 236[2].
    xiii. Endlini yomshado (in the house of christian marriage) Isl. 230[3].
    xiv. Indlu ka Thixo, Isl. 237[2].
    xv. Umuzi we Nkosi enkulu, Isl. 237[5].

Some of these names are mere descriptions and not proper names.
They give a clear indication of the centrality of this place in the minds of
the two Shembes and their adherents as well as with what it is being
associated.

    i. *Eden* is important because the history of rejection started there
as a result of Adam's *breaking* of the laws (Isl. 33[3,4]). Ekuphakameni,
where the whole history of salvation has taken place, is the new Eden.
Shembe does not refer here to the old Adam in the Pauline sense because
the Pauline concept of *metanoia* receives no place in the context of his

theology. The magical effect of keeping the law is salvation; it leads to a complete rejoicing; cf. Isl. 49³.

Lapho sengisondela	When I come near
Ensimini yas' Eden,	to the garden of Eden
Ngiyoja6ula ngiphelele	I will rejoice completely
Sengiya Ekuphakameni.	I am now going to Ekuphakameni.

This verse should be read in conjunction with verse 2 where his request is that his *umoya* be decorated and in need of nothing. Even this gives fullness.

ii. At *Paradisi* the holy water is received which is not only a means of purification but also of strengthening and which is an essential element in the purification rites. The water over which a special prayer has been expressed (*umkhuleko wamanzi*)¹) gives special power and this gives Paradisi, the section where communion is held in Ekuphakameni, great significance. Here they drink from the tree of life (Isl. 9⁵) and the continuous longing is to be at this place of strengthening (Isl. 9⁶). Here is not only healing given but a paradise regained. Gen. 2 and Rev. 22 are interpreted in the context of Shembe's theology.

The words of Jesus Christ expressed to one of the malefactors on the cross (cf. Luke 23⁴³) are interpreted in the Izl. as if Jesus Christ said that He will be with the sinner in Paradise: cf. Isl. 87 chorus:

Lezwakala ilizwi	The voice was heard
Emthini wokudelwa:	at the tree of being despised.
Namhla wena soni	Today you sinner
Ngo6anawe eParadisi.	I will be with you in Paradise. (i.e. He has left)

In Isl. 140² Shembe states that those who partake of the holy communion will have eternal life "which will resurrect them on the last day" (*ko6uvusa ngomhla wokuphela*) and they will be with him in Paradise.

iii. *Jerusalem* naturally takes a prominent place in the *Izihla6elelo*. Juda and *uHlanga*, the myth of Zulu origin, have been the same in that the history of Juda has been repeated in Natal. The scribes (*a6afundisi*) are gathered with the following task:

3. Bahlole* imi6alo: let them investigate into the writings.

* hlola: Inspect, examine, look into, explore, test. For the first time the Scriptures are closely investigated which proves that Ekuphakameni and its history is salvation history.

---

¹) Sundkler, Bantu Prophets, 206.

Now they decide:

chorus: Kunjaloke namhlanje	It is so then today
Emagqumeni as' Ohlange.	at the hillocks of Uhlanga.

In Isl. 101 he calls to mind Jesus' words over Jerusalem:

3. Sikhukhukazi esihle	Beautiful hen
Simi phambi kwakho,	we stand before you.
Akusiyo i Jerusalema kuphela	It is not Jerusalem alone
Owayithandayo	that which you loved.
5. Kufakamele Nkosi	Protect it, *Nkosi*,
Loku Kuphakama,	this Kuphakama,
Njenge sikhukhukazi	like a hen
Sithanda aɓantwana ɓaso.	loving its children.

This metaphor of the hen is important as well as the fact that Jerusalem did not allow her children to be gathered with the result that it has been left in ruin: "Now I leave you in ruin" (*Sengikuskiya uchithekile*, verse 6). It is now Ekuphakameni, the new Jerusalem which is in Natal. Here in Bethlehem their Christ has been born: cf. Isl. 152¹.

Jerusalema Betlehema	Jerusalem Bethlehem
Izazi zisitshelile	the wise have told us,
Umsindisi uselezelwe	the *uMsindisi* has been born already
EBetlehema eBetlehema.	in Bethlehem, in Bethlehem.

The wise man saw his star entering Jerusalem (Isl. 152²; cf. Isl. 7²) and now they are invited to see the *uMsindisi*. This salvation history is Shembe's own history. The star symbol at Ekaphakameni laid out with stones is also significant.

iv. *Bethlehem*, the city of Juda (*muzi wakwa Juda*, Isl. 34²) is in their midst; the city which is small (*muzi omncinyane*, Isl. 80⁴); at which the Saviour sleeps "in a manger of cows" (*ekhombeni wezinkomo*, Isl. 152⁵).

v. *Nazareth*, the place where Jesus grew up, appears only in the Izl. of Shembe I. The prophets of Nazareth came with their *iNkosi* who was enveloped in clouds (Isl. 7⁴) while the saints went out to meet their *iNkosi* (Isl. 7⁵); Jehova loves the people of Nazareth (Izl. 37², 149²); the young women and men of Nazareth are admonished to cry over their sins in front of the *uMsindisi* (Isl. 45³,⁴); to believe takes place at Nazareth (Isl. 143); here they believe to overflowing: cf. Isl. 207².

ENazaretha	At Nazareth
Sokholwa sichichime.	we will believe to overflowing.

This is the only name used for Ekuphakameni in the confessions of faith (Izl. 73, 154). In spite of *this* prominence given to Nazareth it is not often referred to in the *Izihlaɓelelo*.

vi. *Zion* is only once used for Ekuphakameni, while the movement itself is often designated as the *amaZiyoni* (Eng. Zion), and members of the movement are referred to as *i(li)Ziyoni* or *umZiyoni* (pl. aɓaZiyoni). The practices and customs are referred to as *uɓuZiyoni*. The Christian Catholic Apostolic Church in Zion, founded in 1896 by John Alexander Dowie in Chicago[1]), had its influence on 'Zionism' in South Africa. When Shembe uses the name he has himself in mind as "the inhabitant of Zion". cf. Isl. 57[2].

Sifuneleni aɓathunyiweyo	Look for us those who are sent
Ukuhola aɓaningi,	to pull along the many,
Ukuɓayisa kumhlali neZion	to bring them to the inhabitant of Zion
Emzini wokuphumula	at the city of rest.

The "missionaries" of this movement are called to bring the crowds to "the inhabitant of Zion"—this is again evidence of his *centripetal* concept of missionary activity.

vii. The city of *Ntanda* has its own building or temple; cf. Isl. 80[1]. This Isl. may have been written for the commemoration of this building.

viii. The name, city of *uHlanga*, puts Ekuphakameni in the context of the Zulu creation myth.

ix. The designation *Muzi wamakhosazana* (Isl. 80[5]) gives an indication as to the significance of women within the movement.

x. The name Nazarite has not often been used and *Muzi wama-Nazaretha* is only found in the Izl. mentioned above. The movement itself is the *iBandla lamaNazaretha* and Ekuphakameni is the city of the Nazarites: cf. Isl. 10[1].

Umuzi wama Nazaretha[2])	City of the Nazarites,
Lapho siyakhona	where we are going to
Ukhazimula ngaphezu	it shines more
Kwelanga nenyanga.	than the sun and the moon.

This is the case because in this city is the redeemer (*Umkhokheli*, verse 2)

---

[1]) cf. Sundkler, Bantu Prophets, 48.

[2]) This name is not derived from Nazarenes, a movement to which Allan Lea refers mentioned in a book entitled "The task of the christian Church". cf. The Native Separatist Movement. South Africa, 47. Reference is made to Nazarites also in Izl. 68[2], 73[2,3], 83[1-5], 84[1,2], 92[1], 149[1,2], 218[4]. Shembe II states in Isl. 221[6] *amaNazaretha ayingcwele* (the Nazarites are holy). He uses the name also in Isl. 224[1].

who does not buy with silver and gold (verse 3); here is Jehova, and all slaves on the earth should rejoice (verse 5). The true God is thus the one who does not make slaves and he is at Ekuphakameni.

xi. The river Mthwalume is praised by "our dear city" (*Muzi wakithi othandekayo*, Isl. 79[1]) or *is* "our dear city". It is difficult to decide on the correct interpretation. This is also a scriptural reference. cf. Rev. 22[1]. As water is life-giving so this city too, the water of the city, giving life, is the city, i.e. it makes the city what it is. This may be the "logic".

xii. Both Shembe I and II refer to it as the *holy city*. cf. Isl. 148[4].

Bangenile emzini oyingcwele	They have entered into the city
	that is holy
Maka бongwe uJehova.	Let Jehova be praised.

Shembe II states in Isl. 222[5]:

| Ngiyathanda ukuphelela | I love to be always present |
| Kulowo muzi oyingcwele. | at that holy city. |

This is a reminiscence of Rev. 21[2] (*umuzi ongcwele*). The word city is used to translate *umuzi* in the Izl., as Shembe I and II have all the adherents and heavenly hosts in mind when they speak about Ekuphakameni. The Zulu word *umuzi* (pl. *imizi*) could, apart from kraal, also mean a family and a city.[1]) It is sometimes also applied to a whole tribe or nation. For Shembe I and II this city is holy as the kraal, the Zulu temple "where the spirits of the ancestors are thought to linger", is holy.[2])

The following designations could be briefly referred to. Ekuphakameni is truly home in the Zulu sense, i.e. the centre of one's very existence. In Isl. 57[1] the request is for the way to go home (*ikhaya*) to Jehova. This is not a 'supernatural' home but Ekuphakameni itself; the home of the saints. (Isl. 171[3]). The designation *Senzangakhona*, the father of Dingaan, Shaka and Mpande, makes all pre-christian Zulus especially feel at home, as this great Zulu royal family is still held in high esteem. The sins of this royal family have been Shembe's continuous concern, but after he had canonised them, partly due to his nationalistic motives, they were referred to as saintly beings, and now the holy city was honoured with this name. This is especially clear in Isl. 216 where he states amongst others that they drank

---

[1]) Asmus, 15, states that when a kraal-head brings sacrifices to his dead father it is not an individual approaching but the whole family here approaching the whole family there.

[2]) Krige, 42.

of long ago (*kade*) "at that fountain of Sendzangakhona of the *iNkosi*". (*Kulowo mthombo ka Sendzangakhona weNkosi*, verse 5).

Shembe II refers to Ekuphakameni simply as "that city" (*lowomuzi*, Isl. 236²). In his obvious application of the parable of the bridegroom and maids to himself, Shembe II speaks about "the house of christian marriage" (*endlini yomshado*, Isl. 230³), which may only refer to the temple building in Ekuphakameni but could also just as well refer to the whole city. Shembe II calls this city the "house of *uThixo*" (Isl. 237²) and "the house of the great *iNkosi*" (Isl. 237⁵), praising it as the precious thing of their hearts, the door of heaven. (Ibid.).

The contact between *Ekuphakameni* and the supernatural world is so intimate that the kingdom of God is at this place. Its fulfilment is not removed into the distant future but has already taken place and is fully experienced in the "here and now". Some of the Izl. taken by themselves give the impression of an eschatology based on the end of history, but basically Shembe did not think in these terms. When he was still under the influence of his church's eschatology Shembe I looked to the future; but gradually the past, present and future were based on his new eschatological concepts.

Conclusions

An attempt has been made in this book to focus attention on the theological issues involved in the *iBandla lamaNazaretha* as revealed in the *Izihlaɓelelo*. Only when hymns, sermons, liturgical and ritual practices are analysed could a better understanding be reached with regard to the theological disposition of these movements. Bishop Sundkler's analysis of the *Izihlaɓelelo* in his excellent and most valuable study entitled *Bantu Prophets in South Africa* has limited itself only to a few *Izl.* as he kept himself busy with Zulu independentism as a whole. Dr. Katesa Schlosser's book under the title *Eingeborenenkirchen in Süd- und Südwestafrika, Ihre Geschichte und Sozialstruktur* is an attempt at a sociological analysis. Dr. A. Vilakazi in his dissertation entitled "*ISonto lamaNazaretha, The Church of the Nazarites*" is an attempt to give a theological and sociological analysis of this movement. It is a pity that Sundkler has treated this study of a well-known Zulu academician with such contempt in his second edition of the above-mentioned book. His criticism of Sundkler is not always justified but he raises issues which Sundkler either neglects or underestimates.

Two main reasons are given by Sundkler for secession from "mission churches" (a tautology!), namely the colour-bar of white South Africa

and Protestant denominationalism. Vilakazi, again, calls it the African
Reformation and states, "the African is claiming for himself the right to
interpret the Bible as he understands it".[1]) Sundkler's study leaves the
impression that one could also entitle it *The anti-colour-bar prophets in
South Africa*. His emphasis on this aspect, which *is* a tragic contributory
factor to independentism in South Africa, has established a blind spot in
his analysis of the causes for the rise of the movement. It is true that the
Natives Land Act of 1913 and the Act of 1926 limiting skilled labour in
the mining industry, with its Anglo-American capital, to whites only,
had a remarkable influence on independentism *but* there is much more
involved than this simple and popular analysis. Nothing of the truth of
this aspect should however be underestimated because of the harm done
to the witness of the Church. Racial tension does also have its effect
amongst Africans themselves, and this has also led to independentism
and autonomous churches. Independentism starts in South Africa with
the formation of the "Tembu Church" in 1884 by Nehemiah Tile, a
Wesleyan Tembu minister, together with Ngangelizwe, the Chief of the
Tembu. Tile had strong Tembu-nationalistic tendencies which led him to
react against European control and to make the Church truly *Tembu*.[2])
P. J. Mzimba formed his church in 1898 when he seceded from the United
Free Church of Scotland taking the *Fingos* with him while the *Xhosas*
remained loyal. Loram, the famous expert on Native Education, made
the observation that there is often a cordial relationship between those
who seceded and those who remained loyal (i.e. if they belong to the same
tribe) and this has led him to decide that "it shows clearly how racial or at
least tribal considerations rank higher in the Native mind than Church
divisions, and how likely it is that the separatist movement will spread".[3])
Sundkler has made the observation that Zulus belonging "either to the
heathen section or one of the christian groups live "happily (or unhappily,
as the case may be) together"[4]) so that one could deduce that a deeper
factor exists than religious differences and that it also plays its negative
role when different tribes are represented in the one church or movement.
Edgar Brookes maintains in the *preface* to Sundkler's book that nationalism

---

[1]) Vilakazi, Isonto lamaNazaretha, 1.

[2]) Krige, (Social System, 4) states in her chapter on the Zulu history that the vanguard
of the Ntungwa-Nguni in their trek south was the Tembu, and adds that they had a
greater capacity for sub-division than other tribes.

[3] cf. Loram, C. T. The Separatist Church Movement, International Review of
Missions, Vol. XV July 1926, 479ff.

[4]) *Sundkler*, Bantu Prophets, 64.

plays a great part in independentism and that a spirit of separatism prevails.[1])

One may also take Sundkler's thesis further, namely, that the colour-bar is responsible for the resurgence of African religion through independentism. But the resurgence of Hinduism, Buddhism, Mohammedanism and of African animism in countries which had nothing, or very little to do with a colour-bar, refutes this impression. The resurgence of religion has been a phenomenon of extraordinary importance in many parts of the world, especially in countries of rapid social change. Japan experienced the formation of new religions and religions groups since the last century which have grown to more than six hundred. Here also social cohesion was radically disturbed in the most industrialized country in Asia. Here has been no colour-bar but a factor has been at work which Sundkler practically overlooked, namely the *breaking up of a society*. The consequences are a resurgence of the old religions, the founding of new ones; nationalism and self-discovery leads to a reaction to paternalism also in the Church.

The rapid growth of the Christian population since the end of the last century until 1911, when Shembe, the greatest independent leader in South Africa, broke away from an African Baptist Church on the Sabbath issue, has taken place in the period of the development of South Africa's mining industry when thousands of Africans literally swarmed to the cities. The shock of the break up of African society was *one* of the main causes for all kinds of groups and movements, in order to retain social cohesion which is found "in the fountains of Sendzangakhona", as Shembe expresses it. The coming of the white man has disturbed the African society, but this other *new* factor was an even more threatening one. A process to salvage the old in a highly conservative society was consciously set into motion. Sundkler states that the 'Zionists' act as a conservative force with regard to the fundamentals of Zulu society[2]), and in the South African context it will be easy to ascribe this to the colour bar. Furthermore, the process of industrialisation and urbanisation was intensified so that over 30 per cent of South Africa's African population has been absorbed into its cities. Southern Rhodesia, which practised the colour-bar and which had comparatively speaking a much smaller percentage of urbanised Africans and a slower process of industrialisation, experienced very few of the independent movements in comparison with South Africa, the most industrialised country on the continent of Africa.

---

[1]) Ibid., 3.
[2]) Ibid., 98.

If the main causes for the South African independent movements are merely the colour-bar, even if it is the kind practised by Missions, and Protestant denominationalism, an analysis will be simple and easy. But apart from social upheaval there are deep-seated differences in listening to the message, a world view which differs on many points; these issues often go much deeper than even the colour-bar, though that *cuts* deep into the lives of many people. With some it may be due *only* to the colour-bar, but with many the issues are much more complicated and even when it is the colour-bar there are often other issues involved because any religion is an organic whole. Sundkler's statement that after 1945 secessions were "no longer a result of racial tension within the missions, but were due rather to fission among the Bantu Independent Churches themselves",[1]) sounds *strange* for the following reasons:

1. In his first edition he gave the impression that this independentism was *mainly* due to Acts of State affecting land and labour. In the Foreword to the second edition he states that independentism and "the religious ideology on Bantu lines"[2]) were the outcome of such events as the Natives Land Act of 1913, but the idea of an independent African Church was inspired by theories of men like *Rufus Anderson* and *Henry Venn*. The 19th century *bourgeois* sociology, which defined every social environment in terms of "Volk", nation and people, speaking about a people's church (*Volkskirche*), had its influence not only in Churches in the West but also in their missionary activities!

2. Sundkler's statement above is also strange in the light of the fact that one of the main independent movements in South Africa, if not the major one,[3]) was not due to racial tension within the African Baptist Church. Shembe broke away because of the Sabbath issue, and this took place 34 years before 1945. There were thus other factors involved.

3. If independentism was mainly due to "racial tension within the missions" before 1945 one finds it difficult to understand how 2030 churches, sects, movements and groups, to which Sundkler refers,[4]) could possibly have developed only out of the missions. There is enough proof to the contrary, namely that numerous secessions took place within independentism itself before 1945. Although religious tolerance and symbiosis existed clashes over money, racial issues and personality problems often appeared.

---

[1]) *Sundkler*, Bantu Prophets, 303.

[2]) Ibid., 4.

[3]) *Sundkler*, Bantu Prophets, 110, states that probably no other Zulu had such a great influence over so many people as Shembe.

[4]) *Sundkler*, 307.

Paternalism, of which the race issue is one aspect, played its role in its many forms in secessions, e.g., with regard to organization, liturgy and ritual, rejection of everything the Zulu could contribute to the spontaneous development of the church. In Sundkler's list of "Acknowledgements"[1] not even one of his Zulu assistants is mentioned by name, and they had surely contributed invaluable information which enabled the author to write his book. It is these small but significant things, that reveal racial attitudes, which disturbs the sensitive African mind and which so often were contributory factors to independentism.

Protestant denominationalism has often given the impression that each denomination served its own selfish deity and that each of them had their own 'God' as each tribe had its own. But it is an oversimplification to reduce everything to the colour-bar and protestant denominationalism. Vilakazi accuses Sundkler of "a total neglect of the theology of the Separatist Churches".[2] Although this is not a justifiable criticism, one could say that Sundkler neglected major aspects with regard to the causes for separatism in order to justify his main thesis.

For the situation after 1945 his thesis has again to adapt itself—because of the apartheid policy independentism has become a "church apart while" the author has all the time maintained that Zionism, for example, is a *third race*, a group that lives separated from the non-christians and the Christians, a conservative force so far as the fundamentals of Zulu society is concerned. All of a sudden these movements accept the government policy according to Sundkler. The anti-colour-bar prophets have now turned into pro-colour-bar prophets. No, the racial approach was continuously also present with the African and the history of Shaka has much to say about this. Sundkler's book gives the impression that the demons of racialism are to be found only in one section of the South African population. They may be smaller in the other sections but they are big enough to be harmful and did harm the church before 1945.

With regard to the theological issues the following aspect should be considered. Sundkler, interestingly enough, refers *per se* to the independent movements as churches. There are those who have the characteristics of a true church but there are those also who are *not* churches, also according to the Lutheran understanding of what the marks of a christian church are. The nativistic syncretistic interpretation of the christian faith is in many cases not based on the work of Jesus Christ as Lord and Saviour. The

---

[1] *Sundkler*, Bantu Prophets, 10.
[2] Vilakazi, Isonto lamaNazaretha, 4.

christological position of a movement indicates the category in which it falls. The acceptance of a Black Christ leads to a "blood and soil" religion without the Biblical Christ. Shembe wished to restore the Zulu tribe not merely in a nationalistic sense without religion but through the law, especially the magic of Sabbath observance. His reaction against the whites is not simply a nationalistic reaction, but according to him they mislead the people by neglecting the Sabbath law. In Shembe's case the colour-bar issue came later into the picture and was not the cause for the formation of this great movement. His desire for a true Zulu religion based on the Zulu tradition in the light of the Law is basic. His recovery of the Sabbath is an important contributory factor for his development into a Messianic figure and the exclusion of the Christ of the Gospel.

Sundkler speaks in his 2nd edition of a third type of movement after referring only to the Ethiopian and Zionist types of "churches" in the 1st edition. One suddenly discovers in the 2nd edition the following statement, namely "we must point out here that we are now speaking of *a third, a Messianic type*"[1]) after he continually referred to Messianism and the Black Christ in the 1st edition. This "now" in the above statement has already been misleading being interpreted as if the Messianic type has only now started to develop. Instead of admitting the weakness of his first classification this is by-passed with a "by the way" remark. An attempt to classify literally thousands of churches, Christian sects, nativistic movements and groups into three types is idealistic to say the least, even if one takes the extreme phenomena into consideration. To fit these movements into this strait-jacket will need much imagination in many cases. Among them are the African version of the Anglican, Presbyterian, Methodist, Lutheran, Baptist, Pentecostal, Sabbatarian types of churches. Sundkler himself speaks about Ethiopianism, Zionism, nativistic Zionism and African aninism.[2]) Many of the movements which Sundkler would classify under Ethiopianism because of secession from "mission churches" chiefly on "racial grounds" or from "Bantu churches" where "Bantu leaders" follow the policy of these churches,[3]) do *not* fall under the category of racialism.[4]) Are people racialistic when they react after trying without any effect to have an indigenized church, an οἶκος, a spiritual home? Is it not here often a case of the true meaning of Ps. 68[32] and Acts 8[27]ff rather than the

---

[1]) Ibid., 302.

[2]) Ibid., 297.

[3]) Ibid., 53–4.

[4]) For a more realistic classification see H. W. Turner's classification in V. E. W. Hayward (ed.), African Independent Church Movements, Edinburgh House Press,

political meaning the word "Ethiopian" acquired?[1]) People stretched out their hands unto God as the eunuch of Ethiopia did but so often they had no Philip to explain the message in *their* religious world which has more often been treated as so much straw, and when they do react in utter frustration this is also interpreted as "racial grounds"! Any realistic classification cannot be satisfied with three types covering the $\pm$ 3000 independent churches, sects, movements and groups. This fantastic growth is also due, according to Sundkler, to two reasons!

Shembe developed, according to the analysis of the *Izihlaɓelelo*, into a Messiah and his movement is thus a Messianic type. But here again there are different types of Messianic figures. Shembe does not lead his people to a glorious future—they are already in it. He is even more than a Messiah. The singing, the music of drums, the repeated proclamations of grace and forgiveness, have led them to believe that the kingdom of God has been realized. Shembe does not merely know the future but he *is* the future. Their God, whom they possess and who possesses them, is at Ekuphakameni. He is the father, the source of all their material needs and their salvation—a really comprehensive approach. The old Zulu question about who is the strongest is again asked and the answer is clear. It is not the distant God of the missionaries nor of the whites who desecrate the Sabbath and whose messages do not *reach* their very being, but it is their own Supreme Being who has hands and feet and who walks with them. Together with all the weakness Shembe observed in the religion of the whites their racial attitudes contributed to his deep sense of vocation with regard to his people. He has taken the Bible seriously in his own way

---

1963; see also James W. Fernandez, "African religious movements, types and dynamics" *in* Modern African Studies, Vol. 2, No. 4, Dec. 1964; R. Linton, "Nativistic Movements", American Anthropologist, Vol. 45, 1943, 230. For a one-sided emphasis on these movements as political expressions of self realization see K. Symmons–Symonolewics, "Nationalist Movements" *in* Comparative Studies in Society and Religion, Vol. VII, No. 2, Jan. 1965, 221–230. Independent churches or movements is a gross generalisation typical of the telescopic type of 'research' or journalistic approach. There are a) Churches; b) Christian sects; c) Nativistic movements with different degrees of nativism; d) Messianic movements; e) Millenarian movements; f) Nationalistic movements. A clear-cut typology of many of these movements is not possible although, many are basically nativistic and not christian churches or sects. They are *revivalistic* with the emphasis on the old in the light of the new, *vitalistic* as a result of forces within and without or *reformation* movements.

[1]) Ethiopianism is a most unsatisfactory term. Although it was a reaction against "negrophobia", according to Willoughby, its aim was to bring christianity "in harmony with Bantu character and tradition", *Willoughby, W. C.* Race problems in South Africa, O.U.P., 1923, 237; the aim was "to produce a truly African type of christianity suited to the genius and needs of the race, and not to be merely a black copy of any European church", *Wells, J.* Stewart of Lovedale, Hodder and Stoughton, 1908, 289.

on matters of sickness, death, poverty and social conditions. Empirical Christianity has been refuted because it does not give these things and also because it is not understood. Shembe had a different concept of what the fullness of religion implies.

Shembe's doctrine of the *uMoya* cannot be fully comprehended by the analytic mind of a Westerner. He himself is a holy spirit but in the name of the holy spirit he drives out evil spirits. He has the *uMoya* at his disposal. He has no doctrine of the trinity but his theology of the trinity consists of the Supreme Being, Shembe and the Holy Spirit. Shembe however is also the manifestation of the Supreme Being *and* the Holy Spirit. One could also speak of a *Binity* in which the Supreme Being and Shembe, his manifestation, is confessed, keeping in mind that Shembe is also a holy spirit, the one sent, the incarnation of Jehova's Spirit. Zulu ontology differentiates on the basis of vital force. To his followers he is the personification of Supreme Power. Here is not a clear distinction made between man and Spirit as is the case in the churches' doctrine, but identity exists between them which is the basis of all mysticism. As the child is the continuation of the father so is Shembe the manifestation of the heavenly Father. All those who passed away are also holy spirits, called out of the graves through Shembe and are active beings at Ekupha-kameni. Here is the old animism fully at work in *post-christianity*.

What Robinson states about the Holy Spirit in the established churches could perhaps also be applied to Shembe's movement, namely, that the doctrine of the Holy Spirit "is the article of a standing or falling church".[1] The emphasis on spirit-possession is revitalized in the light of the new. The fundamental emphasis is emotive rather than rational. The theology of Shembe is not so much illogical as mystical of which the Nhlangakazi events are the culmination. Shembe's spiritualism has changed into spiritism. He had no problem to accept the Scriptural concept of the Holy Spirit but explained it in his own context. As Jesus Christ could send the Holy Spirit, so Jehova and he himself could use their own *uMoya*. The Holy Spirit and the holy spirits are bearers of power and sources of revelation, and here the angel also has a specific role. The church should have a well-worked out Biblical interpretation in the Zulu society of the Holy Spirit and its work, as well as a clear exposition of the doctrine of the communion of saints, keeping in mind the Zulu religious approach on these matters.

Dancing, singing, ritualism and emotionalism express a desire for a religion vividly experienced. Together with this, sacred sites, regalia and

---

[1] *Robinson, Wheeler*, The Christian Experience of the Holy Spirit, Nisbett and Co.. Ltd., 1952[10], 42.

holy water are of great significance for Shembe. Ritual washing and vomiting, as a way of confession, give sin a formal and ceremonial character. Baptism and holy communion have become purification rites. The concept of sin with Shembe is greatly influenced by the Zulu religion. Confessions play an important role in restoring the harmony in the tribe, and so with the shades. All this shows how Shembe's religion is an *act* religion, which has to do with rhythm, colour, magical elements, acts in different forms. The sacraments also are not merely *symbolic* in the Zwinglian sense but in them two realities come together; they are not mere vehicles of grace but carry *numinous* power. Thus Shembe calls all to come to be baptized and to share the sacrament of the Holy Communion which gives everlasting life. This literalism and legalism in Scriptural exposition, and its understanding, makes the Bible also a magical book so that in the Book of Life one's *name* is written and protected. Magical moralism is basic to literalism and legalism. Here a human product is put in the place of God's word. Man wishes to justify and sanctify himself by influencing the supernatural forces. Shembe himself is a *magical personality*.

Shembe must have faced even in the African Baptist Church the problem of communication. In the Old Testament the *Word* of God is the means of communication, while in the New Testament it is the Incarnated Word which is communication by sight; Word and Image of which the Word is basic. The communication of the message in new cultures with their own myths and social patterns had to take place. With the Jewish world-view the religious principle was in the centre, namely the *Torah*, and with the Greeks the *Logos*, a rational principle. The Gospel with its prophetic and historical background had been translated and transposed by using images, ideas and verbal symbols and language patterns of the Hebrew tradition which had already been adjusted to the hellenistic world. Christ was soon at the centre of the covenant-community and of its history.

Shembe did not experience this privilege in the Zulu culture even after decades of missionary activity. The missionaries have more often reacted against it than exercising the wisdom of understanding it. It is true that they came with different denominations converting *individuals* who became foreign to their own. Shembe, for whom the totality is the object of his thinking, saw this weakness and he had to translate the message of salvation in his cyclical, unhistorical and mythical world, the myths of which remained, theologically speaking, untouched except in preaching which concentrated only on its dangers. Shembe discovered in this situation the Jehova of the law which took precedence in the *Izihlaɓelelo* and communicated the Bible as he understood it. Ritual prohibitions formed the psychological basis for his theology. Texts in the Old Testament pertaining to the Law and the Nazarites played an important role as texts in the New Testament pertaining to the Holy Spirit, water and the spirit and angels were of special significance. The Bible is indeed a 'dangerous' book in Africa and it is at this juncture that the authority of the Church and its doctrine comes into the picture in the African context. It is only a miracle that the message does reach people because there is so much in the Bible, if not carefully treated, which could be associated with the African religion and its emphasis on ritual prohibitions, ancestor spirits, ritual and purification rites.

The problem is that Shembe was no Paul. He was too much involved in his own world-view and could not stand objectively over against it as Paul did over against his world. Such objectivity was disturbed by the tragic history of race. But at the background of this racial feeling was the reaction also against religious foreignness which remained even in churches under African leadership. The Gospel was not translated into Shembe's world. The concept of God, Messiah, Holy Spirit, fellowship of the saints, law and gospel, sin, resurrection received meticulous attention from Paul, and this led to his capturing of the mythical world for Christ. Furthermore, Paul concerned himself with the world of his time and his converts were concerned with the *world*, not with the church. They were not ghettoed into organizations or mission stations.

Although the judgment of God is upon all culture, Christianity cannot be divorced from it as many missionaries tried to do. The meaning assigned to the message is worked out by the culture, which is seen in Matthew's Gospel, directed to a people of Jewish background, and Luke's Gospel, directed to the people of the Greco-Roman culture. Shembe tried to do the same. He tried to translate the Bible and its message into his world and the result is a theology of the Law, of which the Sabbath is the key, as well as the myth of a Black Christ. As the saviour of the Sabbath (he had many difficulties with Jesus on this issue!) he became the true Messiah, further assisted by a socio-economic situation which is fruitful soil for messianic developments. The church to which Shembe belonged did not give satisfaction for those hailing from a culture where ritual is rich and where it has religious and magical significance, for example, dancing before the Lord and repetitive singing are expressions of worship indigenous to the Zulu and foreign to the European. The sacred rhythm wants to come to expression in sacred dance. This is the way contact is made with the supernatural world. The pure expression of *numinous* power is in rhythm,

poetry, music and movements in dance. Rhythm and word go together
in the pre-christian Zulu religion. The turning over and over of one idea
in a sermon is the rhythm of repetition. Much of the singing however is
associated with spirit-possession in its trance effects. The dangers are thus
numerous but the reaction has not solved them. Shembe used it in his
own way without any real theological understanding of what the Scriptural
message demands in this respect, namely, that the judgment of God comes
on these things however important they be; that everything should be
seen in the light of the Cross of Jesus Christ.

The Western liturgy transplanted *en toto* gave to Shembe, as well as
to his followers, no satisfaction. The concreteness of expression in ritual
did not find the necessary attention. Spontaneity and gaiety are characteristics of Zulu worship but the formalism of the denominations did not
understand this. A new way of life had to be implanted by frustrating
everything indigenous, and the extreme reaction is the consequence.
Shembe came forward with his own expression of the new religion in
dance, songs and hymns which contributed tremendously to the growth
of his movement. Not the spoken but the sung word transfer the message,
and Shembe understood this very well.

The *iBandla lamaNazaretha* did not, in the first instance, originate
because of race in spite of the role this issue played later. The *Izihla-
belelo* sufficiently proves that the "fountains of old" were revitalized in
the context of *Nazarethness*. The Church came as a preaching and teaching
institution and Sundkler regrets that the devotional heritage of the Church
Universal was not transmitted to the Church in Africa in the same way.
But why this emphasis on *transmit*? A true *interpretatio Africana* will get
rid of transmitting and transplanting, a basic case for independentism,
and will itself find ways and means under the guidance of well-trained
ministers and theologians to bring the message in the forms most effective
in the specific situations in which the Church finds itself. Sundkler's contention that "the Independent Bantu Churches will be attracted by
Mission Churches with episcopal authority, prestige of liturgical tradition,
and a liberal attitude in racial questions"[1]) should also be analysed in the
light of the fact that the Methodist Church, which has no episcopal
authority in South Africa nor any of the prestige (?) of liturgical tradition,
is the most typical Protestant Church amongst Africans in the whole of
Southern Africa. For this its simple but effective class system and its ministry are responsible and a liturgy which is for many reasons better adapted

---

[1]) *Sundkler*, Bantu Prophets, 299–300.

than those with *prestige*. Furthermore, liberal attitudes in racial questions
have often not characterized these churches, movements or groups. It is
not a question *merely* of more episcopacy, better liturgy and ritual, but a
deep understanding of the anxieties, the needs and aspirations of people
who cannot find a spiritual home in the established churches unless there
is a radical change in their approach. Much of independentism is due to
the lukewarmness of the established churches and is a form of revival. This
is certainly the case in the *iBandla lamaNazaretha* as revealed in the hymnal
of Shembe. Liturgy, ritual, the general form of worship and organization,
need meticulous attention, but all this will not attract the independent
movements if there is not this devotion to true Christian living in every
situation where *the Church* has to give justification of its faith. On the other
hand, with the nativistic movements in their post-christian form, it is not
merely a matter of *development* and *change* but of radical conversion to
christianity. Here one observes that the more something *changes itself* the
more it remains the same.

APPENDIX

*Izl.**

1.

1. *Nkosi* bless uɓaɓa (my father)
Although he wanders in the
      mountains
he not having his place
he sleeping in forests.

2. *Nkosi* bless uɓaɓa
you are his shield
although he wanders in the
      mountains
sleeping in forests.

3. You are his shield
Although he wanders on mountains
he not having his place
he sleeping in forests.

4. Through the prayer of children
Jehova listened to us,
while we were still wandering in
      the mountains
we sleeping in the forests.

5. Disappointed today are our
      enemies,
who caused us to be laughed at,
while we were wandering in the
      mountains
we sleeping in the forests.

6. Even today *Nkosi* let it be so,
let our enemies be disappointed
who were causing us to be
      laughed at,
while we were still sleeping in
      the forests.

7. Even today *Nkosi* it is still thou
who scattered our enemies
while we were wandering in the mountains*
while we were sleeping in the forests.

  * ezintzɓeni in the text should read *ezintaɓeni*.

5.

1. Ye, who wish to live
in the flock of Jesus,
remember the hardship of the road
which goes towards home.

3. The birds have nests
they stay well;
but Jesus has no place
here where he can stay.

* The translations are literal as far as possible literal.

2. The track is small
it defeats the cowards;
Even the gate is small
it is entered with power.

4. Those who wish to follow Him
should repent first of all;
they should not fear the
                    commandments
which bring an end to power.

5. They should take the Cross
on their shoulders,
they should die for the promise
which they were promised.

7.

1. The case has now been discussed
in the whole world;
rest and rejoice
You his people.

3. He shouted with a great Voice
in the midst of four angels;
He said you should not spoil
                    the earth
the case has already been discussed.

2. The angels came out
here on earth;
Here is one angel
coming from the east.

4. There appeared Prophets
they of Nazareth;
they coming with their *iNkosi*
he (was) enveloped in clouds.

5. The saints go out
they of Nazareth;
they met their *iNkosi*
coming by way of clouds.

12.

1. Jehova has left us
We are those who lack and those
                    in need.
Hallelujah, weep for us
Ye hosts of heaven.

4. Oh, Jehova has left us indeed
in such a state of orphanage.
Hallelujah, weep for us
Ye hosts of heaven.

2. We have nothing in the hand
We have come, we are naked
                    indeed *Nkosi* of peace.
Hallelujah, weep for us.

5. We are in need of a piece of bread
of giving rest to our souls.
Hallelujah, weep for us
Ye hosts of heaven.

3. We have no father, we have
no mother.
We have no brother to clothe us
Hallelujah, weep for us
Ye hosts of heaven.

6. You have turned the back on us,
why indeed?
You should remember us our
uNkulunkulu
Hallelujah, weep for us
Ye hosts of heaven.

13.

1. Talents and gifts
may it be used by you *iNkosi*
it should look for me, it should
find me
in the plentiness of your kindness.

2. The ardent desire of your *umoya*
may it look for me and may it find
me;
in the poverty of my *umoya*
let me rejoice today, Oh *Nkosi*.

3. Come all ye people
draw near to the fountain;
that fountain of Jacob
there where the Samaritans were
saved.

4. Come ye today
here is the sun already setting;
the Samaritans all came
with that saying of the woman.

5. And so they arrived then at the
fountain
with that saying of the woman
they said: yes, we have seen for
ourselves
we believe indeed.

6. After that they begged him
and said
Stay with us for three days
and cause us all to drink
like the woman you have caused
to drink.

17.

1. He who is beaten is not thrown
away
let him not despise himself,
rise up, rise up
Ye Africans.

2. The form of the doorway
causes you to bend,

3. The enemies of Jehova
rise up against you
rise up, rise up
Ye Africans.

4. Those are given kingly authority
upon the mountain,

Rise up, rise up
Ye Africans.

5. They already want to deprive
the eternal kingly authority,
Rise up, rise up
Ye Africans.

24.

1. See he comes by way of the
                                    clouds
He will come to call his people,
even those who are asleep will
                                    wake up
from the dust of the earth
Amen Halelujah
Praise ye all.

2. It is coming, it is coming
Ukuphakama
it comes with the saints
of the *iNkosi* of heaven.
Amen Halelujah
Praise ye all.

3. *iNkosi* himself in person
will come down from heaven
Coming with the many
of Ekuphakameni.
Amen Halelujah
Praise ye all.

4. Those who went out, we being
                                disappointed,
Ekuphakameni,
today they are coming
clothed with victory alone.
Amen Halelujah
Praise ye all.

5. Today rejoice ye,
Ye keepers of the laws.
You are going to be anointed
                                    to sufficiency
through having (fulfilled)
                        accomplished the laws.
Amen Halelujah
Praise ye all.

6. What shall ye be rewarded with
Ye transgressors of the laws,
Put your ears and hear
the din of the saints.
Amen Halelujah
Praise ye all.

26.

1. All the sins I have done
stand irremovably in front of me,

3. They said you should not leave me
I would like to go with you,

I cannot conceal even one
that which will not be known.

2. I tried and ended up in the
wilderness
I wished to hide them,
and when I was praying in the
wilderness
they shouted at me in a big voice.

so that I go and hear what you say
in front of *Baba* who is in heaven.

4. It is necessary that you hide
all your sins.
Do not leave me even if you go
to pray,
I would like to hear it
Your confessing it yourself.

28.

1. It comes, it comes
the day of the end,
it will stand in front of you
whether you like it or not;
the hills and the valleys
will be silent.

3. I cry for you
You maidens and young men
At what time will you find
your faith.

2. Oh, those whose power has
ended
in their faith;
they will run looking for it
their faith.

4. The first trumpet
has been sounded
all the earth
quaked.
Where will you run and hide
yourself,
here is the world already being
folded.

5. Your earth, where will you hide yourself,
and all those sinners;
run away ye strangers
Jehova is coming.

35.

1. Our *Baba* who is in heaven
look at me and love me;
do not look at those which I have
brought
they have disappointed me.

3. Our *Baba* who is in heaven
for whom are you throwing me
away
whose am I *Baba*
look at me and love me.

> *Chorus:* They were born with me
> I cannot conceal even one.

2. Our *Baßa* who is in heaven
here I am grinding my teeth
because of the evil which I have
in your face.

4. I have come to you *uMkhululi*
redeem me from all
I am clinging fast, I am now
                        cleansed
at the breast of Abraham.

44.

1. Conscience has left me alone
I have no *uMkhululi* of mine.

2. I look at my brethren
they are all my enemies.

> *Chorus:* Help me Jehova
> Liberate my *umoya*.

3. The hoping of my heart
today has come to an end.

45.

1. I shouted day and night
why did you not hear me?
Nations go to sleep that Zulu may be audible
before the *uMsindisi*.

2. I was stopped by all the nations
which are under the heaven.
Nations go to sleep that Zulu may be audible
before the *uMsindisi*.

3. You maiden of Nazareth
May you cry like a rushing stream
about the disgrace that has befallen you
in the land of your people.
Nations go to sleep that Zulu may be audible
before the *uMsindisi*.

4. You young men of Nazareth
You cry all like a rushing stream,
about the disgrace that has befallen you
You young men of Shaka
before the *uMsindisi*.

51.

1. The *iNkosi* comes with the
                              morning
in the face of the earth,
that the light may increase
in the face of the earth.

2. He will remove darkness
in the face of the earth,
they will shout with joy
his worshippers.

3. Rejoice ye heavens
rejoice ye earth,
the lamentation has stopped
in the face of the earth.

4. The dead will rise
coming from all sides,
Jehova our *uThixo*
will cause them all to rise.

5. All those who are asleep
in the dust of the earth
Jehova will call them,
they will arise with haste.

53.

1. Cause ye this news to spread
May it go to all this earth.

2. They rejoice for Simakade
at all times,
it is not the flesh alone that
                              recovers
even their souls.
Chorus: Why do you stay with this news
all the earth is hungry.

3. Encourage this news
Ye who love him
the testifier of this news
here he is, he has arrived.

58.

1. Our father which is in heaven
I am in your face (in front of you!)
let it be handled with holiness
that name of yours.

2. Your will should be done
here on earth
as it is in heaven
where we are going.

Chorus: Your *umoya* must come *Nkosi*
Cause your people to be healed.

3. That which you promised us
through Jesus Christ, *iNkosi*
You said you would not leave us alone
You will send us *umoya* which is holy (the Holy Spirit).

60.

1. Praise Jehova
because He is righteous
because His kindness remains
                                    forever
because He is righteous.

2. He remembered Africa
because He is righteous,
He did not forget his people
because He is righteous.

3. He created the heaven
and also the earth,
it is the work of His hands
because He is good.

4. You remembered your people
whose hips are naked.
You sent them Isaiah, your Servant
because He is good.

5. During those days
the deaf will hear
that which is preached in this
                                    book
because He is righteous

6. Those who put on nothing
on their feet,
He prepared them to enter
in a place which is holy.

7. Even those who shave heads
shave the heads on the side,
Even those who shave chins
through breaking of the laws.

8. And those who enter with shoes
in the house of Jehova
turning it into a house of play
through the breaking of the laws.

61.

1. Let me not feel sleepy my *iNkosi*
inside (in) your work.

3. My time has arrived
I am now leaving you my progeny

Wake me up from sleepiness
that I may not enter into temptation.

stay like this (Goodbye!)
I am going to *Baɓa*.

2. Thus said Jesus
unto His disciples;
Could you not wait with me
one moment.

4. If you do not wait
You remain in drowsiness.
You will all enter into temptation
keep ye watch and be ye determined.

63.

1. Wake me up *Nkosi* I have been sleeping for a long time
that I may be awake to hear your Voice.
> *Chorus:* Come ye, come ye to Ekuphakameni
> that you may hear his word.

2. The deep darkness before the dawn arrives
the rays of morning will catch many.

3. I may hurry, I may hasten in entering into Ekuphakameni
before the gates are closed.

71.

1. My *Nkosi* you loved me
before the mountains were strong
from long ago you anointed me
I am the beginning of your way.

3. And the fountains and rivers
before they had flowed strongly
Jehova created me
before His way.*

2. I am your work of old,
before the large stretches of land
                                    were strong;
and the fountains of water
they had not yet sprouted strongly.

4. The depth was not yet there
I was already born,
He had not yet created this heaven
and also this earth.

5. The sun had not shone yet
in the space of this heaven.
And the moon had not yet shone
in the space of this earth.

* The *way* came afterwards. If this is a reference to John 14[6] then Shembe was even before Christ, i.e., he is greater than Christ.

74.

1. That which was preached about
at Ekuphakameni,
has caused many to be saved
Come ye and be ye saved.

2. Those who enter disappointed
go out rejoicing;
listen all ye nations
come ye and be ye saved.

3. The intruder of the morning
of the border of Juda
has caused many to be saved
come ye and be ye saved.

4. Tell all the nations
which are under the heaven,
that they may come and hear,
                    here is news
of Ekuphakameni.

80.

1. *Nkosi* it is your happy occasion
the building of the city of Ntanda;
today we are giving thanks
in your face.

3. We expect that which is good
that which is to come of you;
as was in the beginning
you gave birth for us, *uMsindisi.*

2. And you also Bethlehem Juda
the city which is small,
give thanks together with us
through your being built.

4. And you also Bethlehem Juda
the city which is small,
give thanks together with us
through your being built.

5. Yes, Bethlehem Juda
the city of the princesses
be dressed beautifully with skin blankets
dance for Jehova.

81.

1. *Thixo* who is all powerful
give us that grace of yours
that we may throw away all
the works of darkness.

3. Oh, the good fortune of those
who have conquered their straying;
their live-stock cannot be known
its plentifulness.

2. Clothe them with brightness
our hearts,
we wait with hope
oh, our *uMkhululi.*

4. Clothe them with brightness
our hearts
we shall wait with hope
oh, our *uMkhululi.*

5. The angels rejoiced about those
who have good fortune,
they received them with joy
in the city which is holy.

83.

1. We are saved
all we Nazarites;
we shall sing and tell them all
we are saved.

2. We shall be clothed sufficiently
with the pleasure of joy;
to be clothed by those
who hope to be saved.

3. We are saved
all we Nazarites;
we shall drink sufficiently
on top of the mountain.

4. We are saved
all we Nazarites;
we shall be clothed sufficiently
with this pleasure of joy.

5. We are saved
all we Nazarites;
we shall drink from that rock
at mount Sinai.

85.

1. I have sinned in thy face
and in the face of heaven
my eye has caused me to sin
I broke the laws.

2. I was defeated by the first
of the Ten Commandments
the second I may not cling to
oh! *Nkosi* of peace.

3. Those who break these laws
are being hammered with stones
they were never protected
what shall I be (i.e., Woe is me!), me a sinner.

4. I have already sinned even with my tongue
I spoke falsehood
I have already sinned even with my heart,
I got angry by it.

5. I have already sinned even with my hand
I touched that which was not fitting
I have already sinned even with my feet
I walked in shame.

86.

1. Who has pushed me out *Nkosi*
Here from your house *Nkosi*
I saw myself being outside
I not having known.

2. Disappointment always *Nkosi*
brings me back to your house;
that I may praise with the many
in thy face, it is so, you know,
                          Nkosi.

3. The branch does not stay on the vine
It is cut off and thrown away
outside the vineyard
eternal word, let me stay with you.

87.

1. Oh, the blessings of that sinner
who hangs from the tree
blessings that fell on him
hanging from a tree.

2. The sinner looked at the Forgiver
and said: I myself
I am not worth anything
because of what I did in your face.

Chorus: The voice was heard
from the tree of shame:
Today you sinner
I will be with you in Paradise.

3. I confess it (sin) and place myself before Thee
thou Forgiver of sinners;
do Thou remember me
in Thy kingdom.

88.

1. Come ye all ye nations
we go to Ekuphakameni;
(that) we be anointed fully
with the oil of kindness.

3. Come ye, oh ye worshippers
(that) we go to Ekuphakameni,
(that) we may go to worship
iNkosi of heaven.

Chorus: Shall we go, shall we go
to the land above.

2. The nations have all been invited
Ekuphakameni,
let us also go
we may go, and worship Jehova.

4. The long road does not kill
those who worship him,
let us go, oh ye worshippers
(that) we may go to Ekuphakameni.

89.

1. Stay with us our *Nkosi*
this day is passed;
we ask to be helped
we are looking to you.

3. We are still closed off from
the view
of that world of happiness,
where it is not shining
this sun of this time.

2. We have not yet got there
in that land of happiness
there stand the angels
where the sun does not set.

4. Let praise be to you
in earth and in heaven
with all your hosts
to you father *Nkulunkulu.*

96.

1. I am straying in your face
all the days of my life;
the heart leads me astray
I am getting smaller and smaller
in your face.

2. Speak you my *Nkosi*
Speak you to my heart;
I alone, it has already defeated me
I stray from your face.

Chorus: Help Help *Nkosi Baɓa*
Pity my *umoya.*

3. Trying has come to an end
it has not satisfied my heart;
I am going down every day
I am breaking the laws.

100.

1. We shall conceive having hope
through this name of yours;
we shall give birth to them being
                              alive
those who believe in thy word.

3. We shall rejoice through the
                              saints
who come from the clouds;
the weapon of believing
is Jehova alone.

Chorus: We shall wander in the wilderness
        through this fame of yours.

2. The badge of victory
is Jehova alone
the brave one goes with conquering
it is Jehova alone.

4. We shall perform a war dance
                coming from the gate
of the holy city;
we who have defeated
whilst on earth.

5. The angels clap their wings
because of our victory;
ye caused to be pleased, *uThokozwayo.*

101.

1. It is the eagle which has wings,
lift up your wing
that we may enter and hide
                    ourselves in you
rock of the old.

4. Love us and protect us
beautiful hen,
we are in thy face
hen of heaven.

2. No other fortress have we
other than you
where we can hide ourselves
we your little poor ones.

5. Protect it, *Nkosi*
that Ekuphakameni,
like a hen
loving her children.

3. Beautiful hen
we stand in front of you,
it is not Jerusalem alone
that you loved.

6. Jerusalem, Jerusalem
how much did I desire
to gather your children
under my wings
but you did not allow me,
now I leave you scattered.

102.

1. I remembered Ekuphakameni
where it is gathered
the holy congregation
of the people of Nazareth.

2. I remembered Ekuphakameni
where there are fountains
of the water of life
of eternity.

3. I remembered Ekuphakameni,
a drop of *umkholongo*
it is the share of the saints
of Nazareth.

4. All ye that are thirsty
come to Ekuphakameni,
you will drink beautifully
from the fountains of water.

118.

1. Listen ye, here is the Word
oh, all ye nations.
Be converted and be baptized
that ye may be saved.

2. Wash my heart
that it may leave that which I like,
Amen Halelujah
run away all ye sinners.

3. Nobody is wept for
in the hell of fire
nobody weeps for another
in the hell of fire.

4. Amen Halelujah!
Run away all ye sinners;
there is no rest
in the hell of fire.

5. They are staying in this distress
in the hell of fire;
they stay there crying
they cannot be loosened (delivered).

6. The food of there (of that place)
is distress only;
the water of there
is tears.

127.

1. Cause the Sabbath to come quickly
Nkosi of the heavens and earth
that all the nations be saved
that are under the heaven.

2. Cause the Sabbath to come quickly
Nkosi of the heaven and earth
that all the nations be saved
that are under the heaven.

3. They are gathered here
all these nations
they want the truth of your word
so that they observe the Sabbath.

4. Cause the Sabbath to come
quickly
Nkosi of the heaven and earth
even two and even three
are in need of the Sabbath.

131.

1. *Nkosi Baba* hear us
protect your city
the city of Ekuphakameni
destroy all its enemies.

2. All those who have a grudge
         against (this city)
let them be written
in the book of life
their names be destroyed.

3. Remove them, you *Nkosi*
from the book of life
destroy their cities
that no person could stay in them.

4. Those who begrudge
         Ukuphakama
we push them to you,
shut them in, you *Nkosi*
they should not rise up (i.e.
         against us.).

5. For a long time they have laid it
on our necks
that yoke of iron
on our necks.

6. Clothe them you *Nkosi*
with the blanket of weeping,
lift up, you *Nkosi*
this Kuphakama.

132.

Prayer of the suffering servant, Shembe at Ntanda on September 5, 1926.

1. I am going to the vineyard
(where) I shall end up;
many will accompany me
with loving Jehova.

Chorus: It is so beautiful at our home
where we are going
beautiful gold and silver
do not compare.

2. They are invited by the one who hangs from the tree
at the Cross:
on the tree that is despised
the earth quaked.

3. He was confessing my sins
on the tree of disgrace

4. I was rested
by the one who hangs on a tree;

the stars have fallen
the sun dimmed
the earth quaked
the stones burst.

you have already heard, come ye.
Mine were buried with him
in the grave, you have already
heard, come.

134.

There were 8 (people) in Nov. 1926, the suffering servant, he was called *uThumekile*, Isaiah Shembe, spreading the word of the *iNkosi* at Mangethe which is in the wilderness. In a voice this prayer came.

1. The *iNkosi* should bless you, ye servant of the *iNkosi*;
   May you cause it to go, ye servant of the *iNkosi*,
   the nations also are expecting it.

2. The *iNkosi* should bless you, ye servant of the *iNkosi*;
   May you cause your days to be increased under the sky.
   They are waiting, all those nations,
   all which are under the sky.

3. The *iNkosi* should bless you, ye servant of the *iNkosi*;
   May you cause to be spread his word, ye servant of the *iNkosi*;
   these nations are expecting
   all those under the sky.

4. Jehova should build you up, servant of the *iNkosi*,
   that you should spread his word, servant of the *iNkosi*,
   these nations are expecting
   all those under the sky.

5. The *iNkosi* should bless you, ye servant of the *iNkosi*,
   may you wipe our tears in the name of the *iNkosi*
   all these tears are awaiting you
   all these are under the sky.

136.

1. I was called by your voice
I stood up and followed you
I left our land
I stood up and followed you.

4. He left his father Isaac,
he listened to your voice
he despised himself through your
voice
he stood up and followed you.

2. You called me *iNkosi* with
                your voice
I listened to your voice
I left gain through your word
I stood up and followed you.

3. You called him you *iNkosi*
Jacob your *iNceku*;
you called him with your voice
he stood up and followed you.

5. In a certain place
you welcomed your servant,
through the messengers now in
              heaven,
he set off to follow.

6. My father called me
I listened to your voice.
My mother and my sister
I left them and I followed you.

138.

1. All the stubborn ones
are in the hell of fire,
he who refuses to be told he sees
          through a bloody trail
oh, he is surprised.

2. They stand alone, why?
In the valley!
They have been called in the valley
          of distress,
their lights are out.

3. So said the rich man:
I am troubled
in this flame of fire
come and extinguish (it on) me.

4. The rich man looked,
he had very great pain
he saw Lazarus, he was far off
on the breast of Abraham.

5. The rich man shouted
with a great voice.
He said: Father Abraham
Pity me.

6. Send Lazarus
put the top part
of his finger in the water
that he should come and cool my
          tongue
I am in distress.

140.

The name of *iNkosi uNkulunkulu* serving the Supper of the *iNkosi*.
The Supper is served on the 14th day of the month. Joshua 5[10]; Corin-
thians 11[23]; Exodus 12[6]; Matthew 26[20]; Mark 4[16],[27].

1. Ye are invited young men
and ye also young women,

3. He said unto them: Verily, verily
I am the life of eternity (i.e.

who have been destined to eternal   eternal life),
                                            life   who eats of my flesh
Come to the life-giving meal.   will have life of eternity.

2. Those who partake of this food   4. Come ye that have been bought
will have eternal life;   bought with the blood of the
which will resurrect them on the   iNkosi,
                                  last day this meal is prepared for you
they will be with me in Paradise.   it is life of eternity.

153.

1. Here is the word of invitation,   2. Black and white
it invites all people.   it also invites;
It is not selective   it is not selective
it invites all people.   it invites all people.

3. Ye blind and ye crippled
answer, ye are being called.
This invitation is of the heaven
all the nations are being invited,
it is not selective
it invites all people.

154.

1. I believe in the Father   3. But the animals through your
and in the Holy Spirit   word
and in the communion of saints   they followed Noah.
of Nazareth!   But mine stand alone
because I would love to see it   it does not want to follow you
that world which is to come.   because I would love to see it
                                           that world which is to come.

2. My heart is like that of an animal   4. You are the rock of refuge
I do not want to follow you.   you are the shield of believers
Help me you iNkosi   I will be helped by you alone
I would love to believe,   you rock of rest
because I would love to see it   because I would love to see it
that world which is to come.   that world which is to come.

5. Bonds have come down upon me
oh, *uMkhululi*, I am in want
my heart is distressed
uneasy conscience has come upon me
but I would love to see it
that world which is to come.

155.

1. I follow from behind
the road is so long!
My power will end
in going to Ekuphakameni.

2. Many have left me behind
I am in need, I am in want!
Who will help me
to go to Ekuphakameni.

3. They will enter by the gates
the angels so beautiful,
will open for them
at the gates.

4. They will meet with many
being put out of the gates
of Ekuphakameni
on account of their sins.

5. The angels drive them out
those who watch at the gates
of Ekuphakameni
on account of their sins.

157.

1. It has come upon me, the weight
of my sins,
and of my parents
they left them with me.

2. Who is the diviner
my *uMkhululi*!
It is you alone
oh! my *uMkhululi*.

3. The day I am treated
and saved
what shall I praise you with
oh! my *uMkhululi*.

4. The sickness of the heart
is so painful,
I suffer from guilty conscience
of my heart.

5. The soap which is generations
(i.e., of generations)
which is under the sky
may not wash even one
my *uMkhululi*.

6. I washed at sunrise
till sunset,
Not even one was removed
oh, my *uMkhululi*.

159.

1. Today it has been heard
that voice of eternity
the graves of the saints
sing with joy
the pleasure of *uMsindisi*
of the saints, it has been heard.

2. The gates of that city
are being opened for the saints
they sang for them with joy
the foundations of that city,
cry out with joy, ye that are bought
for entering into that city.

3. Here are the messengers of
                                    the saints
Hearken! You are being called.
You that are sleeping on the earth,
the voice of him who lives forever,
cry out with joy, you inheritors,
for the entry of the saints.

4. *Simakade* was happy
because of the opening of the graves,
the trumpet sounded
of opening the gates;
rejoice ye that are bought
for getting into that city.

5. We thank you our *Nkosi*
uThixo of Ekuphakameni,
thank you hosts
who are staying up above
and the crowds of this earth
they will enter up above.

160.

1. So say the word of the cowards
who will fly from Ekuphakameni,
where are you going to, ye people
tomorrow this comes to an end.

4. Grow ye, Kuphakama
that all the nations go down
today we hear them saying
come ye to Ekuphakameni.

Chorus: So are you, Kuphakama
         You shed light upon all nations.

2. The cowards laughed cynically
Saying ha! ha! ha! this is coming
                         to an end
tomorrow it is coming to an end
all will come to an end, there will
                         be nothing.

5. You city that is built on the
                         mountain
you cannot be obliterated from
                         view
you shed light upon nations
which are under the sun.

3. Be determined ye brave ones
and be not caused to fear through the cowards
who will flee from Ekuphakameni
Saying he! he! he! this will come to an end.

161.

1. Greet ye uKuphakama
all ye nations will be saved there.
They entered in ones
they were saved there,
the sting of sin will end up there.

2. Why have our brethren remained
who are in need of being saved;
and with pleasant smell
to save nations,
it will fill up all
the city of there.

3. Call them with his word
he who stays in Ekuphakameni,
whose smell is pleasant
to save nations
many were saved by it
whose good fortune
does not drip to the ground.

162.

The Prayer of Shembe: I was with the *umoya* of the *iNkosi* on the day
of the *iNkosi* on the mountain of Nhlangakazi, January 22, 1929.

I had kept my *umoya* for the proclamation of the *iNkosi*; whilst it was
so a hymn was heard. It came out to me, it came with its being sung, it was
already on the way. He who is fit to be praised I praise and who is fit to
be glorified I glorify. It is he alone who makes heaven and earth. May he
be praised.

1. Amen. Amen. Amen!
Amen. Amen. Amen!
The aloe af the Veld
it is not as bitter
as your word *Simakade*
in the hearts of many.

3. Amen. Amen. Amen!
Amen. Amen. Amen!
They left it just when it appeared
that city that shines
they retreated
it is the heritage of the brave.

2. Amen. Amen. Amen!
Amen. Amen. Amen!
The cough medicine of the mountains
is not as bitter
as your word *Simakade*
in the hearts of many.

4. Amen. Amen. Amen!
Amen. Amen. Amen!
Arm yourselves ye brave ones
(with) the fruits of faith;
have ye forbearance, even if it is so,
it is entered with difficulty.

5. Amen. Amen. Amen!
Amen. Amen. Amen!
Even the gate in there is small
it is not entered into with burdens
leave down there those burdens
it is not entered with burdens.

164.

1. The service of there
peace and kindness,
we enter one by one
and be received with kindness.

3. Ye gates of uKuphakama
rise up that we go in
we have been yearning for you
you home of peace.

2. You home of quietness
rejoice through us,
we are blessed by the saints
we greet you friends.

4. The sun and the moon
it does not shine there,
only *Simakade*
the sun of there.

5. The shining of the sun
it does not compare
with our city
where we are.

165.

1. The soldiers arrived
make a great noise;
the army of destruction is already
out
it goes with strength
armyourselves believers.

4. Inhale *umoya*
fight bravely
so that you may carry the
weapons through this faith
love preserves
it gives strength
go on suffering though it be difficult
it has already been heard.

2. It goes out with a word of
                              destruction
it goes with fire that destroys many
it goes out with weapons
of destroying the believers
who believe in *uThixo*
arm yourselves believers.

3. We see the tent of *uThixo*
which come down from heaven,
we also see the angel
coming down from heaven
our voice was heard in heaven.

5. It comes out with trouble-
                              making
which is going to trouble us,
the mouth of the *iNkosi* has spoken
tell all the nations of the world
hosts of heaven.

6. Rejoice once and for all, with us
hosts of heaven
that the enemies of the nation be
                              completely burned
we will bend knees in front of the
                              great *iNkosi*
to the end of the world.

169.

1. We have been called for, we,
That word of yours,
we now believe
what is said by your word.

2. We do not turn, we,
to the right
nor to the left
we stand to it, by it.

4. We believe in thy word
we have been sent for this,
we believe in thy word
the *uMsindisi* in reality is you.

5. Let us believe in your word
receive you *Nkosi*
the prayers of your word
cause our feet to be blessed.

3. Our hearts
who are shivered by the word
strengthen them so that they say
they will be saved those nations.

170.

1. We are kept by you *Nkosi*
this night
we rise up being alive
by that grace of yours.

2. Let us give praise to you, *Nkosi*,
Your waking us up
let us be kept by your grace
on this day of yours.

3. We have been given it by your grace
this day of yours
let us enter with you, *Nkosi*
into this day of yours.

173.

1. Give way that we enter
that we may serve Jehova
we were shut in
the gates are opened.

2. Give way that he may enter
oh, here is Zulu
the progeny of Dingaan
and Sendzangakhona.

3. Who opened
this door
Oh! *Mkhululi* of prisoners.

4. Come ye with those nations
they lack that word
which is above all.

178.

1. Many are the nations
under the sun
they parted through the law
from country to country.

2. Many are the nations
which are under the sun
who has separated them
from country to country.

3. What kind of a word
which can cause them to come
                        together
those nations.
Come ye Zulus, you have heard.

4. It is *uThixo* alone
who can cause these nations to
                    come together
come ye Mabaca,
ye hear his voice.

180.

This Isl. came to the suffering servant in June, 1931.

1. Come ye all ye nations
that hearth has been kindled already,
all the nations are warming themselves at it
come ye those who are in want.

2. Ye invited, come ye
your heritage is ripe;
why do you cry carrying it,
it is enough, eat ye it.

3. They are being diminished those who do not love it,
those who love it come ye,
the gates of that heritage
have been opened for you.

4. That heritage is kept
it is being kept for you,
the heaven and this earth
it was not here yet (i.e., it existed before
                    heaven and earth).

181.

1. Rise up Kuphakama
in the name of the *iNkosi*
awake all our nations
they are still asleep
in the name of the *iNkosi*.
They should wake up to you
Oh! Kuphakama.

2. We are sorry about our people
Pity us *Nkosi* we are orphans.
We have no other *uMkhululi* than
                                you
Who can liberate us from bondage.

3. Why do you despise us so
                    much *iNkosi*
come back to us and intercede
                    on our behalf
our fathers are no longer here
we are shouldering their sins.

4. Beat *Nkosi* and soothe,
we have sinned, we confess in
                    your face
whose are we if you discard us!
Return to us *Nkosi* of peace.

186.

1. You are not being praised —
you are not being praised,
so greatly!
why is it all ye people.

3. If we are thirsty through this
we shall drink from the tree of life
that tree which is in that city,
why is it all ye people
that you do not spread this name!
Spread it all ye people
this so great name.

2. With this name alone
we have been made inheritors
of this heritage that stands forever.
Why is it all ye people
that you do not spread this name!
Spread it all ye people
this so great name.

4. What do they say, those who
        come from that land of life
they say it is so beautiful!
The city of there lacks no sun
nor the moon,
Jehova he alone
is the sun and the moon.
Why is it all ye people
that you do not spread this name.
Spread it all ye people
this so great name.

188.

1. We all have been invited
we have been invited by the *iNkosi*
        of the Sabbath
that we may be saved
through this Sabbath.
Amen, Amen, Amen!

3. Be steadfast, oh ye worshippers
on this Sabbath.
It is a feast of intercession
it was made for us by our creator
Amen, Amen, Amen!

2. We had all sinned
in your face *Nkosi*
worshipping our gods (idols)
you sifted* us through the Sabbath.
Amen, Amen, Amen!

4. We had all sinned
worshipping our idols
you sifted us, you *Nkosi*
with this Sabbath.
Amen, Amen, Amen!

5. It is the Sabbath today all ye people
come ye to the *uMsindisi*.
The *uMsindisi* rejoices because of them
who keep the Sabbath.
Amen, Amen, Amen!

* The word *hlenga* could mean: i. Sift, clean, separate chaff from core; ii. Ransom, redeem; iii. Escort.

189.

1. Take up your arms
thrust powerfully.
Take ye the shields of faith

3. Love that is firm gives power
it supports and defeats with faith.
Be determined ye brave ones

love strengthens —
it gives power
take and defeat with faith.

2. The army of our enemies should
            be destroyed completely
that the nations may be saved.
The mouth of the *iNkosi* has
                  already spoken
tell the nations the news.

with faith
it defeats with happiness
it loves friends.

4. I ask for bonds, oh *Nkosi* of
                              my heart;
I may follow the believers with
                              faith.
I will praise with praise,
Giver of power.
I must not be in want, I must not
                              lack
you lover of sinners.

191.

1. Come ye friends
you that worship the *iNkosi*
come ye also sinners,
carry ye and leave not even one
                  behind.
The *uMsindisi* wants you
even if you are like that.

3. Listen to the voice of the
                  messengers
all ye people,
it is good fortune to many
to hear that voice
it is heard by only a few
to many it is not audible.

2. The messengers have gone out
to invite many.
Listen ye sinners
come together with the invited,
that voice calls out for you.

4. The time is ended
oh, all ye people,
they passed in a hurry
these messengers,
when shall you hear his voice!
Come ye sinners.

5. They go by hurriedly
those messengers
when will you hear it!
Come ye sinners, the time is ended
oh, all ye people.

194.

1. Come then, ye sinners,
Come even all

2. Do not
be afraid

the feast is ready.   it is all good,
Come ye then   Come ye then
That ye may eat it and live.   That ye may eat it and live.

3. Ye blind
Ye cripples
Come even ye all
the feast of this grace
was already ready.
Come ye then
That ye may eat it and live.

197.

Durban, March 15, 1933

1. If you call me *iNkosi* with your
                              voice
I listened to your voice
I left gain through your voice
I stood up and followed you.

4. When I had heard your voice,
                              iNkosi
whilst I was still in my mother's
                              womb,
I came out with haste
and followed you.

2. You called me *iNkosi* with your
                              voice
I was still in my mother's womb,
I listened iNkosi to your voice
and I followed you.

5. Even today, *iNkosi*, I praise
the day of my birth,
I came out in a hurry
and I followed you.

3. Even today *iNkosi* I would not
                              refuse
if you call me with your voice,
I would leave everything with haste
and follow you.

6. Even today call me with your
                              voice
I will listen to your word.
I will leave my stock* through
                              your word
and I will follow you.

7. Come then my child
I am still standing in the gate;
I will not leave you my child
Come and follow me.

* -fuyo: live-stock, possessions in cattle or domestic animals.

199.

22 April 1933

1. Children of *uNkulunkulu*
they love one another
they will never separate
and they will never quarrel.

2. If they quarrel
whose are they,
there is no quarrel
in the world above.

3. We are children
of one person,
would that we love one another
by the minutes and times.

4. The children of *Baba*
who is in heaven
they love one another
by the minutes and the times.

5. You do not separate
you of the earth
come together and be one
like those of heaven.

200.

26 April 1933

1. So sayeth the voice of *Simakade*
to you his people
do not work on the Sabbath
you, his people.

2. Listen to his word
which is with all people
keep the Sabbath
you, all his people.

3. He who desecrates the Sabbath
let him die;
listen all ye his people
keep ye the Sabbath.

4. Our Maker rested
on this Sabbath
we also must rest
on this Sabbath.

5. He who works on the Sabbath
may he die.
Do not work all ye people
on this Sabbath.*

6. The Sabbath is the city
of rest *iNkosi*
work ye not ye respectors**
on this Sabbath.

7. It is a good thing to respect
the day of *iNkosi*
respect all ye his people
the day of the Sabbath.

* Ex. 31^1.

** hlonipha: i. Respect, reverence, regard with awe, honour; ii. Act respectfully,
-modestly.

201.

1. I have no weapons, I have no
                                              shields
with which to protect my *umoya*.
Here is my name, it is now being
                                              removed
from the book of life.*

2. Pardon *Baba*, pardon *Nkosi*
Protect me, you *Baba*
that my name be not removed
from the book of life.

3. Let not my name be removed
from the book of life,
what shall I be *Baba*
in thy face.

4. Wash me, you *Baba*
cleanse me truly
that my name stand through you
in the book of life.

5. That city which is shining
he does not enter, even one,
whose name is not written
in the book of life.

6. The great day will come
that is fearful,
come ye that we write our names
in the book of life.

7. Come ye quickly
before the sun sets,
whilst you are still allowed to have names written
in the book of life

* Dan. 12.

208.

1. Rejoice ye, rejoice ye
the Nazarethness has come.
Rejoice ye, rejoice ye
the nations will be saved
those which are scattered
wandering in the wildernesses
through your word.

2. Rejoice ye, rejoice ye
the Nazarethness has come.
Rejoice ye, rejoice ye
the nations will be saved
darkness has ended
rejoice and be happy
all ye nations.

3. Many nations
which are under the sky
we see them scattered;
they are singing, they are
                                              disappointed.

4. Increase, increase,
Increase Nazarethness.
Increase, increase
the nations are thirsty.
They want to drink from you
that they may be satisfied, that
                                              they overflow.

212.

1. The Sabbath is a resting-place
it supports *Simakade*,
we have risen now worshippers
let us keep the Sabbath.

2. We have been called by our Maker
call out in answer worshippers.
The Sabbath is the key
the gates may be opened.

3. Those sheep of their Maker
they hear his voice,
they hear his voice.
Hear ye his voice
you his sheep.

4. Call out in reply, it is already
morning
you his sheep,
you know his voice
which is with all worshippers.

5. Murmur and spread
with that kindness of his
sleeping places, sleeping places,
let it be praised.

6. It is not selective of anyone
of those who fear him.
He has soap, their Maker
He will wash them all.

7. Give thanks ye that have been washed
with this soap of his,
you have been washed and it is complete
you no longer lack anything.

213.

This Isl. was composed on the day the suffering servant Shembe met
a young man carrying a young ape to go and sell it. The *iNceku* of the
iNkosi gave the young man five shillings and said he should return the ape
to the forest.

1. Shembe son of Mayekisa
protect me
so said the small ape
he was passing by it.

2. It said: *Mkhululi* of the bound
what will you liberate!
I have left mother and father
I do not know where I am going to.

4. He asked him by saying
how much do you want?
The child answered saying
I want five (shillings).

5. He gave him the five and said:
Return it back.
He took that ape back
to where he took it from.

3. He called the child,
he said: where are you taking the
                                    ape to!
he answered by saying:
I am sent.

6. Awake it is already morning
when shall you awake!
There you are being surpassed by
                                    apes
through recognizing the *iNkosi*.

214.

1. Our *uMkhululi* —
we the progeny of Dingaan
we have heard, he has arrived.
uMkhululi has arrived!
uMkhululi has now arrived!
Ye Zulus, we have heard him now.

3. Our need —
we the progeny of Dingaan
has now come to an end.
uMkhululi has arrived!
uMkhululi has now arrived!
Ye Zulus, we have heard him now.

2. Descendants of Dingaan
they are with Sendzangakhona,
be awake, he has come.
uMkhululi has arrived!
uMkhululi has now arrived!
Ye Zulus, we have heard him now.

4. May you remember *iNkosi*
the work of your hands
of the progeny of Dingaan.
uMkhululi has arrived!
uMkhululi has now arrived!
Ye Zulus, we have heard him now.

5. Confess yourself to him —
you the progeny of Dingaan
they are with Sendzangakhona!
uMkhululi has arrived!
uMkhululi has now arrived!
Ye Zulus, we have heard him now.

216.

1. Rise up with us today
on this morning
Even today
oh! *Nkosi*.

4. We are the progeny
of that root,
we do not lack
we are with Sendzangakhona
oh! *Nkosi*.

2. That you be a journey
to those who are journeying
and even those who are staying

5. We of long ago
we have long been drinking
at that fountain

let it be so
oh! *Nkosi*.

3. That you keep them
in their staying
on that day
of today
oh! *Nkosi*.

of Sendzangakhona
oh! *Nkosi*.

6. Shaka said we are not even
                              beatable
to you Mhlangana and Dingaan
and yet today it is even so
to you Mhlangana and Dingaan
oh! Nkosi.

218.

The Gospel, Dec. 1934.

1. Come, oh ye Zulus
We have seen our *iNkosi*
we come from the world that is to
                              come
we have seen our *iNkosi*.

4. Rejoice ye Nazarites
we have seen our *iNkosi*,
a flower with its colours
does not shine like him.

2. We invite you, ye Zulus,
we invite you for our *iNkosi*,
we come from the world that is to
                              come.

5. Believe ye Zulus
through us alone
we come from the world that is
                              to come.

3. So beautiful is he, Zulus!
we have seen our *iNkosi*
we come from there, the world
                    that is to come
we have seen our *iNkosi*.

6. Eyes do not bring for one another
otherwise we should have brought
                              for you
He is so beautiful our *iNkosi*
ye Zulus, come ye.

219.

1. We have heard it, oh *Baɓamkhulu*
we could not comply
oh! *Baɓamkhulu*,
make soft thy Word (i.e. be not
                              strict)
oh! *Baɓamkhuli*
we shall try to do thy Word
                              (will).

3. The voice of the prisoners
oh! *Baɓamkhulu*
may you hear their voice
oh! *Baɓamkhulu*!
They want one who rests
oh! *Baɓamkhulu*,
these prisoners give them rest.

2. Thousands of generations
stand here
oh! *Babamkhulu*
they found your word difficult
oh! *Babamkhulu*
Make soft thy word
oh! *Babamkhulu*.

4. We are staying in distress
oh! *Babamkhulu*,
in this world
oh! *Babamkhulu*
it is all tears
oh! *Babamkhulu*
in that valley of distress.

220.

This Isl. was written by *iNkosi* Isaiah Shembe May 1939. After his rising from the dead.

1. Wake up it is already morning
the Zulu became dejected in the land.

2. Grow ye Kuphakama
the new city
The Zulu became dejected in the land.

221.

This Isl. was written by J. G. Shembe in Jan. 1938 on the mountain of Nhlangakazi. It should be sung on the day of memory only.

1. At last came this day
the great, which is being feared.
The angels arrived
to fetch *Thumekile*
go well, go well,
my father who is holy.

6. *iNkosi* of the heaven and earth
soon you will call me;
do not forget your people
the Nazarites who are holy.
It was the prayer of the *iNkosi*
when he left this earth.

2. The world was shaking
the Zulus reported to one another
the heaven thundered
the stars wept.
It was frightening, it was
                    frightening
the *iNkosi* departed.

7. Create another in my house
to lead your people.
Give him the heart
which is like yours.
You touch him and you anoint him
with fat of blessing.*

* *This is put in the mouth of his father.*

3. You the city that is chosen
of *Mikhayideni*
may it dress up with blankets
and dance for *uSimakade*.
He is the *iNkosi* of the *amakhosi*,
you my *uMkhululi*.

4. The young women and young
men
they were contrite and cried.
Women and men
they lost hope
uNkulunkulu, nKosi of us,
(with) whom are you leaving us.

5. *Nkosi* of us, *Simakade*
remember us again
we sinners are sad
we fall into thy hands.
Cry maiden, cry young man
cry ye orphan.

8. My flesh is tired;
it is going to lie in the grave
my spirit will rise
and be clothed in new flesh.
From old I was born,
forever I will be there.

9. Put him in a place of
remembrance
in the holy city
wrap him up with skins
that he may rest well.
Sleep well, sleep well
son of Nhliziyo.*

* Nhliziyo is one of Shembe's great great grandfathers.

10. Kuphakama is a rock
which stands for ever;
the bones which are holy
you look after them.
Let the lights be put on
(lit. till) forever.

11. My father who loves me,
me your small child
who is still on earth.
I would like my father
that I be with you.

222.

This Isl. arrived when I was at Veleɓahleke in 1938. I had called to mind a certain girl who very much wished to be converted but the parents stopped her — J. G. Shembe.

1. I come, Nkosi, I alone
I have no escort.
My father and my mother
they refuse that I follow you.

4. I would love to see
where you are and your *iNceku*
call me with your voice
I will follow you again.

2. My brothers and my sisters
they have a grudge against my
umoya,
Close my ears, *Nkosi*
so that I do not hear their voice.

3. I perceive thy voice, *Nkosi,*
in my heart calling me;
let me be given by you *uMkhululi*
a loving heart.

5. My spirit agrees
and you my heart shall not refuse
I would love to end
at that holy place.

5. *Baba* I am thy child
even though the world does not
like it
pull me out of the flames
Nkosi, may I not be refused.

223.

This Isl. came whilst I was at Velaбahleke, Nov. 1938. By J. G. Shembe.

1. I am your follower
and that of the Holy Spirit;
Give *Nkosi* to our hearts
the willingness to hear your voice.

2. In my childhood I follow you,
even at old age I should follow
you;
Give *Nkosi* to my heart
to hear your voice.
to hear your voice.

3. I will acknowledge you whilst I
am still alive
Even in painfulness, it is your will;
Give *Nkosi* to my heart
to hear your voice.

* A term of respect.

4. It will follow you at Ekuphakameni
and also at Nhlangakazi I will
follow you;
agree my heart
agree that I follow him.

5. Yesterday my *Nkosi* I was
following you
even today, *Mhlekazi**, let me be
with you;
even tomorrow, my *Nkosi*
let me follow you.

6. *Nkosi,* it was not in me to
follow you,
you pulled me Baбa with bonds
of love;
even today let it be so
that you love me.

226.

1. Today I have surrendered[a)]
I have left my country,

3. Get away mist[d)] from my eyes
that I may see it again

I will never go back
it is already near Ekuphakameni.

that pillar of that fire
which fetched me from my country.

2. Let me also be given, *Nkosi*
this love of childlikeness;[b]
I shall[c] die here
In your hand.

4. My flesh is dressed up
until it was seven fold;
even today it dances
on the green hillocks.[e]

with material that does not perish;
which is not bought with gold,[f]
which comes from you, *Baϐa*.

[a]) Schlosser's translation uses the word *Steuer* (tax) but *thela* could mean also *surrender, yield*, and this is the sense in which the word is here used.

[b]) *uϐuntwana* is translated in Schlosser's book as *brotherly love* (Bruderliebe) which does not bring out the meaning of a love that leads to subjection to *Nkosi*, in this case his father.

[c]) Schlosser's translation expresses a wish "hier will ich sterben" while Shembe II means more than this – he *will* die here.

[d]) Schlosser's translation has *Schatten* (shadow) while the text has the word *Nkungu* which means mist, rainy mist, fog, and could also mean ignorance.

[e]) *amagquma* is translated in Schlosser's book as *Berge* (mountains) but in Zulu it means a dune, hillock.

[f]) *Engathengwa ngagolide* is translated in Schlosser's book "der ich mit Gold gekauft bin" but this completely misses the point.

228.

Ekuphakameni

1. *Nkosi Baϐa* I love you
but you are hidden;
you are not visible to me;
even if I wish it.

4. This love is great.
It is as powerful as death:
It is pleasant to the heart
even though you are hidden.

2. Where is that stream
through which I can wash,
the dirt will leave
I am then beautiful and complete.

5. For many years
I was living in darkness
you loved me *iNkosi*
and light came.

3. What type of clothing shall I put on
when you visit me:
on which mountains are they found
the scented herbs that are loved by
thee.

6. Come *Nkosi* quickly!
Unwillingness is ended.
Come you beloved one,
today I am yours.

233.

Nhlangakazi, 1946*

This Isl. I wrote when I was at Zibidhlela on 27/10/1945. I remembered my sickness at Them6alim6e in April 1941, when I returned from the grave.

1. I went out of the path
I entered into shame.
My enemies got hold of me,
I was far away from you.

2. The burning fire
devoured my flesh.
I searched for a helper
he was far away from me.

I called *Simakade*,
I was in difficulty;
he heard my voice
in his place.

4. He sent his *iNceku*
who came with the saints,
with the blanket of life,
they clothed me.

5. To trust in *Simakade*
and to hide in him,
it is a good thing
it is satisfying.

6. Let me look unto you, Nkosi,
may I escape from death.
May I hold your hand
so that I come out** of the
                    valley of death.

* This Isl. receives special status through the addition of Nhlangakazi.
** *phume* is conditional.

234.

Nhlangakazi, 16.1.1945

Prayer

1. My *uThixo*, my Rock
why do you forget me?
I cry daily
because I am troubled by my
                        enemy.

2. My evil troublers
they hunt me down continuously;
they say every day,
they say, where is your *uThixo*.

4. Today I thank you
you have allowed me to come to
                            you;
I lie before you,
in that holy place.

5. Let it be a pleasant scent
to you alone who is the Creator;
my praise
on that mountain of yours.

3. What is it my soul   6. Yes, *Nkosi*, let me sprout,
why are you dejected   that I be heavy-laden;
trust your *uThixo*, (text: uThizo)   let me bring forth fruit
there is not one hardship.*   which is loved by you.

  * Schlosser's translation states "Es gibt ja keinen anderen Helfer", *(Ayikho enye inqaɓa)* but *inqaɓa* refers to difficulty, hardship.

235.

Nhlangakazi, 16/1/1945

Prayer

1. You are worthy to be praised   4. Let it be acceptable to you, *Nkosi*
I also praise you;   my praying;
this praise is yours   to begin with I am grateful
in all the earth.   to good fortune as well as kindness.

    Chorus: You are worthy to be praised
              I also praise you;
              let my will be changed
              and be the same as yours.

2. In heaven it is you alone,   5. Your loving me *Nkosi*
the souls are yours;   let it be increased seven times;
you do not choose by the colour   give me *Nkosi* this love
                    of a person   with which to love you.
you do not look at sin.

3. All those who praise you,   6. Even if I do not see you
with love and truth   not hearing your voice;
with contrite hearts   even if I have manifold sins
you accept them.   which trouble my *umoya*.

        7. In my grief
        I spread myself in front of you;
        you my hope
        you are my strength.

237.

Mikhaideni, May, 1947

1. Stay well Kuphakama.
Today we are leaving you,
the time has ended.
We are going to different countries.

2. Remember us Kuphakama
you are our home;
you are the house of uThixo
you are the gate of heaven.

3. We are trusting in you
even here in darkness;
in the dangers of the wilderness
there we are going.

4. We leave the heart with you,
you are our precious thing;
with you is peace,
which is not on the earth.

5. They are blessed those who love
you
the city of the *iNkosi* who is great
they have good fortune the saints
whom you receive.

6. Come back today my soul,
enter Ekuphakameni,
too long you wander about troubled
you having no place to rest.

241.

A song of lamentation of the widow of Khanyama Ziɓane who was hanged on 12/9/1945. This song of lamentation was written on the 23/10/ 1945 in Empumalanga at Eshowe where she came.

1. *Nkosi*, son of *uThixo*,
protect me;
I came from far
I go with suffering.

2. My only son
had his neck broken,
on account of his sin
it spilled the blood of a human being.

3. Protect me *Nkosi* of kindness
I am not worthy of anything,
you do not choose persons by
their colour
you pity those who cry.

4. *Nkosi*, take away the grief
of our widows;
their orphans are imprisoned
even today they stay in misery.

5. Lover of sinners, wiper of tears,
liberate them with your kindness,
protect those who are bounded
bring them back from the chain.

6. There is not a single one who
is good,
you are the only one who intercedes.
Intercede for them *iNkosi*,
all those who come to thee in
trouble.

243.

1. Our *Nkosi Simakade*
We stand before you;
we beg you be here
also with us.

2. Come down holy spirit
come into us,
do unto all
what is loved by you.

3. Let all sins come to an end,
and all disease
purity and goodness
let it stay with us.